Microsoft® Windows™
Multimedia
Authoring and Tools Guide

Written, edited, and produced by
Microsoft Corporation

Distributed by Microsoft Press

PUBLISHED BY
Microsoft Press
A Division of Microsoft Corporation
One Microsoft Way, Redmond, Washington 98052-6399

Library of Congress Cataloging-in-Publication Data

Microsoft Windows multimedia authoring and tools guide / Microsoft Corporation.
      p.   cm. -- (Microsoft Windows multimedia programmer's
  reference library)
    Includes index.
    ISBN 1-55615-391-0
    1. Computer animation.   2. Computer sound processing.
  3. Microsoft Windows (Computer program) I. Microsoft. II. Series.
  TR897.5.M53   1991
  006.6'76 -- dc20   91-15271
                                 CIP

Printed and bound in the United States of America.

  2 3 4 5 6 7 8 9 MLML 6 5 4 3 2

Distributed to the book trade in Canada by Macmillan of Canada, a division of Canada Publishing Corporation.

Distributed to the book trade outside the United States and Canada by Penguin Books Ltd.

Penguin Books Ltd., Harmondsworth, Middlesex, England
Penguin Books Australia Ltd., Ringwood, Victoria, Australia
Penguin Books N.Z. Ltd., 182-190 Wairau Road, Auckland 10, New Zealand

British Cataloging-in-Publication Data available.

Contents

PART 1   Multimedia Authoring Guide

Chapter 1   Introduction

Windows with Multimedia 1-2
The Multimedia PC 1-3
Getting Started 1-4
How This Part is Organized 1-4

Chapter 2   Creating a Multimedia Title

Types of Multimedia Titles 2-2
   Productivity 2-2
   Information 2-3
   Entertainment 2-3
   Creativity 2-4
   Education 2-4
Defining the Title 2-5
   Identifying the Audience 2-6
   Designing the Title's Structure 2-6
   Establishing Design Standards 2-9
Preparing the Data Used in a Title 2-10
Building the Title 2-11
   Using a Programming Language 2-12
   Using a Multimedia Authoring Tool 2-12
Summary 2-13

Chapter 3   Managing Data

The Data Management Environment 3-2

    Storing Data 3-2

    Transferring Data 3-5

Managing Your Library of Data Resources 3-7

    Define a Data Management Methodology 3-8

    Collect and Register Resources 3-10

    Identify and Select Specific Resources 3-10

    Edit Resources and Update database 3-11

    Purging Unnecessary Resources 3-11

Summary 3-11

Chapter 4   CD-ROM

What is CD-ROM? 4-2

Factors to Consider When Designing for CD-ROM 4-3

    Naming and Locating Data Files 4-3

    Storage Capacity 4-3

    Data Transfer Rate 4-4

    Seek Time 4-4

Putting Your Title on CD-ROM 4-5

    Premastering 4-5

    Final Testing 4-6

    Mastering and Replication 4-7

Chapter 5   Images

An Introduction to Digital Images Technology 5-2

    Types of Digital Images 5-2

    What is a Vector Graphic? 5-2

    What is a Bitmap? 5-4

    Resolution 5-5

    Image Depth 5-5

    Image File Size 5-7

Acquiring Images 5-8
   Purchasing Images 5-8
   Creating Original Art 5-8
   Scanning 5-9
   Video Frame Grabbing 5-9
Setting Up the Image Preparation Environment 5-10
   Image Processing Software 5-10
Image Processing Hardware 5-12
   Computer Hardware 5-13
   Scanners 5-13
   Video Digitizing Equipment 5-14
Capturing and Preparing Images 5-15
   Choosing an Image 5-16
   Capturing with a Scanner 5-17
   Capturing from Video 5-19
   Enhancing Images 5-21

Chapter 6   Audio

An Introduction to Digital Audio Technology 6-2
   What is Sound? 6-2
   Making Sound Digital 6-3
   Quality vs. Size 6-4
   Compact Disc Digital Audio 6-5
   Choosing a Fidelity Level 6-6
Acquiring Audio 6-7
   Developing Your Own Recordings 6-7
   Purchasing Production Music Libraries 6-7
   Hiring a Digital Sound Studio 6-8
Preparing Audio 6-8
   Setting Up the Audio Preparation Environment 6-8
   Capturing Audio 6-12
   Converting Audio 6-13
   Edit the Audio 6-13
   Storing Audio 6-14

Chapter 7   MIDI

What is MIDI? 7-2

Basic MIDI Terminology 7-2

MIDI and the Multimedia PC 7-4

    MIDI Ports 7-4

    MIDI Cables 7-4

    MIDI Synthesizers 7-5

    How a Message Becomes Music 7-6

When to Use MIDI 7-7

Acquiring MIDI Scores 7-8

    Purchasing MIDI Music 7-8

    Hiring a MIDI Sound studio 7-8

    Recording Your Own MIDI Scores 7-8

Preparing MIDI 7-9

    MIDI Preparation Software 7-9

    Hardware 7-10

Building a MIDI Score 7-11

    Compose Each Track 7-12

    Build the Composition 7-12

    Edit Each Channel 7-12

    Modify Characteristics of the Score 7-12

    Store the Composition 7-13

Converting Existing MIDI Files 7-13

    Rechannelize the MIDI Data 7-13

    Convert Patch Numbers 7-13

    Set a Volume Level 7-14

Authoring Device-Independent MIDI Files 7-14

    General Authoring Guidelines 7-15

    Prioritizing Your MIDI Data 7-16

    Using Standard MIDI Patch Assignments 7-16

    Standard MIDI Key Assignments 7-18

Chapter 8   Text

Retyping Text 8-2
Scanning Text 8-3
    Getting Better Results When Scanning 8-4
Converting Text 8-6
    Analyze the Destination File 8-8
    Analyze the Source File 8-8
    Convert the Text 8-9
    Tracking the Converted Files 8-10
    Proofing and Correction 8-10
Text Preparation Hardware and Software 8-11

Chapter 9   Animation

Making Movies with Director 9-2
Playing Movies On a Multimedia PC 9-3
Building Movies for Movie Player 9-4
    Movie Player Capabilities 9-5
    Using Palettes and Bitmaps 9-6
Using MCI Within Movies 9-9
    Using MCI Script-Channel Commands 9-10
    How MCI Commands are Processed 9-11
    Tips for Using MCI Commands in the Script Channel 9-11
    About Device Filenames 9-12
    Examples of MCI Script-Channel Commands 9-13
    Using Custom Script-Channel Commands 9-14
Improving Animation Performance 9-15
    Limiting Movie Size 9-15
    Using Cast Members Efficiently 9-16
    Working with Graphics and Fonts 9-16
    Selecting Appropriate Transitions 9-17
    Converting MacroMind Director Files 9-18

PART 2   Data Preparation Tools User's Guide

Chapter 10   Introduction

The MDK Data-Preparation Tools   10-2

    The Convert Tool   10-2

    The BitEdit Tool   10-3

    The PalEdit Tool   10-4

    The WaveEdit Tool   10-5

    The FileWalker Tool   10-5

    Starting a Data-Preparation Tool   10-6

Required Hardware and Software   10-7

Related Documentation   10-7

Conventions   10-8

    Document Conventions   10-8

    Terms   10-8

Chapter 11   Understanding Data Preparation

Data Makes Multimedia   11-2

    Using Rich-Text Capabilities   11-2

    Using Images and Animation   11-2

    Using Audio   11-2

The Use of CD-ROM   11-2

Supported Data Types   11-3

The Elements of Data Presentation   11-4

    Choosing Fonts   11-4

    Using Audio   11-4

    Using Images and Animation   11-4

Preparing Data   11-5

    Preparing Text   11-5

    Preparing Images and Animation   11-5

    Preparing Audio   11-6

Managing Multimedia Data   11-6

Chapter 12   Using Convert

Valid File Formats 12-1

    Audio Formats 12-1

    Bitmap Formats 12-2

    Palette Formats 12-3

    MIDI Formats 12-3

Starting Convert 12-3

Converting a File 12-5

    Specifying the Source File Format 12-5

    Specifying the Source File(s) 12-6

    Specifying the Destination File Format and Extension 12-8

    Specifying the Destination Location 12-9

    Converting the File 12-10

    Using the Select Bitmap Size Dialog Box 12-11

    Using the CGM Import Filter Dialog Box 12-12

    Using the DRW Import Filter Dialog Box 12-13

    Using the Color Reduction Options Dialog Box 12-13

    Using the Input Data Format Dialog Box 12-14

Quitting Convert 12-15

Chapter 13   Editing Bitmaps Using BitEdit

Valid File Formats 13-2

Starting BitEdit 13-2

The BitEdit Menus 13-4

    The File Menu 13-4

    The Edit Menu 13-4

    The Selection Menu 13-5

    The Options Menu 13-5

The BitEdit Tools 13-6

Opening a Bitmap File 13-7

Setting Preferences 13-8

Using the Editing Tools   13-10
   Changing Background and Foreground Colors   13-10
   Drawing Freehand on a Bitmap   13-12
   Drawing Rectangles, Circles, and Lines on a Bitmap   13-13
   Filling in a Bitmap Area   13-14
   Using the Color Eraser   13-15
   Using the Zoom Control Tool   13-15
   Undoing Your Changes   13-16
Selecting Parts of a Bitmap   13-17
   Using the Selection Tool   13-17
   Using the Select All Command   13-18
   Detaching and Moving a Selected Bitmap Area   13-18
Editing an Image Using Edit Commands   13-20
   Pasting from the Clipboard   13-22
Editing an Image Using Selection Commands   13-23
   Cropping a Bitmap Image   13-24
   Flipping a Selection   13-24
   Rotating a Selection   13-25
Working with a Bitmap Palette   13-26
   Pasting a Palette   13-27
   Reducing Bitmap Colors   13-28
   Reordering a Color Palette   13-29
   Selecting Palette Colors   13-30
   Using Transparent Color   13-30
Resizing a Bitmap   13-33
Creating a New Bitmap File   13-34
Saving Your Changes   13-36
Quitting BitEdit   13-37

Chapter 14   Editing Color Palettes Using PalEdit

About Color Palettes 14-2
Starting PalEdit 14-2
The PalEdit Menus 14-4
    The File Menu 14-4
    The Edit Menu 14-4
    The Palette Menu 14-5
    The Effects Menu 14-6
Using Palette Files 14-6
Setting Preferences 14-8
Changing the Palette View 14-9
Selecting Color Cells 14-10
    Selecting Similar Colors 14-11
    Selecting Unused Palette Colors 14-12
    Selecting Colors from BitEdit 14-12
    Flashing Selected Colors 14-13
Changing Color Definitions 14-13
    Editing Color Cells 14-13
    Adding a Color to a Palette 14-16
    Adjusting Palette Brightness 14-17
    Adjusting Palette Contrast 14-18
    Tinting, Filtering, and Fading a Palette 14-19
Changing Palette Structure 14-23
    Reordering an Entire Palette 14-23
    Moving Individual Cells 14-24
    Deleting Individual Cells 14-25
    Pasting Color Cells 14-26
    Merging Selected Color Cells 14-27
    Cycling Palette Colors 14-27
    Consolidating Colors from BitEdit 14-29
    Creating an Identity Palette 14-29
Saving Palette Files 14-30
Applying a Palette File to a Bitmap 14-31
Quitting PalEdit 14-32

Chapter 15   Editing Waveform Files Using WaveEdit

Valid File Formats   15-1
Starting WaveEdit   15-2
The WaveEdit Menus   15-3
    The File Menu   15-3
    The Edit Menu   15-4
    The Effects Menu   15-5
    The View Menu   15-5
Opening Waveform Files   15-6
    Opening a New Waveform File   15-6
    Opening an Existing Waveform File   15-7
    Opening Multiple WaveEdit Files   15-8
Viewing a Waveform   15-8
    Using the Zoom Scroll Bar   15-9
    Changing the Measurement Scale   15-10
    Viewing Channels of a Stereo Waveform   15-10
Selecting Parts of a Waveform   15-10
    Using a Mouse   15-11
    Using the Select Start and Select Size Spin Boxes   15-11
    Selecting an Entire Waveform   15-12
    Using the Zoom Command   15-12
Editing a Waveform   15-13
Modifying a Waveform   15-14
    Changing Waveform Characteristics   15-14
    Inserting Silence   15-15
    Fading a Selection Up and Down   15-15
    Changing the Amplitude of a Selection   15-16
Undoing Your Changes   15-16
Playing Waveform Files   15-17
Recording Waveform Files   15-17
Saving a Waveform File   15-19
Quitting WaveEdit   15-20

Chapter 16   Editing Files Using FileWalker

Valid File Formats 16-2

Starting FileWalker 16-2

The FileWalker Menus 16-3

    The File Menu 16-3

    The Edit Menu 16-4

    The View Menu 16-4

Opening Files 16-5

Viewing a File 16-7

    Displaying an Unstructured File 16-7

    Displaying a Structured File 16-8

    Displaying Offsets 16-9

    Expanding a File Heading 16-10

    Contracting a File Heading 16-11

    Moving Through a File 16-11

    Getting Information About a File Item 16-12

Editing Files 16-13

    Selecting Data to Edit 16-13

    Editing Data Using the Clipboard 16-14

    Editing a Data Field 16-15

    Inserting a Data Field 16-18

    Inserting a RIFF Chunk 16-19

Saving a File 16-20

Quitting FileWalker 16-21

Chapter 17   Questions and Answers About Preparing Bitmaps, Palettes, and Sound Files

Preparing Bitmaps and Palettes 17-1

Editing Waveform Files 17-10

Index

Part 1
Multimedia Authoring Guide

Part 1, Multimedia Authoring Guide, provides an overview of the concepts and technologies involved in developing multimedia applications for the Windows with Multimedia environment. You'll learn specific details about the data used in a multimedia application, and find out how to make the best use of these resources.

The information in this part is oriented towards developing applications for Windows with Multimedia. However, you will also discover in-depth information about many aspects of the multimedia development process and the issues associated with building a multimedia application.

Part 2, Data Preparation Tools User's Guide, describes the data-preparation tools that are included with the Microsoft Multimedia Development Kit (MDK). It provides an overview of each tool, and describes how to prepare data, such as images and audio, for use in a multimedia application.

Multimedia Authoring Guide

Chapters

1   Introduction

2   Creating a Multimedia Title

3   Managing Data

4   CD-ROM

5   Images

6   Audio

7   MIDI

8   Text

9   Animation

Chapter 1
Introduction

The technology of *Multimedia* blends publishing, entertainment, and computers into a medium for information exchange that expands the potential of all three areas. The Microsoft® Windows™ 3.0 graphical environment with Multimedia Extensions 1.0—commonly referred to as Windows with Multimedia—has brought this technology to the desktop personal computer.

This is a guide for developers who want to create multimedia applications (or *titles*) for Windows with Multimedia. Building a multimedia application involves many people—programmers, writers, artists, musicians, and sound engineers—and therefore requires someone to coordinate the activities of these different professionals into a coherent project team. This role is sometimes known as the *Multimedia Producer*.

This book was written to help multimedia producers and their team members to understand the technologies and issues involved in developing a multimedia application. It contains descriptions of authoring processes along with comments and suggestions about using different hardware and software. Multimedia producers should read the entire book for an overview of the technology involved in building a multimedia application. Team members should read the specific chapters relevant to their area of responsibility (such as Text, Images, or Audio). This book assumes some experience with Microsoft Windows and MS-DOS® personal computers.

This chapter introduces the software and hardware involved with building and using a multimedia title.

Windows with Multimedia

Windows with Multimedia provides the underlying software support for multimedia. It does this by providing several significant enhancements to the standard Windows 3.0 platform:

- Audio support for digital audio and MIDI devices. Device drivers are included that can play disc-resident digital audio and MIDI files in the background while an application is running. This includes support for Compact Disc Digital Audio (CD-DA).

- Standard MIDI instrument patch management services allowing MIDI files authored on different MIDI hardware to play back on the Multimedia PC without modification.

- Media control support through the Media Control Interface (MCI) that can accommodate any media-related device including digital audio devices, scanners, video overlay cards, and videotape players.

- Several new VGA video display drivers, including: a high resolution display driver for 8-bit VGA+ (256-color) display adapters with improved performance and new features; a high resolution display driver to display 256-color bitmaps in 16 shades of gray on a standard 16-color VGA display; and a display driver to show 256-color bitmaps at 320-by-200 resolution.

- A new extensible control panel that allows application developers to add custom control panel applications (also known as *applets*). Also included are new control panel applets that allow users to change display drivers, set up a screen-saver, select sounds to associate with system events, and map MIDI instruments so that externally produced MIDI files will play without modification.

- Support for analog joysticks.

These multimedia extensions to Windows 3.0 provide multimedia developers with a standard system software platform on which to build and deliver their applications. You also need a personal computer able to unleash this power. The Multimedia Personal Computer is the component that makes this possible.

The Multimedia PC

Multimedia PCs are a specific class of PCs that meet or exceed the Multimedia PC specification 1.0 (announced at the Microsoft Multimedia Developer's Conference in November, 1990). The "MPC" trademark indicates that the hardware complies with this specification. The minimum hardware requirements in this specification are listed below. (Your system may differ as various machines use more advanced hardware to provide higher quality sound and performance characteristics.)

CPU
80286 or compatible microprocessor running at 10Mhz

RAM
2 megabytes (MB) of RAM

Magnetic Storage
3.5-inch floppy disk drive, 1.44 MB capacity
30 MB hard drive

Optical Storage
CD-ROM with compact disc digital audio outputs and a data transfer rate of 150 kilobytes (K) per second

Audio
8-bit DAC (digital-analog converter), 22.05 and 11.025 kHz rate
8-bit ADC (analog-digital converter), 11.025 kHz rate, microphone level input
Music synthesizer capable of four or nine instrument synthesis
On-board analog audio mixing capabilities

Video
VGA color graphics adapter (16 or 256 color)

Input
101-key Keyboard
Two button mouse

I/O
MIDI I/O ports
Serial port
Parallel port
Joystick port

A variety of hardware manufacturers provide fully integrated Multimedia PCs with these components already built in, or supply upgrade kits to transform a current 80286 computer into a Multimedia PC. The MPC trademark is one easy way to recognize whether computer hardware or software is compatible with Windows with Multimedia.

Getting Started

You'll need to set up a development environment for creating multimedia titles. This involves acquiring the right software and hardware:

- The Multimedia Development Kit (MDK) is the critical software package you'll need. The MDK includes multimedia extensions to Microsoft Windows, simple data preparation tools for editing/manipulating audio, images, and other data files, and the Multimedia Viewer for building text-based multimedia titles. You should also consider acquiring additional data preparation and development tools as necessary.

- The system you use to build your application should be powerful, based on a 80386 microprocessor with at least 4 MB of RAM and at least an 80 MB hard drive. While you will use the same hardware components for sound, MIDI, and image display as those present in the standard Multimedia PC, all other components should be as high-performance as you can afford.

In addition, each chapter in this book discusses the types of hardware and software needed to prepare the different types of data used in your application.

How This Part is Organized

The rest of this part covers the following topics:

Chapter 2, "Creating a Multimedia Title," describes the authoring process you'll follow to produce your multimedia application.

Chapter 3, "Managing Data," discusses storing and managing the data used in your application.

Chapter 4, "CD-ROM," highlights CD-ROM technology and production issues.

Chapter 5, "Images," describes digital images and their preparation.

Chapter 6, "Audio," explains digital audio technology.

Chapter 7, "MIDI," presents an overview of the Musical Instrument Digital Interface (MIDI) technology.

Chapter 8, "Text," discusses the conversion and preparation of text.

Chapter 9, "Animation," describes authoring issues with animation.

Chapter 2
Creating a Multimedia Title

An electronic document differs substantially from a printed one. Books have existed for centuries and people understand how they look and work. Books have substance and weight and texture. Everyone knows what to expect from books.

A multimedia title exists electronically. It lacks the tactile qualities of print. Simply transferring the internal design of a book to an online medium fails to take advantage of the potential power a computer can offer.

This chapter briefly discusses some of the issues associated with developing a multimedia title. The process of creating a multimedia application usually begins when an idea germinates and one person or a team of people comes up with a marketing rationale and an action plan for producing the product. There are three general rules that apply in every case:

1. Know exactly what you want the product to be

2. Establish what you want your title to contain

3. Prepare the data you'll be using

The purpose of this chapter is to discuss the issues associated with these rules in enough detail so you can develop a specification for your title. This specification should be a full, detailed description of the images, sounds, structure, and user interface features of your product.

Types of Multimedia Titles

The best multimedia applications are interactive. Unlike turning pages in a book, a multimedia application can shift the information focus at the viewer's whim. If the scene presented isn't desirable, the user can choose another. The focus remains the information provided; graphics, audio, and animation help make that information more accessible. When applied creatively, these multimedia capabilities can greatly enhance software applications. The acronym PIECE stands for the five basic areas where multimedia might be successfully applied:

- **Productivity**

- **Information**

- **Entertainment**

- **Creativity**

- **Education**

You can build applications specific to each area, or you can create multimedia presentations with aspects of each. The only limit is your creative application of the technology. The following pages briefly describe each area; the discussions are meant to start you thinking.

Productivity

One major reason that computers swept through the business world was the many applications designed to improve worker productivity. Standard productivity applications include word processors, presentation packages, spreadsheets, and databases. As a multimedia producer for a company that offers these kinds of products, you should consider how Windows with Multimedia and the Multimedia PC could enhance or improve the user's productivity.

For example, a spreadsheet could provide support for such enhancements as voice annotation of specific cells. It could also offer the capability to include photographic images with generated graphics.

Another area that could be enhanced by multimedia is documentation. Tutorials could include graphics, voice, and animated information as well as the standard text and branching mechanisms. The degree of detail within a tutorial could be greatly expanded with the increased amount of storage available on the CD-ROM. For instance, a compiler might include complete source code examples.

Information

Most information products—such as encyclopedias, dictionaries, atlases, and medical references—still come packaged as paper. The massive storage capacity of CD-ROM, coupled with the advanced graphic and audio capabilities of Windows with Multimedia, offers opportunities for innovative information products.

For example, Microsoft now offers Bookshelf for Windows, a complete set of reference resources including *The American Heritage Dictionary*, *Bartlett's Familiar Quotations*, and the *U.S. ZIP Code Directory*. Bookshelf for Windows includes the text for these and other popular reference works, and it also provides animations, audio, and high-quality graphics.

Entertainment

A major reason for the success of personal computers is their potential for fun. Computer games have often stretched the limits of computer hardware and improved user interfaces. Now, with the capabilities available through the Multimedia PC, computer entertainment can take gamers down more exciting and realistic paths than ever before.

The first computer games relied mainly on interactive text and the player's imagination. The second stage offered colorful, interactive graphics. Multimedia games can incorporate live action photos, animation sequences, and sudden bursts of movement and sound. A trip to the bottom of the sea could show schools of fish darting in multiple directions as the hull creaks from increasing water pressure. In maneuvering the ship, the gamer would contend with a vast reservoir of statistics against which every action is measured and responded.

Entertainment comes in many forms beside games. Multimedia creates interesting opportunities for literature. Along with plot and character, authors can now consider appropriate images, animation, and background material. A novel about two lovers during the U.S. Civil War might include historical maps, music from the period, Matthew Brady's photographs, and the text of the Gettysburg Address.

Creativity

One of the ways computers make people more productive is to provide tools that support the creative process. Word processors make writing easier by reducing the drudgery of typing and retyping. Paint and drawing programs enable non-artists to produce elegant illustrations. Better tools let you focus on the act of creation itself.

The Multimedia PC supports many different creative endeavors. The MIDI interface provides a link to music composition. The CD-ROM can store extensive amounts of information with which an artist can work. Huge libraries of generic multimedia objects will emerge from which multimedia producers can choose during development:

- Audio clips (hit songs, classical, jazz, sound effects)

- Clip art (icons, cartoons, figures, and graphs)

- Photos (wire photos, nature scenes, famous people)

- Boilerplate text (quotes, speeches, definitions)

- Typefaces (for word processing and graphic design)

Multimedia PCs can be used to create and deliver desktop presentations for business, education, or even for home viewing. Incorporating the elements of multimedia enhances existing applications and creates entire new genres of tools for creative development.

Education

Multimedia adds a fresh splash of color to the palette of educational alternatives. The strengths of computer-aided instruction—interactivity, personalized instruction, and multiple layers of complexity—can be further enriched through audio, live animation, and music. Opportunities for educational multimedia products exist in several categories:

- *Elementary and Secondary Education.* The compelling nature of multimedia applications offer opportunities for creative instructional materials for youngsters in grades K–12. At lower grade levels, the courseware might resemble interactive games with flashy graphics, animation, and sound effects. At higher grade levels, these properties would still exist, but the information content would increase, taking advantage of the CD-ROM's extensive data storage.

- *Adult Education.* This broad category includes many areas where multimedia applications can better serve to improve learning. For example, many adults want to learn a foreign language. A multimedia application could provide the student the phrase in both the native and foreign tongues, phonetic spelling, and an audio clip of correct pronunciation. Hypertext links could pop up windows with synonyms or related verb tenses.

- *Career-Oriented Self-Paced Instruction.* The increasingly complex requirements of business mandate continuous retraining throughout a career. For example, you could produce a tutorial on giving oral presentations. It could explain the principles of public speaking, and also provide recordings and footage of great speeches. Other windows might display the text of the speech, with annotation to highlight conceptual techniques. An animated slide show could explain the pros and cons of different types of presentation graphics.

The quantity of information available from a CD-ROM fulfills the concept of information browsing. A student could explore the learning environment by strolling from one topic to the next. The gentle voice of a supportive, yet non-intrusive guide, might come along as the student examined an archive of fiction, photographs, and song.

Defining the Title

The first step in developing a multimedia title or application is to define the reason for building the title and describe its potential. The inspiration for a title can happen from a single idea, such as "wouldn't an online tour through the USA be neat?"

Defining a title involves the following processes:

- Identifying the audience

- Designing the structure

- Establishing design standards

Eventually, the product definition should materialize into a high-level product description and business plan. The following pages offer some basic tips on how to design a multimedia title and describe some of the processes you must go through during development.

Identifying the Audience

Understanding the audience is critical to the success of the title, as this definition drives nearly all aspects of the title's design. When you define the audience for your application you should ask yourself such questions as:

- How much do they know about computers?

- What information should the title provide?

- How is the information presented useful?

- How much work is the user willing to do to access this information?

- How often will they need this information?

- When they need information, do they need it immediately, or will they feel they can leisurely browse through the material?

- Are images appropriate? Are sounds and music appropriate?

Asking these and other questions help to focus the discussions associated with the design process. When doing this exercise, try to identify everything possible about the subject, the data resources available, the software tools available for producing it, and the team necessary to produce it.

Now that you know your title's purpose and audience, you can define its structure.

Designing the Title's Structure

Once you decide on the purpose and content of the title, you must determine how to structure this information for the most effective presentation. Remember that a multimedia title differs from a printed text. You aren't limited to a purely sequential, front to back structure—the title should provide an interactive experience to the user. The choices a user makes while viewing a title should directly affect what they see. Incorporate the concept of interactivity into the structure of your title's design.

Once you have discussed and made decisions concerning these issues, you can start working out scripts, storyboards, sample screens, and prototypes. This is also where the real designing occurs. To prototype your application, you can choose from the traditional scripting and design methods, such as copyboard drawings and typed scripts, and from software tools such as Asymetrix ToolBook or the MDK's Multimedia Viewer.

The Contents Topic

One classic navigational landmark within text-oriented multimedia applications is known as the *Contents topic*. The Contents topic serves as the entry point into the title and as a safe haven for users whenever they become lost in information. The sample Viewer application uses the following Contents topic:

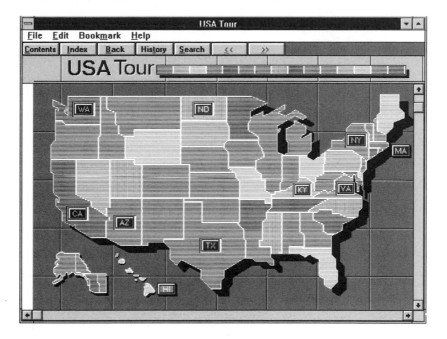

This Contents topic reflects good design. The United States map provides an instant summary of the structure of the title. It offers access to all elements in the title. It clearly distinguishes areas of interest graphically (through buttons with state names). And it presents an attractive opening screen for the title.

The Contents topic sets the tone for all other topics and therefore should establish a consistent and meaningful design that underlies the entire title. It acts as the center of navigation for the title just as a table of contents helps the reader identify the parts of a book.

In many cases, the Contents topic lists all the categories covered in the title and provides a cross-reference jump to each category.

Creating a Hierarchy and Browsing Sequences

Another aspect when structuring text-oriented information to consider is the hierarchy of related topics and how this affects the sequence in which the title presents information. For example, a typical newspaper story works with an underlying pyramid structure. The opening paragraph explains the key issues of who, what, when, where, why, and how. Subsequent paragraphs explain the story in ever-increasing detail, expanding upon the points made in the first paragraph by offering additional related information.

The information in a multimedia title may take the same structural form as this hypothetical news item. You could set up the first level of your topics with the core material, and then offer additional levels through cross-topic jumps to related topic screens. This establishes a hierarchy of information much the same as the pyramid.

In some cases, however, the information represents a continuation of prior screens, and not an additional level of thought. In these situations a *browse sequence* would probably prove beneficial. By establishing linear browse sequences, you tell the viewer that the information contained in a series of topic screens should be read sequentially from start to finish for maximum understanding.

Identifying Cross-Topic Jumps

Most authoring tools can connect related topics through cross-topic jumps. You can choose images or words as jump areas and specify the topics to which those jumps lead. You can place jumps to multiple topics within a single topic.

This power requires a certain amount of thought. A large number of jumps lets the viewer browse through information in a totally random manner. The benefit of this is that the user can access a vast amount of information easily. Cross-topic jumps, however, have some drawbacks:

- Large numbers of jumps can make navigation overwhelmingly complex

- It takes time to test large numbers of jumps to ensure they work correctly

The Multimedia Viewer, and other authoring tools, provide built in navigational aids to help a user re-establish position within the title. Nevertheless, as designer, you should make sure that all jumps you include in a title serve a useful purpose.

Establishing Design Standards

Printed books have a certain look, an underlying graphic design that helps to promote consistency and clarity. It's important to make sure your multimedia titles adhere to a consistent internal design—topic screens look alike, typefaces are consistent, and multimedia elements such as audio, graphics, and animation should integrate cleanly into the overall feel of the title.

Given the large and varied number of text, audio, and graphic resources that could come together in your title, take the time to identify some basic design standards at the beginning of the development process.

You should decide on an overall concept or metaphor for your title. For example, in the Viewer's sample USA Tour, since the basis of the title is information about the United States, the basic metaphor was a map—other visuals in the title build on and reinforce that basic metaphor as they provide information and guidance.

The Design of Topics

As you divide the information in your title into separate topics or screens, you should strive to ensure they maintain a consistent style in terms of written voice, content, and breadth of information.

For example, decide whether you intend to require the user to scroll through the information in a topic, or whether instead you'll limit topics to only the amount of information that can appear in a standard window. This decision affects the design of your title—shorter topics can require a greater number of browse sequences or cross-topic jumps (possibly not a good idea with CD-ROM as this increases the number of times the software has to access the optical disk).

The Use of Fonts

The fonts you choose for your text play an important part in ensuring the readability and aesthetic qualities of a title. Some typefaces are easier to read online than others (for example, some research indicates Sans Serif fonts work better online than Serif fonts). Even though Windows with Multimedia provides flexibility in your choice of fonts, font size, and font colors, inconsistency and poor design in the use of these typefaces can detract from the information content of your title.

The Use of Audio

Audio samples can substantially enhance the usefulness of a multimedia title. You must make sure, however, that any audio used is easy to understand, not too loud or too soft, and of consistent quality with other sound samples used.

Various factors affect audio samples: the number of bits used to store the sample (typically 8 bit or 16 bit), the quality of the equipment used to obtain the sample, and the sampling rate at which the original sound was digitized (11.025 kHz, 22.05 kHz, or 44.1 kHz). The higher the sampling rate, the better the quality. Of course, the better the quality, typically the more disk space required for storage.

If you decide to include audio with your title, make sure you take the time to understand the associated issues and establish some guidelines.

The Use of Images and Animation

Images and animation add tremendous value to any title. The use of graphics and animation can help clarify relatively obscure texts. Good graphics communicate efficiently. If you choose to use graphics with your title, make sure to include their usage into your design standards.

Establish guidelines for all aspects of how your title will display graphics: their placement, whether to use borders, number of colors, size of the graphics, and many other factors.

Establishing a quality design standard before development takes some time, but adherence to professionally developed standards not only makes your title look better, it helps make it easier to use. And easier to market as well.

Preparing the Data Used in a Title

One of the more involved and time-consuming aspects of multimedia product development is gathering all of the text, sound, and image data you plan to use in your product. Animations, images, text, and sound must be digitized from various sources, edited, and eventually converted to the final storage and presentation formats required by Windows with Multimedia.

The cost for data preparation tools, systems, and labor is significant. Digitizing and editing the data for your application are time-consuming and costly aspects of product development. For example, to digitize, convert, touch up, and crop a single image can take from several minutes to an hour. Scripting, recording, mixing, and editing a few minutes of sound can be as demanding. Consequently, you'll want to always be looking for tools and methods that allow you to automate and improve the production process. Your efficiency in this process directly affects the overall cost of development.

One key point to always consider: plan for the future. You should always prepare data for a title with the objective of recycling it within other titles. Spreading the data preparation costs across multiple titles is simply a smart way to maximize your return on investment. Look for ways to use the same information in different products—for instance, a multimedia encyclopedia and a series of educational titles.

Chapters 5, 6, 7, 8, and 9 in this part describe some of the issues associated with preparing five basic types of multimedia data resources—images, audio, MIDI, text, and animation. Each chapter presents an overview of the processes involved.

Caution   Never digitize music from professional recordings, or images from magazines, books, movies, or other recording media if you plan to use these resources in your final product—most are protected by copyright. If you find something that you must have, ask permission to use it or you will be violating copyright law. The "Multimedia Producer's Legal Survival Guide," by Stephen Ian McIntosh, is a good source available on this subject.

Building the Title

When you know what content and features you want your product to have, how you want it to look, and how you want the user to navigate through it, you're ready to decide on the tools and methods you'll use to create it. Multimedia software products can be simplistically divided into two categories:

- Products created using a programming language such as C

- Products created using high-level authoring tools such as Multimedia Viewer

In almost all cases, the authoring method you use imposes certain restrictions on the scope of your design. To design the product, you'll need to know the limitations of the tools you have available. However, to create a truly innovative product, you won't want to box yourself in by these limitations.

Using a Programming Language

The Multimedia Development Kit includes a complete set of functions for building Windows-based multimedia applications. Developing a multimedia title through this approach offers the most flexibility in the design of a title; it also requires the highest level of technical skill.

Should you decide to go this route, obtain the services of experienced Windows programmers. The prerequisite experience for this would be a working knowledge of both the C programming language, and the Windows development environment.

The *Programmer's Reference* and the *Programmer's Workbook* describe in detail the use and content of the application programming interface (API) included with the Multimedia Extensions to Windows.

Using a Multimedia Authoring Tool

Tool-built titles are created using a specialized tool, or set of authoring tools, that provide the basic building blocks and framework for creating an application. These tools can be used by non-programmers, though some programming knowledge generally helps.

Authoring tools are typically best suited for content-rich applications—those loaded with text, images, and sound. Because they are specialized for data delivery, they are often not as flexible or efficient as programming languages. Their benefits lie in their ease of use, fast development cycles, predictable characteristics, and reliability.

The MDK includes the Multimedia Viewer authoring tool. Viewer was designed primarily to develop mainly text-based titles, however, it does support images, animation, and audio. Viewer requires Microsoft Word for Windows to create the source files for the title. You then use these source files to build a title for display with the Viewer runtime engine.

The *Multimedia Viewer Developer's Guide* describes the capabilities of the Multimedia Viewer and explains how to use it to build multimedia titles.

Summary

This chapter explained some of the issues connected with creating a multimedia title. It described some of the following topics associated with designing a title:

- Identifying its purpose and audience
- Defining its content (text, graphics, and audio/visual)
- Deciding on its overall structure
- Establishing standards for its internal design
- Preparing the data it uses
- Building the title

You should now have a general understanding of what to do once you decide to create a title. With a design in hand, you can start to put the pieces of your title together.

Chapter 3
Managing Data

Introducing multimedia data resources creates additional challenges for application developers. A key issue in creating multimedia titles is managing the many data elements—text files, audio files, bitmaps, and animations—used within a title. Multimedia data resources are expensive in many ways:

- Copyright costs for text, images, audio, and animation

- Workhour costs of preparing the resources—converting from analog sources, translating different file formats, editing the resource, and the time involved in each step

- Storage costs since audio, images, and animations require lots of disk storage

Effectively managing the data used to build a title can help control the costs of multimedia application development. Data management is a key part of creating multimedia applications, but it isn't really a step in the process—it underlies the process. You'll want a data management system in place when you start collecting your first set of images and sounds.

This chapter introduces some of the concepts and issues you should consider when figuring how to manage the data used in your multimedia title.

The Data Management Environment

You'll need to establish a hardware/software environment to handle the storage, transfer, and management of the data used in creating a multimedia title. There is no one right way to set up this environment—many different hardware and software solutions are available and new solutions arrive on the market almost daily. This section simply discusses some of the issues involved in setting up such an environment and offers some guidelines you can use when building yours.

Storing Data

Storage is a major consideration. Data resources such as images, audio, and animation consume awe-inspiring amounts of disk space. As you set up a multimedia development system, ponder your data storage and transfer requirements. Once you start working on multimedia applications, you will quickly learn that the resources that make a title compelling also require a lot of storage.

- Audio digitized at 22.05 kHz eats up storage at about 1.3 MB per minute.

- Full screen, 256-color images can easily require 200-300K each.

Since you'll want to capture original data to preserve maximum fidelity, you will probably be storing 16-bit audio files at 22.05 or 44.1 kHz, and 24-bit images. You can convert to lower quality levels for delivery with your title, and avoid having to recapture the data when more powerful equipment appears in the future. Recognize, however, that higher quality data typically requires substantial storage.

When you set up your development system, you face many data storage options. There are conventional hard disks of various types and capacities; removable hard disks; tape drives; and optical media, including WORM (Write Once, Read Many) drives and erasable optical drives. Each type of storage device has advantages and disadvantages. Each can play specific role as storage media:

- *Working Media*. Used during working hours to process data.

- *Archival Media*. Used for the long-term storage of images, audio, etc., in the highest resolution possible (24-bit images, 44.1 kHz audio).

- *Backup Media*. Used for day-to-day backup of data.

Working Media: Hard Disks

Your computer's hard disk is your active working storage area. It has to have enough capacity to hold your development software and current data resources. It also has to be fast enough for efficient use.

Two main factors determine the performance of a hard drive: *average access time* and *transfer speed*.

■ Average access time, measured in milliseconds (msec), is how long it takes the drive to find the data the computer has requested. A reasonable range for average access time is 10 to 28 msec, with larger hard disks usually being faster.

■ Transfer rate is the speed at which the drive can move data in and out of the computer. This is really a critical factor when dealing with large files, animation, or audio. Transfer rate is typically measured in bytes per second. A fast hard disk will transfer data at about 2 MB/sec; a slow hard disk can be as low as 40K per second.

Hard disks are available in sizes from 20 MB to 1.2 gigabyte. (One gigabyte (GB) equals one billion bytes.) You will probably want to consider 150 MB as a minimum size. Although the development process can be distributed among several computers, at least one station should have a hard disk able to hold the assembled application and any associated software.

Archival Media: Optical Discs

The critical elements for archival media are storage space, long-term viability, and cost. Optical media, specifically WORM discs, are excellent choices for this purpose.

The basic distinction between types of optical drives is whether you can only read data from it (CD-ROM), write data one time and then read it as many times as you want (WORM), or write and read to it as you would to a hard disk (erasable or rewritable). Each format has strong points: CD-ROM is a great distribution medium, WORM is good for archiving data, and erasable optical (which is often also removable) is ideal in a development system and for transferring data between computers.

Erasable optical drives usually have a slower access time than magnetic drives; typically ranging from 35 to 180 msec. The transfer rate, however, is quite often comparable. Removable cartridges for erasable optical drives extend in size up to about 600 MB.

Backup Media: Tape Drives

For daily backup you want a highly reusable media. One that offers adequate storage and retrieval capabilities, and also provides reasonable performance at low costs. Magnetic tape has long served this need.

There is probably more computer data stored on 9-track magnetic tape than on any other medium, and it has long been the standard medium for transferring information around the country—for example, to CD-ROM mastering plants. But it is certainly not a fast or convenient method of getting to your information. And 9-track tapes typically only hold between 30 MB to 80 MB of data.

New developments in magnetic tape technology, however, allow it to remain viable as a storage, transfer, or backup medium. New formats have come out that are smaller, faster, and store more data. One excellent format for digital back-up is (Digital Audio Tape). Various implementations of this format store from 1.2 to almost 3 GB of data and have an average access time of less than a minute, or sometimes a lot less. These drives aren't cheap, but the price is dropping.

DAT is also an ideal format for recording high-quality audio. With its high storage capacity and excellent fidelity, it can hold almost 4 hours of audio digitized at a 44.1 kHz sample rate with 16 bits per sample.

There are a variety of tape drives filling the gap between 9-track and DAT. These range in capacity from about 20 MB to 120 MB and are relatively cheap and slow.

Connecting Storage Devices

Simply obtaining a single massive storage device isn't necessarily the right solution for you. In many cases, you'll want to have the files distributed throughout your site on different types of devices. The exact details of resource flow will have to be determined for each site.

For example, you might perform all image collection, registration, and editing functions on a local workgroup of personal computers. Other PC workgroups could be dedicated to audio enhancement and text preparation. The central fileserver would only come into use after the resources have been prepared for final incorporation into the application.

Connecting these different types of storage devices to the different computers used at your site can be a complicated process, as various hardware interfaces exist. A SCSI interface is probably the best interface choice for a variety of reasons.

SCSI (pronounced "scuzzy") stands for Small Computer Systems Interface. The power of this interface lies in its versatility and expandability. A single SCSI interface card lets you attach up to seven devices to a computer—such as hard disks, tape drives, CD-ROM drives, and scanners. And it will typically move information between them at a higher rate than any other interface.

Note, however, that all SCSI interfaces aren't 100% compatible. If you decide to base your development system on a SCSI interface, make sure you purchase your equipment from a dealer who either knows the subject or is willing to let you experiment and take back what doesn't integrate properly.

Transferring Data

Since it is likely that you'll be developing your multimedia titles using a distributed workgroup of different computers, you'll have to choose a method for transferring information between these computers. This used to be a considerable problem, given that most sites have a hodgepodge of different computers of various incompatible operating systems.

Fortunately, it is now relatively easy to pass information back and forth between computers with different operating systems and hardware architectures. There are three basic ways to move files between computers:

- Removable media

- File-transfer software across a serial port

- Local area network

All three methods can be used to transfer information between different personal computers. Each method has its pros and cons, but generally you will find that speed and efficiency are directly proportional to cost. The following sections discuss each method.

Removable Media

One time-honored traditional way to move information between computers was to transfer the data to a floppy disk and running down the hall to the other machine—often referred to as "sneaker net." When floppy disks only held 360K of data, this wasn't extremely efficient. But with the increasing availability of high-capacity removable media, this approach has become practical in many situations.

Removable media is available in capacities ranging from 360K floppies to 600 MB erasable optical disks. The most practical mid-range entry is the 44 MB removable hard disk, usually marketed under a variety of brand names. Although removable media is not as convenient as a local area network (LAN), it can be an economical alternative in a small operation, particularly if you install a SCSI card in your PCs and simply move the drive between machines.

But if you want to move big chunks of data between different types of computers, and don't want to use a LAN, you should combine your mass storage needs with your data transfer needs and get one of the high-capacity removable media drives previously described.

Serial Port

Possibly the least expensive method of moving files between computers that sit fairly close together is to run a cable between their serial ports and use specialized communications software. This method will transfer files too large to fit on a floppy disk, and can be fast enough to satisfy small production needs. However, it is difficult to connect more than two computers this way.

Local Area Network

Networks are probably the most effective way to transfer files in a production environment. They are also expensive, potentially more complicated than the other methods, and require setup, training and maintenance. However, if you are serious about creating an efficient production environment, invest in a network.

Several network systems, such as Microsoft LAN Manager, are available to connect PCs with other types of computers. They allow any machine to access the storage devices attached to any other machine to open or transfer files. Since you will probably use a distributed system of several machines to produce and manage your data, be sure you have a network up to the task.

Since the size of multimedia data resources can grow quite large, multimedia developers must identify the most logical points in the network to place the data resources. For example, clip art images belong on a fileserver close to those individuals that work with images. Audio waveform files belong next to the audio experts. Recent developments in technology allow for the creation of distributed databases, where individual servers contain only that portion of the database necessary to control the type of data for which they are responsible.

The subject of deciding which network to purchase, assembling the network, and managing the flow and storage of information on the network could easily fill several massive books. Issues such as backup, security, and access times across the net must be considered and addressed during design. Look for experienced, professional help before making any decisions regarding the acquisition, design, and maintenance of a network.

Managing Your Library of Data Resources

One major advancement for software development during the 1980s was the notion of re-usable code. Development groups made every attempt to share tools, source code, and development libraries whenever possible to reduce the need to reinvent the wheel for each new product cycle. This will accelerate during the 1990s, but a new requirement will arrive: re-usable resources.

Multimedia developers will begin developing libraries of data resources. Such libraries become extremely valuable for vendors who produce many different products and progress through multiple iterations of a product's life cycle. The ability to coordinate and share expensive resources among different product groups can increase overall efficiency and reduce costs.

The type of library you build and the method in which you implement it depends on the needs and workflow at your site. The following sections discuss some of the issues associated with creating and managing such a library:

- Define a data management methodology

- Collect and register resources

- Identify and select specific resources

- Edit and update specific resources

- Archive or purge resources

Define a Data Management Methodology

Before you start working with the various data resources, you should devise and put into place your strategy for managing them. Without a strategy in place, you may find yourself quickly overwhelmed by the large volume of resources necessary to build a full-featured multimedia title.

There are many different ways to manage this data. You should consider incorporating either or both of the following approaches:

- Using a Database Management System (DBMS)

- Establishing a specific logical directory structure

Using a Database Management System

A DBMS enables you to control quantities of resources that could number in the tens of thousands for single applications, and far more in environments where multiple applications are being developed.

A DBMS records both the existence of resources and the relationships between different resources. You can run reports showing the type, number, and status of the different resources. Such reports could identify usage patterns (for instance, you don't use any images from a certain photographer). As another example, by including royalty/copyright information with data resource records, you could derive the royalty costs associated with development.

When deciding which DBMS to acquire, make sure to check whether it has the following capabilities:

- Able to handle multimedia resources

- Compatible with standard networks

- Supports the relational database model

- Provides a forms utility to support easy development of front end screens

- Works under a standard environment (such as MS-DOS or Windows)

- Provides adequate backup and purge capabilities

- Includes an easy to use report generator

- Configurable to meet different requirements

The reason a DBMS is so useful is its ability to consolidate and report information. As producer, you will have your own specific areas of interest in managing the project. For example, you may want to know the total cost of the copyrights used, the distribution of images vs. text vs. audio, or the number of total images scanned vs. the number of images actually used.

This and other types of information can be recorded in the database and made available both during and after a development project. A good DBMS should provide the configuration and reporting tools necessary to let you obtain and distribute the types of information most important to you.

Setting Up an Appropriate Directory Structure

Another useful tactic to consider when establishing your development environment is to create a directory structure that supports your data management system. For example, if you're using Multimedia Viewer to create a title, you may want to set up a structure that divides all the different source files and data resource files into separate directories. Such a structure appears below:

\Viewer contains all necessary directories and files to build and run a Viewer title

\Viewer\title contains the directories and files relevant to a specific title, such as the project file and the final title itself.

\Viewer\title\dib contains the 256-color image files for a title

\Viewer\title\bmp contains the 16-color image files for a title

\Viewer\title\wav contains the audio files for a title

Viewer\title\mmm contains the MacroMind Director® animation files for a title

\Viewer\title\rtf contains the source text files for a title

Many other logical and equally useful structures could exist. If you're using a network, make sure to decide how to share information between workstations. The effectiveness of setting up such a logical structure depends on how easily it allows you to find and access specific resources.

Collect and Register Resources

You can gather data resources from many sources. You can get images from clip art, scanned photographs, or original computer artwork. Audio can be created, copied, or taken from analog/digital recordings. And tremendous volumes of text exist in multiple formats. There's no shortage of available resources.

The problem is sorting out what you need from what you don't. Using a DBMS to register resources as they're collected can be extremely helpful.

You should design your database to ensure it contains the information about each resource you want to record. Details associated with each record may depend on the type of resource registered. For example, the database record for an audio resource may include whether it's been recorded at 22.05 kHz or at 44.1 kHz. The database record for an image resource might instead include the number of bits used for the image depth.

Another area helped by the use of a DBMS is tracking data resources built from parts of several different resources. This situation will not be uncommon. Your database design should let you register the new resource into the database. For example, say you register an image showing all U.S. presidents. You then use an image editing package to pull out all presidents elected during the twentieth century. You now have a new image to enter in the database. You may want your database to identify the relationship between the original image and its derivative image.

Identify and Select Specific Resources

Associating a database record with each resource can help support the creative process. By pulling information together in different ways, a designer can examine multiple potential creative avenues before coding and implementation.

For example, say you want to put together an application about whales. Instead of having to remember the filenames for everything relevant to whales, you can instead use a database query to identify resource records that relate to whales, the ocean, and sailing. The database query could then collect all the resources that match these characteristics. Such resources might include pictures of whales, audio clips of whale songs, and text references to articles about whaling.

Edit Resources and Update database

The MDK provides various editors to view and enhance different data resources. Each time you change a resource, you should record the time and type of changes made.

For example, PalEdit lets you create a merged palette for use with several images displayed simultaneously. You could use the database to identify which images share that common palette. Later on, when you incorporate the images into the application, the database identifies that the images share a common palette.

Another use for the database is when you have several different resource types that belong together. For instance, you might want to link a picture of a sperm whale with the sound of waves crashing against a beach. Your database should let you identify which data resources belong together, greatly simplifying the final act of linking them into the controlling application.

Purging Unnecessary Resources

Finally, after you've finished your title, the time comes to decide what to do with the resource files used during development. You can either archive the files for later use, or you can purge them entirely. Both archive and purge processes are critical to effective data management.

Summary

This chapter discussed in broad terms some of the concepts associated with managing the large quantities of data involved in developing a multimedia title. As the project manager, you should be aware of these issues and enlist the aid of professionals before deciding on a specific approach.

Chapter 4
CD-ROM

You can often trace an industry to a single invention. Publishing started with the printing press; Recording started with the phonograph; Motion Pictures began with the movie camera. The heart of the Multimedia PC is its CD-ROM drive. Every Multimedia PC has a CD-ROM drive, which enables it to deliver large scale, content-rich titles quite easily.

CD-ROM stands for Compact Disc-Read Only Memory. The information used by a multimedia application is stored on a compact disc identical in size and appearance to an audio CD. You can only read data from a CD-ROM disc; you can't write information to it. The information contained on a CD-ROM is defined before the disc is manufactured. Once created, the CD-ROM disc remains unalterable for the rest of its existence.

This chapter discusses the following topics:

- A brief discussion of CD-ROM technology

- How CD-ROM technology should factor into title design

- The process of publishing a title on a CD-ROM

Computers without a CD-ROM drive—even though they may provide marvelous technical capabilities—are limited to the reduced storage available with floppy disks, or to the expensive option of removable magnetic media. CD-ROM is cheap, it holds lots of information, and it is easy to distribute. CD-ROM makes the Multimedia PC an excellent platform for the delivery of multimedia titles.

This discussion is meant to provide an overview. For more detailed information, read through the CD-ROM series of books published by Microsoft Press®.

What is CD-ROM?

CD-ROM uses the same basic technology as the audio CD with which you're already familiar. An audio CD contains music translated from analog into digital information and pressed onto a plastic disk as a sequence of pits and level areas. A laser beam from the CD player scans the CD surface and translates this information into digital data. This data is converted back to an analog waveform and then amplified. Eventually, beautiful music comes out your speakers.

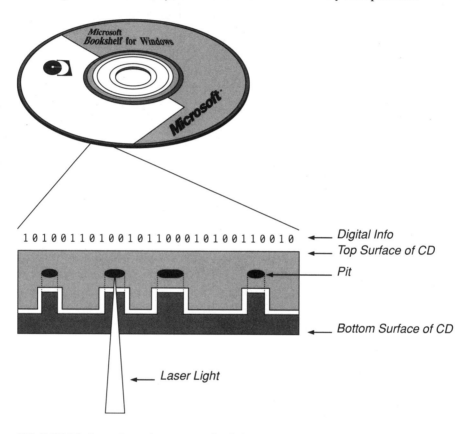

CD-ROM is based on the same principle. But along with audio, it can also hold other types of digital information, such as text, graphics, and animation—the data types that make a multimedia title special.

Factors to Consider When Designing for CD-ROM

Once you decide to build a CD-ROM based title, you need to consider how certain capabilities of CD-ROM affect your title's design. For example, since a CD-ROM is Read-Only, the user of a title will never be able to write anything directly to the disc. If your application requires information from the user be stored, you'll have to establish a file or files on the hard disk for this purpose.

Here are some other factors you should think about during design:

- Naming and locating data files

- Storage capacity

- Data transfer rate

- Average seek time

Naming and Locating Data Files

The CD-ROM standards prohibit the use of punctuation (such as periods or hyphens) or lower-case letters as either directory names or filenames. The only characters allowed for CD-ROM are A-Z, 0-9, and the underscore (_). For example, the filenames FILEONE.TXT and FILE_ONE.TXT are OK, but FILE-ONE.TXT and FILE-1.TXT won't work.

Also, when laying out the file and directory structure of your title on the disc, make sure to limit the number of files in a directory. If you have a large number of files in a directory, this can significantly increase the time necessary to open a file.

Storage Capacity

A single CD-ROM disc can hold up to 680 MB of information. You could conceivably store 150,000 printed pages or about 250 large books on one disc. This amount of storage seems almost limitless compared to the 40–100 MB hard drives currently popular.

This isn't quite true. Even though ASCII text requires relatively minimal storage, a full-featured multimedia title probably includes not just text but animations, audio sequences, and full-color images—all of which require substantial storage.

So don't fool yourself in thinking that CD-ROM offers a panacea to all storage restrictions. If you plan for your title to be more than just text, you better also plan how to best use the space on your disc. Images, audio, and animations will quickly take over the space available.

Data Transfer Rate

A key issue to always consider when designing a title is the rate at which data transfers from the CD-ROM to your computer. The Multimedia PC standard establishes a minimum transfer rate of 150K per second. That doesn't mean much until you consider the numbers involved with multimedia data.

An uncompressed 256-color, full screen image (640 by 480 pixels) is about 300K in size. Transferring this image from the CD-ROM to the computer at 150K per second takes about 2 seconds—and this doesn't include any seek time or processing time by Windows to display the image.

Compression and read-ahead techniques can reduce the time involved, but the issue remains intact: you have to factor transfer rate into your product design. You might decide to use smaller images with fewer colors. Or you could transfer large images or audio while text is being displayed for the user to read. There are many different ways to work around this issue, but you need to consider them during design.

Seek Time

Another issue associated with CD-ROM drives is the time it takes to find what you want to read from the disc. This is known as *seek time*. The Multimedia PC standard states that the average seek time must be 1 second or less. Remember, this is time added to the time required to transfer the data. Your objective when designing a title, regardless of the authoring method used, is to reduce the number of seeks the drive has to make to access your data.

One way to do this is to have your program retrieve commonly used information on its first seek to the disc—for example, an index to all the text in your title—and then write that information in a temporary file on the hard disk. This temporary file is known as a *cache*. Since hard disks have faster access times than CD-ROM drives, the program would look in the cache rather than waste time performing another seek to the CD.

Putting Your Title on CD-ROM

You have gathered your data—text, images, audio, animations, and so on—and built your application. Now you want to put it on a CD-ROM for distribution. The process of turning an application and its associated files into a CD-ROM disc loosely divides into the following stages:

- Premastering

- Final Testing

- Mastering and Replication

These stages often merge and overlap. Premastering, testing, mastering, and low-quantity replication are activities you can perform in-house if you want to invest the time and effort. Large-scale replication, however, which requires an enormous capital investment, will probably be done by a company that specializes in this service, such as 3M.

Premastering

Premastering is the stage of production in which the data is organized as it will be on the final CD-ROM disc. The primary activity is building the logical structure that allows your application to locate and retrieve data from the disc. Premastering involves the following steps:

- Physically interleave audio and images as required by your application

- Build the logical structure required by the file system/operating system

- Build the final disc image

- Block the data to mastering facility requirements

- Store the data on a medium acceptable to the mastering facility

Note Windows with Multimedia doesn't currently directly support interleaving data (such as audio and images) on a disc. You can, however, use interleaving if your application requires it for performance reasons and can handle the de-interleaving. If interleaving is required, it is important that the facility premastering your disc understands and can accommodate your application's interleave format.

If you decide to do your own CD-ROM premastering, the equipment required can cost $40,000 or more. Companies such as 3M sell premastering systems to produce an exact disc image of your data. This image can be stored on optical disc, DAT, or 9-track tape, and sent off to a mastering plant for final production.

If you don't want to invest in the equipment, many companies are available to do the work for you. Contact them directly for information on the range of services they offer, the cost, and the preferred transfer medium—usually 9-track tape, DAT, or some form of optical media such as WORM (Write Once, Read Many).

Final Testing

Testing is an ongoing process. By the time you reach the premastering stage you should be positive that your text is flawless, the images and sounds look and sound perfect, and the overall application is just as you want it. Performance testing is particularly important in multimedia applications, especially where you load images and sounds—perhaps even with some degree of synchronization.

There are two main ways to test the performance of your application: you can press a disc and run it, or you can run the application in a simulated CD-ROM environment. Both methods have their advantages. Some premastering systems offer you a choice. For a nominal fee they will create a *one-off* disc for you to test until you are totally satisfied. If you have extensive testing to do, this is a good approach as it won't tie up a lot of expensive equipment at a high hourly rate.

Premastering systems can often simulate a CD-ROM environment by storing the data on a large hard disk that has had its access time and transfer rate reconfigured to simulate that of a CD-ROM. The advantage of simulation is that you can usually do some fine-tuning. If you find a problem area, you can make corrections and repeat the test.

Mastering and Replication

Mastering and replication is a mechanical process, and if you deal with an established facility they have probably done it thousands of times. Very few errors creep in at this point. If your disc doesn't work, it is likely because there was something wrong with the data or format sent in. The mastering steps include:

- Verifying that the tape is readable

- Adding synchronization data, header data, error detection codes (EDC), and error correction codes (ECC)

- Writing data to magnetic disc

- Creating a glass master

- Creating a metal stamper

- Replicating the discs

You don't need to understand all the details of this process. You do, however, need to know exactly what the mastering facility expects to receive. Work with their representatives to ensure you provide the data in the proper format.

The cost of mastering and replication can also include the printing of a simple label on the disc, and the insertion of the disc and printed material into a jewel box. You must supply the printed material and the film for the label, usually several days before supplying the data to be mastered.

Chapter 5
Images

The word multimedia naturally implies graphics—photographs, drawings, animation—that add variety and life to the application. This chapter discusses several key items about preparing and using images in multimedia applications:

- It introduces digital image technology

- It identifies alternative ways to acquire images for multimedia titles

- It describes software and hardware components for image acquisition and preparation

- It provides a brief description of the image capture and preparation process

The process of transforming an image into a form that can be displayed in a multimedia application requires both ingenuity and a working knowledge of the available tools. This chapter presents an overview of the technology and the issues involved.

An Introduction to Digital Images Technology

Mankind has produced images for thousands of years. Images have been produced with such materials as paint, ink, and chalk and transferred onto such media as canvas, paper, or stone. The development of photography in the early 1800s provided the means to capture reality permanently on paper. Today's technology can now store and display images electronically.

Types of Digital Images

Images and computers were for many years totally separate. Over the last decade, however, a variety of different digital imaging technologies and tools have evolved. Such systems can create and display graphics comparable to anything previously prepared by hand. It's this capability that makes the use of images in a multimedia title both feasible and necessary.

The images used in a multimedia application will either be *bitmaps* or *vector graphics*. Which format you use depends on the needs of your application. You'll probably combine both types of images in any multimedia titles you create. The next few sections describe some characteristics of bitmap and vector graphics.

What is a Vector Graphic?

Vector graphics are stored as a set of instructions. These instructions describe the dimension and shape of every line, circle, arc, or rectangle that makes up a drawing. When an image displays, software reads these instructions and converts them to shapes and colors to display on the screen.

The following illustration shows an example of a vector graphic:

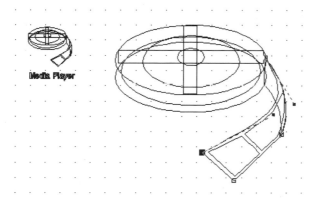

The programs used to create vector graphics are often called *Draw* programs, as they require you to create the image by drawing lines, circles, and other geometric shapes. Since vector graphics images are built from lines, arcs and circles, they can't duplicate the same painted or photographic effects as bitmapped images. Vector graphics are most commonly used for line drawings, newspaper-style clip art, and architectural drawings.

The main advantage to vector graphics images is that you can manipulate each piece of the image separately. You can move the individual objects around on the screen, and you can shrink, enlarge, rotate or twist them without introducing the distortion that often occurs when doing the same thing to bitmaps. Vector graphic objects also maintain their unique identities when overlaying other objects.

The main disadvantage of vector graphics is that as the images get more and more complicated, they take the computer longer to render. Developers often create complex images as vector graphics, then convert them to bitmaps for use in an application.

Many Windows 3.0 Draw programs now store images in the Windows metafile format. Windows automatically knows how to display graphics files stored as Windows metafiles. For other formats you will either have to convert them to metafiles or provide your own software to display them.

What is a Bitmap?

Bitmapped Images (or *bitmaps*) are composed of a set of bits in computer memory that define the color and intensity of each pixel in an image. Bitmaps are typically used to reproduce images that contain lots of detail, shading, and color. Photographs, film negatives, and other illustrations are commonly stored as bitmaps. The following example shows how a bitmap is formed.

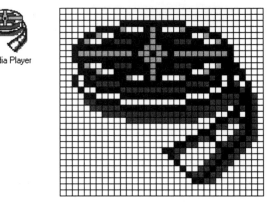

Media Player

You can create bitmaps by using paint software, by scanning photographs or flat art using a color scanner, or by digitizing video frames using a video camera and frame grabbing equipment.

The software tools used to create bitmaps are often called *Paint* programs, as they require you to build the image by painting individual pixels a specific color. The standard bitmap format used by Windows is the Device Independent Bitmap format (DIB). Generally, you'll create the images in some other industry standard format (such as PCX) and then convert them to DIB for incorporation into your application.

Bitmap images often display more quickly than complex vector graphic images. Bitmaps can load directly into memory for display, eliminating the time needed by a rendering engine to build a vector graphic image.

Bitmaps, however, require more disk space than vector graphics, since bitmaps have to specify information about each pixel displayed on the screen.

Using bitmaps can also cause your application to reach limitations of the PC display system, unless you recognize the factors associated with Resolution, Image Depth, and File Size.

Resolution

Several kinds of resolution can affect bitmap quality: screen resolution, image resolution, and pixel resolution. You should understand the differences between all three when working with bitmap images.

Screen resolution is the maximum image area of the computer screen, expressed in horizontal and vertical pixels, for a particular video mode. The standard video mode for the Multimedia PC is 640 pixels by 480 pixels. You'll have to consider screen resolution when establishing a target image size for a scanned photograph.

Image resolution is the size of the digitized image expressed in horizontal and vertical pixels. The image resolution can differ substantially from the screen resolution. For example, say you display a 320-by-240 pixel image on a 640-by-480 pixel display. In this case, the image size is one-half the screen resolution, so the digitized image only fills one-half of the screen. When the image size and screen resolution are identical, the image fills the screen. When the image size is larger than the screen resolution, the screen can display only a portion of the image—requiring the display software to support scrolling to see other portions of the image.

Pixel resolution can become a factor when you move images between different graphic display modes or computer hardware. Pixel resolution refers to the ratio of a pixel's width to its height (also known as the pixel's *aspect ratio*). This can cause unexpected distortions in an image that's transferred between machines with different pixel resolutions. For example, if you capture an image on a device that uses rectangular pixels with an aspect ratio of 1:2, and later display it on a device that uses square pixels with an aspect ratio of 1:1, the image will be distorted. Fortunately, pixel resolution inconsistencies don't occur frequently as most displays use square pixels with an aspect ratio of 1:1. Also, most capture devices let you adjust the pixel aspect ratio for your system.

Image Depth

A second limit involves the maximum number of colors used in a bitmap. Each pixel on the screen can have one or more bits of color information attached to it. The number of bits associated with each pixel in a bitmap is known as the *image depth*. Using one color bit per pixel in a bitmap allows the pixel to be either on or off—producing a monochrome image. Using four color bits per pixel allows the bitmap to support 16 different colors; and using eight color bits per pixel allows the bitmap to support 256 colors.

Note   A bitmap that uses one color bit per pixel does not necessarily display images in just black or white; it just limits the image to using two hues or colors.

Simple drawings and cartoons can get by with just 16 colors. Natural images, however, normally require at least 256 colors. Some software packages can now create 24-bit bitmaps that contain 16 million different colors.

As the tones in the image are sampled to create a bitmap, a color palette—a table of distinct color values—is also created. Each color in a palette is identified by components of the colors red, green, and blue (RGB). The digitizing software assigns an entry in this palette to each pixel in the bitmap. The number of colors in the palette depends on the image depth.

A Multimedia PC equipped with a standard VGA display can support 16 colors in 640 by 480 resolution mode, or 256 colors in 320 by 200 resolution mode. A Multimedia PC equipped with an enhanced VGA display can support 256 colors in 640 by 480 resolution mode.

This disparity of quality creates somewhat of a dilemma—if you want to develop your applications for the broadest market, you can use 16-color (4-bit) bitmaps. However, Windows with Multimedia automatically maps each color to the closest fit when displaying 8-bit images on 4-bit displays. Two 4-bit display drivers included with the system software can yield good results with this 8-to-4 bit mapping:

- The 16-color grayscale driver works with a fixed palette; results are good but color is lost since the image appears in tones of grey, black, and white. You can suggest that customers with 4-bit systems use the grayscale display driver.

- The palettized VGA driver supports custom color palettes; results are good if the optimal palette is used. You can include a custom palette giving good results displaying 8-bit images on 4-bit displays.

A color enhancement called *dithering* can also improve the appearance of bitmaps, whether they're monochrome, 16-color, or 256-color. Dithering is a technique for representing an image using fewer colors than it originally had. Using a subset of the colors defined for a bitmap, dithering varies the grouping of pixels to best re-create the effect of the colors lost. A good dithering method can create the illusion of having additional colors in a bitmap. You can create dithered 4-bit versions of your 8-bit images with BitEdit.

If you want your applications to have the greatest allure, use 256-color (8-bit) bitmaps. To guarantee you cover all bases, include both 4-bit and 8-bit images and have your application identify the display capabilities so it knows which to use. The MDK provides the BitEdit and PalEdit tools for use with bitmaps and their color palettes. Use BitEdit to modify and enhance the bitmap image itself. Use PalEdit to display and modify a bitmap's associated color palette.

Image File Size

The limitation associated with bitmap file size is the transfer time needed to find and copy an image file from a CD to computer memory (RAM) and display it on the screen. Note that this often must happen simultaneously with other events (such as playing music or responding to keystrokes). You have to take image size into account during the design of your title.

Here's why. It takes a full screen, 256-color image 2 seconds to transfer from the CD to the screen. A full-screen, 16-color bitmap requires at least 1 second of transfer time. You need to consider both the seek time and the transfer time for an image when you define the context in which the image will display. For example, to make the time less noticeable, you can pre-load images into memory while something else is happening (for example, while the user reads text).

The size of the bitmap file directly relates to the number of bits in the image. The following formula shows how to calculate the storage needed for a bitmap:

```
Size in bytes = (Height x Width x ColorDepth) / 8
```

Height is the number of pixels displayed vertically
Width is the number of pixels displayed horizontally
ColorDepth is the number of bits of color information stored per pixel

Say you have an full screen bitmap at 1 bit per pixel (black and white only). The display has horizontal resolution of 640 pixels and a vertical resolution of 480 pixels.

Size = (640 pixels x 480 pixels x 1-bit) / 8 = 38,400 bytes

This number represents the storage required for uncompressed images. Scan an identical 8-bit color image, the size substantially increases:

(640 pixels x 480 pixels x 8-bit) / 8 = 307,200 bytes

Obviously, the easiest way to make an image appear quickly is to reduce its size. You can do this by reducing the width/height of your images, or by using images with a lower image depth value. Data compression techniques, such as Run-Length Encoding (RLE), can also be used to reduce the image size.

Acquiring Images

You have a lot of flexibility in how you acquire images for your multimedia titles. Alternatives range from purchasing images from an image bank or professional photographer to capturing images yourself. Costs, image quality, and licensing/copyright issues can affect your final decision. The following methods identify four common alternatives:

- Purchasing—buying digital images

- Creating—creating electronic images using specialized software

- Scanning—digitizing photographs or flat art using a color scanner

- Digitizing Video—digitizing video frames using a camera and frame-grabber

Purchasing Images

Digital image libraries are becoming quite popular. The quality, variety, and resolution of computer-generated and digitized or scanned images are going up as fast as the price is going down.

Note   Think twice before digitizing images from magazines, books or television—most of them are copyrighted. If you find some images that you can't do without, ask permission to use them or you will be violating copyright law. The best places to start are the public relations or marketing departments of the companies claiming copyright ownership. Plan ahead as it can take several months to obtain permission.

Creating Original Art

If you plan to become seriously involved in electronic multimedia publishing, acquire the skills in-house for creating images from scratch using paint programs. Finding qualified electronic artists is the most efficient and economical way to create your artwork. Most artists given an electronic stylus and graphics tablet have little trouble learning paint programs.

When you use a paint program to create artwork, you have access to many electronic tools equivalent to those found in an artist's workshop, such as airbrushes and paintbrushes. Paint programs also support smearing, mixing colors, rotating shapes, editing pixels, and many other features that only a computer can provide. All paint programs also provide tools for drawing simple shapes, selecting a portion of a picture, or cropping and resizing the picture.

There are advantages to creating your art:

- You have total control over the palette used

- You don't have to worry about royalties or copyright concerns

- You get exactly what you want

Original artwork is particularly useful for icons, buttons, small graphics, and animations. It is also the only effective way to get good 16-color images. Artists used to working within the constraints of 16 colors can do very impressive work—just look at video games.

Scanning

Many bitmaps used by a multimedia application will come from photographs. A photograph uses continuous tones and shades—colors that blend smoothly from one to another. By using a scanner or special digitizing equipment, you can transform photographs into bitmap images.

Scanning is the most common way to rapidly create full-color electronic images from photographic prints, slides, or pieces of flat artwork. The main drawback of scanners is that the scanning process is time-consuming. Scanning a large image at high resolution can take up to a minute or more of processing time. This adds up when you have a few thousand images to digitize. If a speedy production cycle matters more than having the highest quality, consider buying a good video camera and a frame grabber.

Video Frame Grabbing

You can use a video camera hooked to a digitizing board in your computer to capture images. The digitizing board, often called a *frame-grabber*, converts the analog signal from the camera to a digital format that can be read and enhanced by software the same as a scanned image.

The biggest difference between a scanner and a digitizer is that a scanner can only capture an image from a two-dimensional source, such as a photograph or slide, while a digitizer can capture any video image. A digitizing board usually captures two-dimensional images faster than a scanner, but it doesn't necessarily provide the best quality for the money. So, unless you're willing to get the best equipment, you might be better off buying a scanner to capture two-dimensional images.

Setting Up the Image Preparation Environment

Preparing images for your application places more demands on your system than displaying the images. You'll need to perform the following types of tasks:

- Touching up images to remove imperfections

- Adjusting an image's brightness and contrast

- Cropping images for the application

The following sections describe issues to consider when setting up an image preparation environment. This section describes particular categories of software and hardware, without recommending any specific products.

Image Processing Software

After you've scanned or digitized an image, you may have to do additional processing to prepare it for use in your product. This is where image processing software and paint tools come in.

There is often a fine line of distinction between digitizing software, image enhancement software, and paint software. Some products have all three capabilities built in, while others specialize in one capability or another.

Digitizing Software

At its simplest level, digitizing software controls the scanner or digitizer you are using to capture an image. It may allow you to set the image size, select the portion of the image to digitize, specify the resolution and number of colors, and select the format in which to save the image file. Most of the high-end digitizing software also includes image enhancement and painting features.

You can probably get by just fine using simple scanning software and the MDK's BitEdit and PalEdit tools if you don't need to do extensive editing to enhance your images.

Image Enhancement Software

Image enhancement software is designed to convert images to different formats, spatial resolutions, and color resolutions; to modify saturation, hue, tint, contrast, and brightness; to sharpen or blur edges; to modify palette assignments; and to flip, rotate, crop, and resize. Think of the image enhancement software as a digital photo-retouching product. You normally use it to make global changes to an entire image, such as blurring the background, changing all blues to greens, and so on.

One function that you will probably use on every image you scan or digitize is color reduction. When you scan or digitize a natural image at high color resolution, you capture millions of colors. Most of these colors, however, are simply subtle shades of a relatively few colors.

If you want to display the image on a computer screen that supports only 16 or 256 colors, then you will have to merge or delete most of the captured colors. Scanning and image enhancement software provide a variety of ways to do this algorithmically and manually.

BitEdit and PalEdit from the Multimedia Development Kit provide simple edit functions for images and image palettes. See Part 2 of this guide for descriptions of these tools.

Paint Software

Paint software is used to actually edit the contents of an image. Paint software is sometimes used in the scanning process to add special effects to an image or to work on color gradations and hues at a pixel level.

Use paint software to make minor changes to images. You can cut, copy, and paste segments of the image, or use tools such as a paintbrush or airbrush to add elements to the image.

File Conversion Software

The images used in your multimedia application can come from a variety of sources and computer platforms. Although your application may be designed to import any graphic format, it will run most efficiently if it imports graphics in Windows DIB format. The MDK's BitEdit and Convert utilities let you convert from a number of the most common graphic formats to DIB and back.

The following table shows the different formats supported by BitEdit and Convert.

Format	Extension	Capability
Apple Macintosh PICT	.PIC	Read, Write
AutoCAD Import	.PLT	Read
CompuServe GIF	.GIF	Read
Computer Graphics Metafile	.CGM	Read
Encapsulated PostScript	.EPS	Read
HP Graphic Language	.HGL	Read
Lotus 1-2-3 Graphics	.PIC	Read
Micrografx Designer/Draw	.DRW	Read
Microsoft RIFF DIB	.RDI	Read, Write
Microsoft RLE DIB	.DIB	Read, Write
Microsoft RLE RIFF DIB	.RDI	Read, Write
Microsoft Windows BMP	.BMP	Read
Microsoft Windows DIB	.DIB	Read, Write
Microsoft Windows Metafile	.WMF	Read
PC Paintbrush	.PCX	Read, Write
Tagged Image File Format (TIFF)	.TIF	Read
Truevision TGA	.TGA	Read, Write

If your images are stored in other formats, you may need to use a two-step approach, first converting them to one of these standard formats and then to the final format.

Image Processing Hardware

Additional hardware for an image preparation system is needed to capture a digital version of an image. Scanners are more commonly used to capture images for a personal computer; the other alternative is a video camera with a digitizing board. The following paragraphs describe the hardware needed for both of these image capturing techniques.

Computer Hardware

Many excellent image creation and enhancement solutions exist for MS-DOS and Windows. Note that such systems typically require adequate horsepower to do the job of editing images.

CPU   Look for at least an 80386 or better processor. You should also consider configuring your PC with plenty of additional RAM.

Hard Disk   Image files are large and fill up a hard disk quickly. Provide your system with sufficient disk storage (at least 300-600 MB) to capture, edit, and convert the images used by your application.

Display   You should have at least a 256-color VGA monitor and card (8-bit) to review and edit images effectively. You may want to invest in a 24-bit monitor and card to view and edit higher quality images.

Scanners

Anytime you want to turn a photographic print, slide or flat artwork into a digital image, use a full-color scanner and scanning software. The scanner builds a digital representation of the photograph and creates a corresponding image file. Scanning software can typically store images in PICT (Apple Macintosh) or PCX (PC Paintbrush) formats. Scanners can produce a far higher image resolution than most cameras. The best scanners digitize at least 300 dots per inch resolution with various color depths per pixel (1 to 24 bits per pixel).

Scanners come in two basic varieties: flat-bed scanners and slide scanners. Flat-bed scanners are used to scan printed materials and photographic prints. Slide scanners are used to scan photographic slides. Use a flat-bed scanner if the bulk of your images are flat art or prints. If most of your images are slides, use a slide scanner for quality reproductions.

Many different types of scanner hardware and software are available. If possible, use a scanner that can capture at 24 bits per pixel and at least 300 dots per inch resolution. You'll probably want to edit and archive your scanned images in the original 24 bit format, and then reduce the images to either 8-bit or 4-bit for the actual application. This lets you work with the highest quality image until satisfied it's ready for conversion to the lower resolution.

Video Digitizing Equipment

Video digitizing equipment consists of several devices and is more costly than a scanner; however, this image capturing method provides additional features such as directly capturing images of three-dimensional objects. The equipment used in video digitizing is identified and described in the following section.

Cameras

The digitizing camera you select can make or break your final product. Cameras come in a range of prices, from the inexpensive consumer variety to the $40,000 broadcast variety.

When shopping around for a camera, look for these qualities:

- Resolution: While you can use almost any camera to digitize your images, look for cameras with high resolution—the higher the better. Remember, you want to end up with an image that comes as close to 640-by-480 lines of resolution as possible. The typical consumer-quality VHS camera produces only 240 lines of resolution, which is not adequate. SVHS cameras produce over 400 lines when properly calibrated.

- Output: High-end digitizer boards accept RGB input, which will generally provide the best image. Some boards also accept S-Video and composite video inputs. Of these two, S-Video is the best. Avoid a camera that has only a composite video output.

- LUX: The lower the LUX value, the less light a camera needs. You'll want a camera that has a low LUX value, but this doesn't mean you want to under light your subjects. Low light means lower quality images. Although natural daylight is the best light for shooting video, it isn't necessarily the easiest to work with, nor is it always available.

Lenses

You'll want the lenses that come standard with the camera, but more often than not you'll also want a macro-lens for close-up work. A zoom lens is a good choice for general use.

Camera stand

The best camera stands are expensive, but you'll probably find that a good one is worth the investment. Here are few things to look for in camera stands:

- Moving platens to center and orient the images

- Quartz halogen lamps to get good light at low wattage

- Back lighting source for slides

- Motorized column for moving camera up and down

- Glass plate

Digitizer Interface Boards

The most popular and broadly supported digitizer boards can capture images at a number of resolutions. Choose a board that allows a resolution of at least 24 bits per pixel for color information. There are several products on the market—shop around before you buy. Some of the less expensive boards give you a lot of power for the money, and may be quite adequate for your needs.

Monitors

You may want a video monitor to view the video image before it is digitized. Either black-and-white or color monitors are acceptable, but color monitors have the added benefit of letting you see the color settings before you grab the frame.

Capturing and Preparing Images

Although scanning and digitization are both relatively straightforward processes, the quality of your final images and the amount of work required to produce them can vary drastically, depending on how well you plan the project. The next few pages describe the following aspects of the image preparation process:

- Choosing images with the proper characteristics

- Capturing images with a scanner

- Capturing images with a video camera

- Enhancing captured images

Choosing an Image

All pictures are not created equal; some are just better suited for digitizing than others. For example, an image with a large section of clear blue sky may look like a good candidate in its original form, but a picture with less sky showing may be a better choice. Here's why: The sky is actually composed of dozens of shades of blue. The conversion software that converts this 16 million color image (24 bits) to 256 colors (8 bits) will probably reduce these dozens of blues to four or five shades. The result is a striped or blotchy sky.

A good image enhancement program will let you blend this handful of colors so that the blotches are barely noticeable, but remember, every extra step adds more time (cost) to the overall production process. Making a good choice will save touch-up time later in production. This is especially true when the application's runtime palette size is limited to 16 or 256 colors.

Another important characteristic of the original image is its physical size. If the original image is too small, you may have to enlarge and distort the image. If the original image is too large, there may be too much detail and you'll have to shrink it. The best size is between 3-by-5 and 8-by-10.

Here are some other important factors to consider when choosing images:

Images to use have . . .	Images to avoid have . . .
Consistent lighting with balanced contrast	Hundreds of wildly varying colors
A moderate number of bold, mixed colors	Deep, dark shadows
Image components that look good blended	High contrast such as bright whites or blacks
Low level of detail	Large sections of a solid color (such as sky)
Human or complex subjects with simple backgrounds	

The texture of the original will affect the final quality. Use high-quality prints whenever possible.

Capturing with a Scanner

The best way to describe the scanning process is to explain the steps involved in converting a photographic print to a Windows DIB (Device Independent Bitmap). The DIB format is the standard format for all Windows bitmaps—it is the recommended target format for all your bitmapped images.

Each image starts out as a separate photographic print with its own unique palette. The process of getting an image ready for the final application goes something like this:

Adjust Your Monitor

Your images may look great on your display, but if your production monitor is improperly adjusted the final image may not look right when displayed on other monitors. Since you can never be sure how well adjusted the delivery system monitor will be, make sure you have at least created the image in the truest, most accurate color.

The best way to adjust a production monitor is to buy a color bar generator that outputs pure RGB and plug it directly into your monitor. You can also look for software that generates a color bar, and then adjust your monitor settings accordingly. Without these tools, adjustments are purely subjective as they rely solely on your ability to visually evaluate color.

Choose the Image Depth

Many scanners offer several image-depth settings. Because Windows with Multimedia supports 1-bit, 4-bit, and 8-bit bitmaps, any palette can contain up to 256 unique colors. The quality of a scanned bitmap depends on how well a system can re-create the effect of a continuous-tone image using these 256 colors. Whenever possible you should always create and enhance bitmaps using large image depths.

Good color scanners can scan with a color resolution of up to 24 bits per pixel, allowing 16 million colors in the palette. Most scanning programs let you reduce the colors in the image from 24 to 8 bits or less. If you want to scan an image once and store the highest quality image possible, scan it at 24 bits and reduce it after you're totally satisfied with the results. If you don't need the original high-quality image, you might as well reduce it as you scan, since it will require far less space to store.

Adjust image to proper size

Set the size or resolution of the screen image by specifying the number of dots per inch (DPI) in the image. Adjust the DPI setting (sometimes called the *scanning resolution*) to be as close to the desired image size as possible. VGA screens with 640 by 480 resolution display images at about 72 DPI; a scan setting of 72 DPI produces approximately a 1:1 ratio in size.

You control the size of the screen image with the scanning resolution. To shrink the screen image of an illustration, set the scanning resolution to less than 72 DPI. To enlarge the screen image, set the scanning resolution to greater than 72 DPI.

A quick way to determine the desired scanning resolution is to divide the number of pixels you want to cover on the screen in one dimension by the same dimension of the area of the picture you want to use. For example, say your original image is 10-by-8 inches and you want it to fill half the screen (320 by 240). Divide 320 by 10 and you obtain a scanning resolution of 32 DPI.

Hint   Although paint programs allow you to resize images, building a digitized image of the correct dimensions with the digitizing software gives you a better image. Paint programs make intelligent guesses when reducing or enlarging an image. In contrast, digitizing software doesn't guess; it uses information from the original illustration to build the digitized image.

Identify Cropping Boundaries

Always pre-scan the image. Pre-scanning takes only a few seconds and provides a quick, low-resolution scan of the entire scanning bed. Pre-scanning your image lets you set cropping boundaries for the digitizing software and saves time during scanning. Pre-scanning is present in all decent capturing programs.

After pre-scanning, eliminate the portion of the picture you don't want. This not only limits the size of the image file, it also reduces the total number of colors included in its color palette. Since you'll probably have to adjust the image's palette if you want to display it with other images, a smaller palette can simplify this process.

Scan the Image

Now scan in the image. After you've scanned the image, look at it and see what adjustments you might like to make. Scanner software sometimes includes a paint or draw package to clean up any problems introduced during the scan. If you have the time, cut out all unnecessary elements of each image, especially in the background. Again, this makes for a smaller image file and a smaller palette.

Transfer the Image

If you capture digital images on a different computer than your multimedia application development system, you'll need to transfer your images to the development platform. There are several ways to move images from one system to another, but using a network is probably the fastest and most efficient method if you are moving lots of large files, such as images.

Capturing from Video

Along with a scanner, you may want to capture images with a video camera. The camera focuses on the image and then transfers that image to the PC through a special interface board that converts the analog video signal to a digital format. This digitizer simplifies the image by combining palette values and setting the resolution. It also converts the digitized image into a standard graphics format such as TGA or PICT, which can be easily converted by the MDK's Convert tool. This setup lets you grab images with the video camera that can be read and enhanced by software the same as a scanned image.

Many different types of cameras exist and they can deliver images in many different formats (such as direct video, composite video, and National Television Standards Committee (NTSC)). After you've captured the image, you still must convert and enhance the image for incorporation within your application. The following paragraphs summarize the steps involved in this process.

Note   A video camera usually digitizes images faster than a scanner, but it doesn't necessarily provide the best quality for the money. So, unless you're willing to get the best equipment, you might be better off buying a scanner for your basic image capturing.

Set up Your Copy Stand and Lights Properly

A proper setup and lighting can cut hours of image processing time. Using a copy stand as it comes out of the box invites trouble because quite often the lights are set to light the center of the stand. Often, one strong light (say, 1000 watts about five feet from the picture), will give you the proper, even illumination levels. Sometimes it is quite effective to tack the image to the wall and shoot it using a tripod-mounted camera.

Connect the Camera to the PC

To digitize images, you must plug a digitizer board into your computer, install the digitizer software, and connect the camera to the PC through the board. You may also want an extra monitor for viewing the camera image and some test equipment to ensure the best quality. Make sure all video equipment used is properly calibrated for color accuracy and reproduction.

Digitizers only accept RGB input, so you'll need to ensure your VCR or camera can output RGB. If you are capturing an NTSC signal, you'll need to convert it to an RGB signal first by using a special NTSC decoder.

Use a video camera whenever possible as it provides a more stable and higher resolution signal than a VCR. The next best signal is usually a live feed from cable, broadcast TV, or videodisc. Use VCR images only as a last resort. They produce highly unstable signals and low resolution output (around 240 lines of resolution).

Capture Frames

Focus the camera on the object(s) whose image you want captured. Use the video capture hardware and software to grab the image and store it to disk.

All frame grabbers tend to distort the image slightly due to motion. The frame grabbing software is designed to compensate for this to some degree, however, for best results use still or slow moving images. Avoid grabbing in pause as the image is the most unstable in pause mode.

If you are capturing an entire sequence of video frames for an animation sequence, you'll have to shrink the original frames to a size that can be played back at a particular rate by the hardware. The standard Multimedia PC can play back at approximately 10-15 frames per second, with a frame size of approximately 100 pixels by 150 pixels by 8 bits. Reducing the frame size is probably best done with the original videotape before digitizing since the entire sequence will then be a consistent size. Some video boards can shrink a full screen video source. Otherwise, you may need to hire technicians in a TV studio at a greater cost.

Correct the Aspect Ratio

Your targeted aspect ratio is the VGA monitor at 640:480 (or 4:3). The resolution of your camera or video image is bound to be different so you'll want to be sure the capture software you use can convert and correct the aspect ratio.

Enhance the Image

You'll need to crop the image to size and perform any necessary color, edge, or contrast enhancements. Edit the image to clean up any problems introduced when captured. Use the greatest color or monochrome depth possible. For instance, when touching up a 24-bit color image, use a software package capable of handling 24-bit colors. The Windows with Multimedia tools only handle 8-bit color manipulation.

Scale the Image

By scaling the image down to less than full screen, you won't notice the lower resolution of the original video image. If you capture multiple video frames for an animated sequence, you'll have to shrink the original frames to a size that can be played back at a particular rate by the hardware. Contact a television studio for details as this requires professional expertise.

Transfer Images to PC

If you capture digital images on a different computer than your multimedia application development system, you'll need to transfer your images to the development platform.

Enhancing Images

After you've captured the image and transferred it to your multimedia development system, you might still need to convert it to the Windows format. You might also want to make some minor changes to the image. For example, the scanner might have introduced minor distortions into the bitmap that you'd like to correct.

The BitEdit and PalEdit tools provided with the MDK let you enhance images in two basic ways:

- You can edit the images and their color palettes

- You can build a merged color palette for use with several images

You'll find the BitEdit tool acceptable for simple enhancements to 8-bit images. You may find you need more elaborate tools for image enhancements. You should consider touching up the image before converting the file to DIB format. Many excellent tools exist for both MS-DOS and Windows. Choose the tool that provides you with the best mix of features and capabilities.

Convert the Image to DIB format

The standard Windows bitmap format is called a Device Independent Bitmap, or DIB. Windows knows how to read this and display this format without any extra conversion. You should convert all images to this format as soon as they are final. Microsoft multimedia applications can display bitmaps of a limited number of other formats, but to manipulate and merge palettes of multiple images, you must first convert them to DIBs.

Conversion to DIB happens automatically whenever you load an image into BitEdit. If you want to convert several images simultaneously, however, use the Convert tool. Convert provides batch processing capabilities, so you don't have to manually open and save each image file. For more information about the Convert Tool, see Part 2 of this guide.

Crop and Size the Image

The preparation of your images for your application should be close to completion. You may need to make final adjustments to one or more of your images with gentle cropping, resizing, or other minor pixel and color edits. BitEdit can do cropping and sizing along with simple pixel editing and color adjustment.

Enhance the Image

Image enhancing software lets you touch-up imperfections in digital images. If you started with a good original illustration, you may have to do nothing more than adjust the brightness. This operation can be done on a section or on the entire image. You might also consider smudging and blending colors around the edges to produce a softened effect, or transposing or replacing certain colors with others to brighten or enhance the image. Always cut unnecessary elements from an image.

When you edit an image, always use the greatest image depth possible. For instance, when enhancing a 24-bit color image, use a software package capable of handling 24-bit colors. You should make all image enhancements and color changes to the original 24-bit image before you convert it to an 8-bit image, since information is always lost during conversion.

When you finish making your enhancements, you may want to save two versions of the image: a 24-bit version and an 8-bit version. You'll use the 8-bit file for the titles you deliver today. Inventory the 24-bit file for the future—hardware able to display such images is just around the corner from being commonplace.

If your application can only display 16-color images, and you want to use full color or black and white photographs or artwork, you should consider dithering your images if you want them to look good. BitEdit provides the capability to dither an image based on a targeted number of colors.

For more information about the BitEdit Tool, see Part 2 of this guide.

Adjust the Color Palette

Even though the content of the bitmap is ready to drop into your multimedia application, its palette may need some adjusting. For example, if you plan to display several images simultaneously, you'll need to edit or replace the palettes associated with those bitmaps. Your goal in this case is to create a color palette that makes all its associated images look good.

For additional information about PalEdit and the process of creating a merged palette, see Part 2 of this guide.

Inventory the Image

At this point you are ready to build these images into your application. Store the image for use. We recommend using some sort of data management system to organize and track the images and other data items associated with your application.

Chapter 6
Audio

Audio rounds out multimedia applications by enriching the environment with music, sound effects, and speech. Each audio element can play a different role in a multimedia application. Music sets the mood and provides emphasis to an application. Sound effects add variety and dash. Speech offers yet another way to present information.

This chapter presents four aspects of using digital sound:

- It introduces digital audio systems technology

- It identifies alternatives for acquiring sounds for applications

- It identifies software and hardware components for a sound preparation system

- It offers a brief overview of the sound preparation process

With a Multimedia PC, you have all the computer hardware and software needed to play digitized sound; and with a few additional components, you can record and merge digitized sound into multimedia applications.

This chapter explains some of the issues involved in creating audio files for playback from Windows with Multimedia. It describes in broad terms how to prepare audio files and offers suggestions for an audio preparation system. Creating good audio is as much art as it is science—nothing can replace expertise and experience. If you want good advice, find a good audio technician.

An Introduction to Digital Audio Technology

Alexander Graham Bell first transmitted sound using analog techniques. The principles he discovered are still widely used to capture and play diverse types of sound that include music, narration, and special sound effects. In recent years, however, digital techniques have also been developed for consumers to record and playback sound.

What is Sound?

When something causes molecules of air to vibrate, your ear perceives this vibration as sound. For instance, when lightning strikes, the air around the flash becomes superheated and expands rapidly. This rapid expansion of molecules produces the change in pressure that eventually reaches your ears as thunder.

Sound is typically represented as an analog (continuous) waveform. The waveform describes the vibration of the air molecules. For example, the plucking of a guitar string not only visually resembles a waveform, it produces them as well.

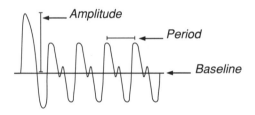

The distance between the top (or bottom) of the waveform and its baseline is known as its *amplitude*. Amplitude indicates the volume of the sound. The points in a waveform with the greatest amplitude sound the loudest. Points in the waveform with little amplitude sound the quietest. A flat line in a waveform indicates silence.

All waveforms divide into *periods*. A period is the distance between two consecutive peaks in a waveform. The *frequency* of a waveform is determined by the number of periods that occur in one second. One period per second equals one hertz (Hz). One thousand periods per second equals one kilohertz (kHz).

Making Sound Digital

The audio CD that contains digital sound has become the fidelity standard of the music industry. But before digital sound, there were phonographs. Phonographs produce audio from LP albums recorded in analog format. The audio waveforms are physically represented as grooves in a record. Playing the record is accomplished by spinning the album with a crystalline phonograph needle resting in the grooves.

The flexing of the needle produces a small electric current which is converted into an audio waveform and amplified until it comes out your speakers as music. This process works wonderfully when you have perfect needles and absolutely clean grooves. Anything less than perfection, however, causes the inevitable distortion all phonograph users hear as pops, clicks, and skips. This distortion of sound is the reason that digital audio has become so popular.

Translating an analog waveform into a digital form works by taking tiny (discrete) samples of the waveform at fixed intervals as the sound is captured. This process establishes the frequency of the waveform. At the same time, the values for the waveform's amplitudes are also captured defining the amount of information stored per sample.

Each sample is mapped to an integer value, which is then stored. These integer values can then be used to re-create the original waveform. The result: quality sound practically indistinguishable from the original.

Compact disc audio is the highest quality format, but produces the largest files. Other formats store sound files more economically, but with some trade-off in quality.

Quality vs. Size

Three characteristics can determine the quality and size of a digital waveform: the frequency of the samples, the amount of information stored per sample, and the number of channels recorded.

Frequency

Samples are taken at the same frequency to divide the waveform into identically sized portions. The more portions (i.e., the higher the frequency), the more quality and disk storage required. More portions also means higher tones in the sound will be recorded; 11.025 kHz sampling only captures tones lower than 5.513 kHz in frequency.

Of course, this is only an approximation; inevitably some information present in the original waveform gets lost in the process. This is why the frequency of the samples affects so directly the quality. The more frequent the samples, the less information lost in approximation.

The three standard sampling frequencies are 44.1 kHz, 22.05 kHz, and 11.025 kHz.

Amount of Information

The amount of information stored per sample specifies the precision with which sample is measured. Information per sample is derived by vertically dividing each waveform sample into equal units. An 8-bit sample divides each sample into 256 equal units. A 16-bit sample divides into 65,536 equal units.

The greater the number of vertical units used to describe the waveform characteristics in the sample, the more accurately the sample resembles the original analog waveform. Of course, more information also requires more storage.

The number of units between the baseline and the upper limit of the waveform is sometimes referred to as its *dynamic range*. For 8-bit samples to divide the waveform into 256 units, the waveform must have a dynamic range that covers all (or most) of the 256 units. If the waveform's dynamic range only covers 128 units, precision (and quality) is reduced—as though only 7-bits were used per sample.

Number of Channels

The number of sound channels specifies whether a recording produces one waveform (referred to as *monaural* or *mono*) or produces two waveforms (referred to as *stereo*). Stereo sound can offer a richer listening experience than mono, but also requires twice the amount of storage.

How Much Storage is Required?

Digital sound files are large, no matter what quality you choose, but the lower sampling rates produce much smaller files than the higher sampling rates. Use this formula to estimate storage needs for audio:

```
(sampling rate * bits per sample)/8 = bytes/sec
```

For example, a one-minute monaural sound clip requires the following space:

One minute of monaural music

Bits/sample	Sampling Rate	# Bytes required
8 bits	11.025 kHz	0.66 MB/minute
8 bits	22.05 kHz	1.32 MB/minute
16 bits	44.1 kHz	5.292 MB/minute

Compact Disc Digital Audio

The digital sound format used by audio CDs can also be used in Windows with Multimedia applications. Compact Disc Digital Audio (CD-DA), known as *Red Book audio*, uses a sampling rate of 44.1 kHz and stores 16 bits of information for each sample.

Multimedia PCs can play standard Red Book audio CDs. Windows controls the audio playback, but the audio is not played through the computer, it is played through special chips in the CD-ROM drive. This capability provides a potential source of high-quality sound for Multimedia PC title developers.

You can include CD-DA with other information in a CD-ROM multimedia title for use with Windows with Multimedia. This lets you use the highest quality audio in your applications without requiring any special hardware or software. Before making this decision, however, you need to weigh the increased quality against the following factors:

- Red Book audio requires the entire processing power of the CD-ROM drive—your title can't transfer any other data when CD-DA is being played.

- Red Book audio uses a lot of space on the disc. Fifteen minutes of CD-DA sound digital can require about 80 MB of storage.

CD-ROM titles that use Red Book audio are often called *mixed mode* CD-ROMs. Sound stored in CD-DA format is separated from the other data on a CD-ROM and requires a separate access when retrieved. Your title must pre-load program, image, and other data into memory (or into a cache area on the hard disk), and then dedicate the CD-ROM drive's circuitry to access the CD-DA sound as the application runs.

Choosing a Fidelity Level

Choosing the sound fidelity level of an application means that you must balance sound quality against the space needed to store the sounds for your application.

- From an audio perspective, you need to have a reasonable fidelity level for the sound used

- From a resource management perspective, you have a limited amount of storage space for sound files

The best quality sound you can use in the Multimedia PC is CD-DA (44.1 kHz) format. This format is particularly well-suited for music or language applications where nuances of pronunciation are critical. Red Book audio requires the most space on a CD and it uses up the entire bandwidth of a CD-ROM drive to play it. You will always have to pre-load images and other data off the CD before you start playing a Red Book passage.

Audio captured with 16-bits per sample at 11.025 kHz or 22.05 kHz offers very good quality, but requires more support from your application. To play 16-bit data on an 8-bit Multimedia PC, you'll need to use the low-level audio functions documented in the MDK's *Programmer's Workbook* and *Programmer's Reference*—your application must include code to convert the data to 8-bit during playback. The benefit to doing this is that your title will sound superior to 8-bit titles when run on a Multimedia PC that support 16-bit audio data.

A good general-purpose sound quality to use is the 8-bit, 22.05 kHz format. If you use good recording techniques, you should be able to get quality comparable to AM radio.

At the low end of the Multimedia PC sound spectrum is the 8-bit, 11.025 kHz sound. Generally, you'll want to use this sampling rate when sound is not a critical or prominent feature of your application. This is adequate for prototyping, applications that use voice narration, or for low-frequency sound effects. However, even the best recordings can sound dull and fuzzy at this sampling size/rate. You'll fare better if you choose recordings that don't use bright, high-pitched sounds.

Whatever format you choose, always start with the highest quality you can record—48 kHz or 44.1 kHz—and then later convert the sound to the lower sampling rates with Microsoft's conversion utilities (WaveEdit). This way you'll always have a high-quality archive file to go back to.

Acquiring Audio

Narration, sound effects, and music often originate as studio-recorded analog data, although they can also be recorded digitally. No matter how it originates, all sound data destined for multimedia applications must eventually be digitally sampled and stored in the Microsoft waveform format for playback.

You find that no one method of acquiring audio will meet all your needs. Experiment with different approaches and tactics until you find the best mix for your situation. The following three alternatives are worth exploring:

- Developing your own sound recordings

- Purchasing production music libraries

- Hiring a digital sound studio to produce digital recordings

Developing Your Own Recordings

Digital audio sampling can be painfully accurate: it picks up every sound blemish you introduce during the recording session, even those subtle distortions caused by analog electronics.

If you're planning to use 11.025 kHz or 22.05 kHz samples, you can get by using a desktop audio recording system. With a desktop audio system, you can remove or alleviate some of the subtle glitches in the original with editing or when you convert the original recording to the lower resolution formats.

If you intend to use full bandwidth CD audio, hire a studio that specializes in digital audio recording.

Purchasing Production Music Libraries

Professional sound libraries are available from a number of companies. Originally intended for radio, television, and motion picture industries, these libraries include a wide range of digitally-mastered music clips and sound effects.

Music libraries include fully-orchestrated entries as well as narrated versions that cut-out lead instruments to allow voice-overs. The distribution medium for these libraries is audio CD, which provides a direct path to your Multimedia PC sound preparation system. Purchase options for sound libraries vary by company and may include individual CDs, entire libraries, and subscription services.

Hiring a Digital Sound Studio

Hiring a digital sound studio allows you to obtain Red Book-quality sound clips from scratch and provides you with at least two advantages over the previous alternatives: you have total control over content; and you can use the clips as you see fit without regard for royalties and copyright concerns. The downside: be prepared to pay for these benefits. This type of expertise isn't cheap.

Preparing Audio

This section describes various issues associated with preparing audio files. Sound is one of the most critical elements of a multimedia application because it can have such a positive or negative effect on the perception of your product.

You can divide the audio preparation process into several phases:

- Setting up the audio preparation environment

- Capturing audio

- Converting audio

- Storing audio

Setting Up the Audio Preparation Environment

The standard Multimedia PC can handle the playback of audio quite well. But to prepare this audio for use in a title, you'll need more powerful software and hardware. The following sections describe some of the factors to consider when setting up your audio preparation environment. As with other sections, specific product recommendations are avoided.

Sound Preparation Software

When choosing your sound preparation software, first decide exactly what you need. Some products perform standard functions for recording and editing waveforms. Other products provide a digital signal processing laboratory that includes the standard functions, as well as advanced capabilities that can include cross-channel mixing and frequency analysis.

The MDK includes WaveEdit—a simple sound editor with recording capabilities to let you record in the 8-bit and 16-bit waveform format. WaveEdit also includes conversion utilities for Macintosh AIFF and PCM formats. The Convert tool also supports the conversion of audio formats.

Features included with sound preparation products appear in the following table. The left column shows standard features found in all the products. The right column identifies advanced features found in higher-end products:

Standard Features	Advanced Features
Digital waveform recording up to frequencies of 22.05 kHz	Digital waveform recording of frequencies up to 44.1 kHz
Visual waveform editing (cut and paste waveform sections)	Cross-channel mixing
Mixing waveforms together	Adjusting waveform tempo without pitch change
Inserting Silence Fades (in and out)	Adjusting Pitch
Adjusting Amplitude	Defining Amplitude envelopes for a waveform
	Mixing more than two channels of waveform data
	Frequency Analysis
	Defining playlists that sequence waveform segments for playback

Once the sound file is complete, the file may need to be converted to a format supported by the multimedia software. Both the WaveEdit and the Convert applications provided with Microsoft's Multimedia Development Kit includes conversion capabilities for several types of digital sound files.

Sound Processing Hardware

The primary concern when putting together an audio preparation system is that it handle digital audio. Windows with Multimedia only works with digital audio, so if you have any source audio in analog format, you'll first need to translate the analog signals into a digital format. After you have completed this process, you can then begin to clean up and embellish the audio for your application.

Another major concern you'll have when acquiring the hardware for your audio preparation system is performance. Audio preparation requires a lot of horsepower and disk space, so you better buy plenty of both.

Other issues to consider when acquiring a system:

- Picking the right central processing unit (CPU)

- Getting enough hard disk space

- Choosing an Analog-to-Digital Converter

- Picking a microphone

- Acquiring tape backup

CPU Editing audio data is a processor-intensive operation, and requires quick CPU and disk controller performance to handle the volume of data managed and collected. The base level Multimedia PC specifies an 80286 processor running at 10 MHz. This would not be adequate for the audio preparation. Look for at least an 80386 or better processor. You should also consider configuring your PC with plenty of additional RAM and using a RAM disk to store temporary data during the data capture phase.

Hard Disk Sound files are large and fill up a hard disk quickly. Provide your system with sufficient disk storage (at least 300–600 MB) to record, edit, and convert the sound clips used by your application.

Analog-Digital and Digital-Analog Converters

These devices are often delivered on a PC interface card. An Analog-to-Digital converter (ADC) converts incoming analog signals to discrete samples at regular time intervals. A Digital-to-Analog converter (DAC) converts outgoing digital signals to analog, for use by an amplifier, speakers, or other analog devices. The Multimedia PC specification establishes both an ADC and a DAC as standard equipment.

Capabilities of various available ADCs and DACs vary. For example, the interface card containing the converters may also contain additional circuitry for digital signal processing, especially in high-end products. A digital signal processor (DSP) chip provides added punch for such tasks as frequency analysis.

If you plan to record and play Red Book quality sound clips, verify that the capabilities of the converters can support a 44.1 kHz frequency.

Microphone and Cables

A good original recording source and good acoustics are part of making a good sound. But, if you are planning to record anything live with a microphone, purchase a good one—it can make a distinct difference in your final recording.

Microphones are very specific to their application. When you're ready to buy a microphone, tell the experts how you intend to use it and have them recommend the best type of microphone for that particular job.

Additionally, don't go bargain hunting when picking out cables for your audio equipment. Cheap, thinly-insulated cables pick up static from the equipment, which makes your audio sound worse. Buy quality cables—they're well worth the investment.

DAT Tape Deck

If you are recording full bandwidth Red Book audio and you are using a 100 MB hard disk, you're going to run out of space in about 19 minutes of recording. With all data you need a backup recording system, but this is particularly important with audio data, just so you can get all your work done.

Capturing Audio

Your goal is to acquire or record all the necessary voices, sound effects, and music. After you've collected all the pieces, you can then prepare them for use in the application. You can collect the different audio elements in two ways:

- You can use pre-recorded digital music and sound effects. This method offers high-quality audio at low cost, but it limits your ability to tailor the content to your application.

- You can create and record the audio yourself. This lets you control the music and sound effects, however, you also have to invest in specialized equipment and professional staff. You'll need to hire professional audio engineers, or contract with recording studios, to do the job properly.

To record using the WaveEdit application included in Windows with Multimedia, load and run WaveEdit. You can record in several formats and perform simple edits on the final waveform. The file can then be saved in the Microsoft Waveform format. To record using another recording system, you'll need to run the recording application and set the recording rate. You'll end up with a waveform that you can edit and mix with other sound.

One of the best ways to ensure a clean, distortion-free signal is to record the sound directly from the source.

Caution   Don't forget that you are breaking the law if you record and use copyrighted material, without securing the rights from the publisher.

One of the nastier elements of digital recording is a distortion, called "clipping," that occurs at loud segments (high amplitudes) of the music. It happens when you record with too much volume, or when you digitize an analog source outside the tolerable range (analog electronics tolerate this sort of distortion much better than digital electronics). Several recording applications display the clipped region when the amplitude of the source waveform is too high. Other products show gauges or waveforms going off the scale or outside the display region. Pay attention to these signs and reduce the amplitude of your sounds as necessary.

It is best to record your sounds at the highest possible sampling rate to preserve the maximum information, the highest quality being either 48 kHz or 44.1 kHz samples at 16 bits per sample. Sounds stored in this format are generally referred to as linear PCM (Pulse Code Modulation) files. PCM files are basically uncompressed, raw sound data.

Converting Audio

Some of you might already have Macintosh-based audio preparation systems, and you may want to continue to create and edit audio with these systems. The most common format for Apple audio files is AIFF. After you finish editing the files, you'll need to transfer them to a PC and convert them to work in the Windows with Multimedia environment.

The Convert and WaveEdit tools include an AIFF to Waveform format converter. After you transfer the audio files from the Macintosh to the PC, run the converter to translate your audio files into Waveform format. Waveform format can use either 11.025 kHz or 22.05 kHz samples, storing 8 bits or 16 bits of information per sample. The 8-bit 22.05 kHz sound is high enough quality for most applications, and is often compared to AM quality radio.

Once in Waveform format, your multimedia application can access and use the audio files just like any other resource.

Edit the Audio

When you have captured all the audio pieces, edit them to achieve the results you want. The editing process involves such aspects as mixing sounds together and eliminating distortion.

Various software packages for music creation, sound effects, and digital mixing exist. These packages let you edit the audio—either as entities or as an integrated soundtrack—and then output the finished product as files on disk.

WaveEdit provides some of the following editing capabilities: setting volume, fading-in and fading-out during transitions, and mixing several channels. WaveEdit can get you started, but it isn't intended to serve as a full-featured audio editing tool. Other sound recording applications contain a fuller set of audio editing capabilities.

Storing Audio

After you create and enhance the audio files, store and inventory the files. Note that sound files are very large. You'll need a very large hard disk if you plan to do a lot of recording. You should consider using digital audio tape as well.

Chapter 7
MIDI

Along with the rich capabilities of waveform audio and CD-DA, Windows
with Multimedia supports the use of MIDI files within multimedia titles. The
standard Multimedia PC platform can play MIDI files through either an internal
synthesizer, or through an external synthesizer attached to the computer's
MIDI port.

This capability expands your options in including sound with your titles. A variety
of different MIDI files exist, from popular music soundtracks, to special audio
effects. The minimal storage requirements of MIDI make it a welcome addition
to your menu of audio alternatives.

This chapter introduces MIDI terms and technology, describes the characteristics
of MIDI in the Multimedia PC environment, and offers some brief guidelines
for authoring MIDI files for use in your titles. If you adhere to the guidelines
in this chapter, the music you compose will work on all classes of Multimedia
PCs—from those that only meet the base level of the specification to those that
include extended MIDI capabilities.

What is MIDI?

MIDI stands for Musical Instrument Digital Interface. Established in 1982, MIDI specifies an international standard for digital music:

- It specifies the cabling and hardware for connecting electronic musical instruments and computers from different manufacturers

- It specifies a communications protocol for passing data from one device to another

Any musical instrument can become a MIDI device if it has a microprocessor to process MIDI messages, and includes the appropriate hardware interfaces. MIDI devices communicate with each other by sending *messages* through this interface. MIDI messages are actually digital descriptions of a musical score—complete with the sequence of notes, timing, and instrument designations called *patches*. When a set of MIDI messages is played through a music synthesizer chip, the synthesizer interprets these symbols and produces music.

Basic MIDI Terminology

MIDI has sprung from both music and computing, and uses terminology that can seem intimidating to the uninitiated. Here is a short glossary of some of the terms you'll encounter in this chapter.

MIDI File
A standard file format for storing recorded MIDI information. A MIDI file contains notes, timing, and instrument designations for up to 16 channels. The file contains information about each note, including the key, channel number duration, volume, and velocity (how quickly the key travels to its down position when struck).

Channels
The MIDI Specification provides for 16 channels of data—each channel addressing a separate logical synthesizer. Microsoft uses channels 1 through 10 for Extended synthesizers and uses channels 13 through 16 for Base-level synthesizers.

Sequencer
A computer program or electronic device designed for MIDI composition, which allows recording, playback, and editing of MIDI events. Most sequencers can import and export MIDI files.

Synthesizer

An electronic device that uses a Digital Signal Processor (DSP) or other type of chip to make music and sounds. A DSP creates and modifies waveforms and then sends them out through a sound generator and speakers. The quality and range of sounds made by a synthesizer depend on several factors: the number of individual waveforms (or *instruments*) the synthesizer chip can play simultaneously; the capabilities of its control software; and the memory size in the synthesizer circuitry.

Instrument

A specific sound that a synthesizer can reproduce. The patch number and sound quality of an instrument may vary from one synthesizer to another. For example, most synthesizers can play a piano sound, but it is likely to sound quite different and use a different patch number on different synthesizers.

Polyphony

This refers to the maximum number of notes that can be sustained by a synthesizer at once. For example, a four instrument synthesizer with six note polyphony can simultaneously play six notes distributed among four different sounds—perhaps producing a four note piano chord, a flute, and a violin.

Timbre

Pronounced "tamber." This refers to the tone quality of a sound, which is determined by the combinations of frequencies from which it is formed. In more casual usage, it refers to the unique sound associated with a particular instrument. Bass, piano, or violin sounds are each examples of timbres.

Track

A MIDI file concept of separate, parallel groups of MIDI data, usually separated by channel. Format 0 MIDI files merge these tracks into one track; Format 1 MIDI files preserve the different tracks.

Patch Mapper

Software that reassigns an instrument patch number associated with a specific synthesizer to the corresponding standard patch number specified in the Microsoft standard MIDI patch assignments. The Windows with Multimedia MIDI Mapper maps instrument patches to any MIDI devices.

Channel Mapping

Channel mapping translates a MIDI channel number from a sending device to an appropriate channel for a receiving device. For example, drums authored on channel 16 can be mapped to channel 6 for a drum machine that only receives on channel 6.

MIDI and the Multimedia PC

The MIDI specification allows MIDI devices to communicate in a prescribed manner. One of the key elements to this is a standardized set of physical connections to provide a single cabling and communication port standard.

By definition, a Multimedia PC includes an internal synthesizer along with standard MIDI port connections.

MIDI Ports

A MIDI device may have one or more of the following ports: MIDI In, MIDI Out, and MIDI Thru. Each port has a specific purpose in sending, receiving, or relaying MIDI messages between devices. This design enables you to connect multiple MIDI devices that can be controlled simultaneously.

MIDI In	MIDI Out	MIDI Thru
Receive MIDI messages sent from other MIDI devices	Transmit original messages generated from the device	Propagate messages received on MIDI In ports to other connected MIDI devices
	Send MIDI messages to other devices	Send MIDI messages to other devices

MIDI Cables

The MIDI In/Out/Thru ports all support the standard MIDI cabling. A MIDI cable consists of a shielded, twisted-pair wire with a male 5-pin DIN plug connected to each end of the wire.

MIDI Synthesizers

Although it is difficult to clearly measure differences between synthesizers, you need some guidelines so you can create MIDI files to play on all Multimedia PCs. For this purpose, two types of synthesizers have been defined: *Base-level synthesizer* and *Extended synthesizer*.

All Multimedia PCs provide at least a Base level synthesizer. Users can enhance their computer by adding internal or external synthesizers, which can be either Base-level or Extended synthesizers.

The distinctions between Base-level and Extended synthesizers depend solely on the number of instruments and notes it can play, not on its quality or cost. The following table shows the minimum capabilities of Base-level and Extended synthesizers:

Synthesizer	Melodic Instruments		Percussive Instruments	
	Number	**Polyphony**	**Number**	**Polyphony**
Base-Level	3 instruments	6 notes	3 instruments	3 notes
Extended	9 instruments	16 notes	8 instruments	16 notes

Polyphony is the number of notes the synthesizer can play simultaneously. The polyphony expressed above applies to each group of instruments—melodic and percussive.

Melodic instruments are each on different MIDI channels; percussive instruments are key-based—all on a single MIDI channel.

When a user adds a synthesizer, the user must configure the MIDI Mapper to use the new device, or the instrument sounds will not be correct when playing MIDI files. The MIDI Mapper Control Panel applet allows a user to configure the MIDI Mapper as needed.

How a Message Becomes Music

In addition to physical connections, the MIDI specification defines standard messages that MIDI devices use to communicate with each other. These messages identify the events to define and reproduce music with one or more MIDI devices. The message content defines events such as striking a note or changing an instrument from a flute to an oboe.

The set of MIDI messages and data values that define and reproduce a song are stored in a file called a *MIDI file*. Each MIDI file can store up to 16 music channels of information. You build a MIDI file with a *sequencer*, which captures MIDI messages and stores them in a file.

When you play a MIDI file, the sequencer sends MIDI messages from the file to a synthesizer, which converts messages into sounds of a specific instrument, pitch, and duration. A synthesizer generates music and sound with a DSP or other type of chip by creating and modifying waveforms and sending them out through a sound generator and speakers.

Timbre is the tonal quality that distinguishes instruments from one another. Some synthesizers synthesize sounds from parameters that define the timbre of an instrument. Other synthesizers use digitally recorded samples of the original instruments and modify these sounds in memory for volume and pitch changes. Sounds produced synthetically are not as realistic as those produced from the original samples. Multimedia PCs may use either type of synthesizer.

The MIDI message sent to the synthesizer identifies which timbre to use. To find the timbre, look at the patches defined by the MIDI Manufacturers Association (MMA) General MIDI Mode specification (shown later in this chapter).

If a synthesizer is polyphonic, it can play several sounds at once. Polyphony differs slightly from the number of timbres a synthesizer supports. A four-voice synthesizer with six-note polyphony can play six notes simultaneously, but must distribute the sounds among a maximum of four timbres—for instance, a four note piano chord, one note with a flute, and one note with a violin.

When to Use MIDI

With all the capabilities inherent to waveform audio, you might ask: Why bother going through the trouble to understand and use MIDI? The reason is that MIDI files offer some very compelling benefits over waveform audio.

- Since a MIDI file is a series of instructions and not a waveform, it requires much less disk space. For example, a typical 8-bit, 22.05 kHz waveform lasting 1.8 seconds might require 41K. A typical MIDI file lasting two minutes could require less than 8K.

- Because the size of the MIDI file is so much smaller, you can pre-load MIDI files much easier than you can waveform files. This gives you flexibility when you design your title and specify when music occurs.

There are several situations where using a MIDI score is preferable to using waveform audio. The following table offers some general scenarios where you'd choose one form of audio over another.

Use Waveform Audio when . . .	Use Compact Disc Digital Audio when . . .	Use MIDI when . . .
You need to play voice-over narration or natural sound effects	Your title requires full CD-DA quality audio.	You need to play music of more than a short duration of reasonable quality.
You need to load other data from the CD drive simultaneously.	You need the full CPU bandwidth for some task other than using the CD drive (when CD-DA audio is playing, you can't load anything from the CD drive).	You need to load other data from the CD-ROM simultaneously.
You want to store less than one minute of sound on the hard disk.	No hard disk storage of sound is needed.	You want to store more than one minute of music on the hard disk.
You have plenty of space available.	You have plenty of space available.	Space usage on your CD-ROM disc is limited.

Acquiring MIDI Scores

Like voice and special sound effects, music is critical to a multimedia application because of the effect it can have on the end user's perception of your product. People are extremely sensitive to any type of sound and are unforgiving if the music composition isn't constructed well. It's critical to pay attention to quality.

You can acquire MIDI scores in several ways:

- Purchasing MIDI compositions
- Hiring a MIDI sound studio
- Recording your own MIDI scores

Purchasing MIDI Music

Just as with digital audio, a variety of different MIDI libraries are available. These libraries include sound effects, transitional music, and full-fledged re-creations of popular melodies. Like anything else associated with building a multimedia title, make sure you have the legal rights to sell and distribute any MIDI clips used in your title.

Hiring a MIDI Sound studio

Hiring qualified electronic musicians on a contract basis may prove more effective for individual projects. The professional expertise will be reflected in composition quality. In addition, professional musicians will have their own equipment (keyboards and synthesizers) and may prefer to use it.

Recording Your Own MIDI Scores

If you plan to use MIDI extensively, you may want to develop the expertise in-house to create and refine musical compositions with MIDI. With this approach, you gain complete control over the development of the music. You also eliminate royalties and copyright issues that accompany the use of existing music.

Along with qualified personnel, you'll need tools: a keyboard synthesizer to compose and play the original score and a computer with a MIDI sequencer program to record the timing, instrumentation, and multiple tracks of the composition. The next section discusses the types of hardware and software you'll need.

Preparing MIDI

The following software and hardware lists identify the types of equipment you'll need if you intend to create MIDI scores for your product. You'll need fewer software and hardware components to prepare MIDI than you'd need to prepare digital audio. MIDI sequencers, keyboards, composition programs, and other MIDI equipment abound in the market. In addition, MIDI files are extremely efficient in terms of disk space usage. You don't have the massive additional disk storage requirements with MIDI that you have with digital audio.

You should, however, consider hiring a knowledgeable musician before you invest—he or she may have a suitable system already. That way you not only gain the benefit of experience, you also might save money on equipment.

Even if you are purchasing complete MIDI files from a supplier, you should test your application including MIDI playback on a Multimedia PC.

MIDI Preparation Software

MIDI software applications for the PC consist of one primary application—a sequencer. Rudimentary characteristics for sequencers and other supplemental applications follow.

Sequencer

Sequencer programs provide MIDI message recording, editing, and playback capabilities—making it essentially a multi-track tape recorder for MIDI instruments. The following list identifies the base functions a sequencer should provide:

- Can import or export a sequence as a MIDI file in formats 1 and 0.

- Settings to control individual tracks; controls for each track should operate independently of other tracks.

- A *Current Position Indicator* to indicate the current position in the MIDI file.

- Recording and editing capability in real time and step time. Real time operations capture data as it's played on a synthesizer keyboard. Step time operations capture individual MIDI instructions as you enter them from the Multimedia PC keyboard.

- *Quantizing* to correct timing and synchronization inconsistencies.

- Support for external MIDI devices and the ability to accommodate extensive MIDI configurations.

MIDI Patch Mapper

To help ensure that MIDI files authored on one synthesizer sound the same when played back on another, Windows with Multimedia includes MIDI mapping functionality as part of its core system capability. The MIDI Mapper lets you identify the MIDI devices in the system and performs the following functions:

- Re-map or mute channel data

- Independently route channel data to any MIDI port in the system

- Re-map patch numbers

- Re-map key numbers (intended primarily for key-based percussion)

- Scale channel/volume controller messages

These standard patch services enable Windows with Multimedia to provide device-independent MIDI file playback for applications.

Hardware

All Multimedia PCs provide Base-level or Extended synthesizer capabilities. In developing MIDI compositions for your applications, you'll also need a MIDI keyboard and may want to include one or more synthesizers in your development system. The following pieces of hardware will provide your system with the capacity to develop MIDI compositions for your applications.

Base-level MIDI Synthesizer

The standard Multimedia includes a MIDI interface, and at least a Base-level synthesizer is included in the hardware and supported through Windows with Multimedia.

Using the synthesizer in the Multimedia PC is the most direct approach for developing MIDI compositions. You can compose exactly what the user will hear. Testing your MIDI files on a several Multimedia PC synthesizers will give you a good idea of how playback sound can vary depending on synthesizer capability.

A MIDI keyboard

The MIDI keyboard will generate MIDI commands to produce music. MIDI keyboards are packaged in at least two configurations: a master keyboard that connects to other MIDI devices and a keyboard-synthesizer.

A master keyboard connects to the synthesizer in your computer and supplies the synthesizer with MIDI messages to produce sound. Master keyboards generally can control several MIDI devices.

In comparison, the keyboard-synthesizer can perform the base functions of a master keyboard. It also can operate as a self-contained unit.

Building a MIDI Score

You'll most likely use a keyboard and MIDI sequencer software to create a MIDI score. A MIDI sequencer is very much like a multi-track tape recorder. When you create a MIDI song using one instrument, you can overlay this song with more instruments to produce the melody, harmony, and percussion.

When creating a MIDI file for a Multimedia PC, make sure that your create a Base-level version on channels 13–16 and an Extended version on channels 1–10. See "Authoring Device-Independent MIDI Files," later in this chapter, to find out why this is important and how to create a proper file.

Here are the general steps involved in creating a MIDI score for Windows with Multimedia:

- Compose each track in the score

- Build the composition track by track

- Edit each channel until you're satisfied

- Modify the characteristics of the score

- Store the composition

Compose Each Track

Most musicians develop the melody, bass harmony, and percussion of their composition from a keyboard by playing, recording, playing back, and editing each component until it sounds just right.

Build the Composition

To create the final composition, each track must be recorded using a sequencer. Certain designated channels must be used to ensure device-independent playback in the Multimedia PC. The section, "Authoring Device-Independent MIDI Files," discusses this topic in detail. In general, you'll need to build your composition to work for both Base-level and Extended synthesizers.

- Build channels 1 through 10 for the Extended synthesizer; use nine melodic tracks and one percussive track.

- Build channels 13 through 16 for the Base-level synthesizer; use three melodic tracks and one percussive track.

You'll want to make the songs sound consistent on both Extended and Base-level synthesizers. To accomplish this, it's recommended that you duplicate the dominant melodies and harmonies of the song in the first three channels for Extended synthesizers (channels 1–3) and Base-level synthesizers (channels 13–15). You may need to reduce the polyphony for channels 13–15.

Edit Each Channel

Sequencers typically maintain each channel's data as a separate track, allowing you to play them back and edit them independently. Go through and edit all the channels until satisfied with the quality of each.

Modify Characteristics of the Score

If you compose your MIDI score using the synthesizer in a standard Multimedia PC, you can be reasonably certain that the instrument patches and volume levels will work fine for other Multimedia PCs. Otherwise, you should translate your patches to the standard MIDI patch specifications defined in the section, "Authoring Device-Independent MIDI Files," and test playback on a Multimedia PC synthesizer.

Another modification you might want to make at this stage is to specify whether notes in the channel play on the Left or Right speakers, or in between. The general process for modifying a channel message and include stereo goes like this:

1. Set the instrument patch to the appropriate patch number as defined in the General MIDI Mode standard (shown later in this chapter).

2. Set the volume of the channel.

3. If you want stereo, set the Pan Controller Message to the appropriate value between Left or Right.

Store the Composition

MIDI files can be stored in three file formats: 0, 1, and 2. Most sequencers can export data in MIDI file format 0 or 1. Save the sequence as a format 0 or format 1 MIDI file—Windows with Multimedia supports only file formats 0 (single track) and 1 (multiple track). It is recommended that you use format 0—especially for CD-ROM since it minimizes both RAM usage and the number of seeks. Once you have saved the MIDI file, you are ready to play it from your application.

Converting Existing MIDI Files

You can also use MIDI files composed on a different system. Here are the general steps to prepare and convert these files for Windows with Multimedia.

- Rechannelize the MIDI data

- Convert patch numbers to the General MIDI Mode specification

- Set a volume level

Rechannelize the MIDI Data

Duplicate the most important melodies and harmonies of the song in the first three channels for both the Extended and Base-level synthesizers. Make sure the channel numbers and polyphony match the guidelines for Windows with Multimedia MIDI files. (Channels 1 through 10 for an Extended synthesizer; channels 13 through 16 for the Base-level synthesizer.)

Convert Patch Numbers

The final MIDI file must have patch numbers that match valid Microsoft MIDI patch assignments.

Set a Volume Level

The relative volume levels may be different in every synthesizer, and so, to get a truly accurate reading, you'll want to play the file through the synthesizer in the Multimedia PC.

Start with a volume setting of 80 for normal listening levels. For quieter or louder playback volume, change the value accordingly. Volume levels range from 0 through 127. You will want to adjust the volume in every channel. This is especially important when authoring your MIDI sequence on a system different from the final playback system.

Authoring Device-Independent MIDI Files

MIDI specifications show a coordinated effort to provide standard communications protocol and connections, and allow devices manufactured by different manufacturers to communicate with each other. Although the MIDI specification addresses several issues, individual manufacturers have had to define their own instrument patch definitions, resulting in a lack of numbering standardization among MIDI devices.

The "MIDI 1.0 Detailed Specification" doesn't define any standard patch assignments for synthesizers. Therefore, when you create a MIDI file, it won't be reproduced correctly unless it is played back on the same MIDI synthesizer setup used to create it. For example, if you create a piano concerto on one synthesizer and try to play it back on another, it might be played with a flute instead of a piano.

One solution to this problem is to map all the MIDI device patches from a common set of patch definitions. The Microsoft MIDI Mapper, included with Windows with Multimedia, maps one instrument patch number to another so that the synthesizer knows which instrument is intended to be used, even though the original file uses standard patch numbers.

The following pages offer the following aids to creating MIDI files usable for the different synthesizers that may exist in Multimedia PCs:

- A list of general authoring guidelines

- How to prioritize your MIDI data

- The standard MIDI patch assignments

- The standard MIDI key assignments

These guidelines include a list of standard patch assignments and standard key assignments for percussion instruments. Using the MIDI Mapper, MIDI files authored to these guidelines can be played on any Multimedia PC with internal or external MIDI synthesizers.

General Authoring Guidelines

Most sequencer programs available today include a channel mapping option that lets you direct that single channel to any of the other 15 channels available. This mapping capability lets you specify the exact channel on which you want to record. This is an important feature for MIDI authoring in Windows with Multimedia, since, to ensure device independence, only designated channels may be used.

Follow these guidelines to author MIDI files for Windows with Multimedia:

■ Author for both base-level and extended synthesizer setups.

■ Use MIDI channels 13 through 16 for base-level synthesizer data (reserve channel 16 for key-based percussion instruments).

■ Use MIDI channels 1 through 10 for extended synthesizer data (reserve channel 10 for key-based percussion instruments).

■ Prioritize MIDI data by putting crucial data in the lower-numbered channels.

■ Limit the polyphony of non-percussive channels to a total of 6 notes for base-level data and 16 notes for extended data.

■ Limit the polyphony of percussive channels to a total of 3 notes for base-level data and 16 notes for extended data.

■ Use the standard MIDI patch assignments and key assignments.

■ Always send a program-change message to a channel to select a patch before sending other messages to that channel. For the two percussion channels (10 and 16), select program number 0.

■ Always follow a MIDI program-change message with a MIDI main-volume-controller message (controller number 7) to set the relative volume of the patch.

■ Use a value of 80 (0x50) for the main volume controller for normal listening levels. For quieter or louder levels, you can use lower or higher values.

The following illustration summarizes the use of the 16 MIDI channels in a standard MIDI file authored for Windows with Multimedia.

Channel	Description	Polyphony
1	Extended Melodic Tracks	
2		
3		
4		
5		16 Notes
6		
7		
8		
9		
10	Extended Percussion Track	16 Notes
11	Unused Tracks	
12		
13	Base-Level Melodic Tracks	
14		6 Notes
15		
16	Base-Level Percussion Track	3 Notes

Prioritizing Your MIDI Data

Synthesizers don't always fall cleanly into the Base-level and Extended designations defined earlier. It's up to the end-user (or the manufacturer of the Multimedia PC) to determine how to use synthesizers capable of more than the Base-level requirements, but not fully meeting the Extended requirements.

For this reason, it's important to prioritize the melodic data by putting the most critical data in lower-numbered channels. For example, a user may have a synthesizer capable of playing six melodic instruments with 12-note polyphony. The user can use this device as an Extended synthesizer by setting up the MIDI Mapper to play only the first six melodic channels and ignore any information on channels seven, eight, and nine.

Using Standard MIDI Patch Assignments

The standard MIDI patch assignments for authoring MIDI files for use with the Multimedia extensions are based on the MIDI Manufacturers Association (MMA) General MIDI Mode specification. The following illustration shows the standard MIDI patch assignments.

Piano		Chromatic Percussion		Organ		Guitar	
0	Acoustic Grand Piano	8	Celesta	16	Hammond Organ	24	Acoustic Guitar (nylon)
1	Bright Acoustic Piano	9	Glockenspiel	17	Percussive Organ	25	Acoustic Guitar (steel)
2	Electric Grand Piano	10	Music box	18	Rock Organ	26	Electric Guitar (jazz)
3	Honky-tonk Piano	11	Vibraphone	19	Church Organ	27	Electric Guitar (clean)
4	Rhodes Piano	12	Marimba	20	Reed Organ	28	Electric Guitar (muted)
5	Chorused Piano	13	Xylophone	21	Accordion	29	Overdriven Guitar
6	Harpsichord	14	Tubular Bells	22	Harmonica	30	Distortion Guitar
7	Clavinet	15	Dulcimer	23	Tango Accordion	31	Guitar Harmonics

Bass		Strings		Ensemble		Brass	
32	Acoustic Bass	40	Violin	48	String Ensemble 1	56	Trumpet
33	Electric Bass (finger)	41	Viola	49	String Ensemble 2	57	Trombone
34	Electric Bass (pick)	42	Cello	50	SynthStrings 1	58	Tuba
35	Fretless Bass	43	Contrabass	51	SynthStrings 2	59	Muted Trumpet
36	Slap Bass 1	44	Tremolo Strings	52	Choir Aahs	60	French Horn
37	Slap Bass 2	45	Pizzicato Strings	53	Voice Oohs	61	Brass Section
38	Synth Bass 1	46	Orchestral Harp	54	Synth Voice	62	Synth Brass 1
39	Synth Bass 2	47	Timpani	55	Orchestra Hit	63	Synth Brass 2

Reed		Pipe		Synth Lead		Synth Pad	
64	Soprano Sax	72	Piccolo	80	Lead 1 (square)	88	Pad 1 (new age)
65	Alto Sax	73	Flute	81	Lead 2 (sawtooth)	89	Pad 2 (warm)
66	Tenor Sax	74	Recorder	82	Lead 3 (caliope lead)	90	Pad 3 (polysynth)
67	Baritone Sax	75	Pan Flute	83	Lead 4 (chiff lead)	91	Pad 4 (choir)
68	Oboe	76	Bottle Blow	84	Lead 5 (charang)	92	Pad 5 (bowed)
69	English Horn	77	Shakuhachi	85	Lead 6 (voice)	93	Pad 6 (metallic)
70	Bassoon	78	Whistle	86	Lead 7 (fifths)	94	Pad 7 (halo)
71	Clarinet	79	Ocarina	87	Lead 8 (bass + lead)	95	Pad 8 (sweep)

Synth Effects		Ethnic		Percussive		Sound Effects	
96	FX 1 (rain)	104	Sitar	112	Tinkle Bell	120	Guitar Fret Noise
97	FX 2 (soundtrack)	105	Banjo	113	Agogo	121	Breath Noise
98	FX 3 (crystal)	106	Shamisen	114	Steel Drums	122	Seashore
99	FX 4 (atmosphere)	107	Koto	115	Woodblock	123	Bird Tweet
100	FX 5 (brightness)	108	Kalimba	116	Taiko Drum	124	Telephone Ring
101	FX 6 (goblins)	109	Bagpipe	117	Melodic Tom	125	Helicopter
102	FX 7 (echoes)	110	Fiddle	118	Synth Drum	126	Applause
103	FX 8 (sci-fi)	111	Shanai	119	Reverse Cymbal	127	Gunshot

Standard MIDI Key Assignments

The standard MIDI key assignments for percussion instruments are based on the General MIDI Mode specification. The following illustration shows the standard key assignments for MIDI files authored for Windows with Multimedia:

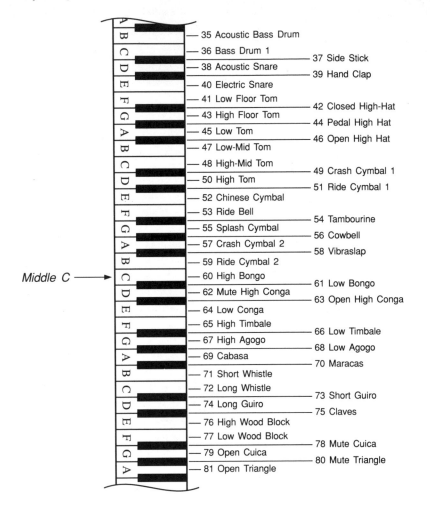

Chapter 8
Text

The one portion of multimedia that everyone feels familiar with is text. Text files form one of the largest segments of the multimedia developer's base of information. Many multimedia applications will be mainly text driven—developed by converting a book into an online multimedia application.

The target format for Windows with Multimedia is either straight ASCII or Rich Text Format (RTF—output by Word for Windows). Whenever you convert text files, however, you invariably lose some original formatting. You still must add the proper formatting, indexing, and other referencing tags to make the text useful. This chapter provides an overview of the three main ways to get your text into a form compatible with Windows with Multimedia.

- Retyping it
- Scanning it in from print
- Converting it through the use of a computer program.

With the proliferation of word processors, desktop publishing programs, and electronic typesetting systems, almost everything currently being printed also exists in one electronically readable format or another. If the issues associated with text preparation seem overwhelming, you have another alternative: pay someone else to do it. There are a number of data preparation houses that will gladly take your money and your text and return a finished product.

Note The Rich Text Format (RTF) is documented in the *Word for Windows Technical Reference*, available from Microsoft Press.

Retyping Text

Although typing is labor-intensive, it is often the most economical method to get large amounts of printed material into a computer. You can either have your staff re-key the text or you can contract with a service bureau. Typists enter the text directly into the system from the printed material.

There are a number of companies offering such a service. These companies generally claim 99.9% or higher accuracy through the use of double or triple key verification (also called double or triple blind typing). This means that they have two or three people type the same material, and then use a computer program to spot differences. The assumption is that several people won't make the same mistake at the same place in the file.

The cost of this service typically varies with the volume and complexity of the original material and the accuracy, turn-around speed, and extra services (such as format tagging) provided by the service company.

The following table lists some of the benefits and drawbacks associated with re-keying the text.

Benefits	Drawbacks
Re-keying printed documents is an established type of service, and you can reliably estimate the costs and time associated with such a project.	Re-keying usually takes longer than scanning.
The typists can include formatting and structural information into the text as they re-key it. This can reduce the time necessary to prepare the text for the retrieval software.	A labor intensive job such as this can become costly. (However, the cost of verifying scanned data is also high.)
	You still must schedule time for proofreading and correction.

Scanning Text

The concept of feeding printed material into a machine that recognizes each letter and feeds it into a text file sounds ideal. Fortunately, such technology exists and is called optical character recognition (OCR). Under the proper circumstances it can be a very efficient way to get text into a computer.

An OCR system consists of a scanner (quite possibly the same one used to scan images), a computer, and some software. The scanner converts a page of text into a bitmapped image, and the software analyzes the letter shapes and converts them into ASCII letters. The number of predefined typefaces is usually limited to less than a dozen, although many systems have a learning facility to include new characters and typefaces.

You scan every page and then you run various utility programs (such as a spell checker) to detect misreads and other scanner errors. For the final step, print and proofread the text. The following table lists some of the benefits and drawbacks associated with using OCR technology.

Benefits	Drawbacks
Scanning requires little upfront labor.	Some scanners can read only a limited set of typefaces. Other scanners read more typefaces, but you first have to train them by running samples through the scanner and then calibrating its interpretation of the text.
An OCR scanner can quickly convert large amounts of printed information into electronic files (less than a minute per page).	Assuming an accuracy rate of 99%, scanned text contains an average of one error for every two lines of text. This error rate can mean hundreds of thousands of errors for long texts. Make sure to schedule time for editing and proofreading.
Scanning usually costs less than re-keying.	You can lose special symbols (such as Greek or other foreign characters) and complex formatting (such as tables, mathematical formulas, or special fonts).

Getting Better Results When Scanning

Here are four ways to get the best results with OCR:

- Quality of the original text

- Type of scanner

- Speed (power) of the computer

- Quality of the software

Start with High-Quality Printed Material.

The process of optical character recognition is much like a person reading. Like a person's eye, the scanner analyzes light reflected from a page to create a pictorial representation of what is black (the ink) and what is not black (the paper). This picture of the page is stored in the computer where the OCR software tries to chop the black parts up into individual letters and then guess what each one is.

Generally anything difficult for a person to read will be impossible for an OCR system to convert. This includes such things as smudged text, small type, strange fonts, characters that are too close together, and typewritten characters created with an old ribbon or dirty keys.

The bottom line to OCR efficiency: always start with high-quality printed material.

Choose an Appropriate Scanner.

Given good clean text, the next critical element in the system is the resolution of the scanner. Typical scanner resolutions range from 75 to 450 dots per inch (DPI). The higher the resolution of the scanner, the higher the likelihood of accurate recognition by the software. Although some companies claim to be able to accurately recognize text at 200 DPI, 300 DPI is probably the lowest practical resolution.

Another factor that influences the suitability of a scanner for OCR is its method of feeding. The two standard methods are flatbed and roller-fed.

■ Flatbed scanners are like photocopiers in that the artwork to be scanned is placed on a glass plate, covered by a lid, and then passed over by a light.

■ Roller-fed scanners are like a typical FAX machine, in that artwork is scanned after being fed in through rollers.

Flatbed scanners are well-suited for bound, oversized, or especially small pages. Roller-fed scanners are good for bulk scanning of material with a consistent format. A flatbed scanner with an optional document feeder offers the best of both worlds.

Use a Fast Computer.

The power of the computer used in an OCR system doesn't effect the accuracy of conversion. Nevertheless, we recommend the computer have at least an 80386 processor running at 25 Mhz. Also, since most OCR programs require large amounts of memory, having 4 MB of RAM or more can make life a lot easier.

Select Fast, Accurate OCR Software.

There are dozens of OCR programs on the market. Most of these are simply software programs that you load into a computer and run, though some high-end programs work with a board that plugs into the computer. These hardware and software combinations are usually faster, more accurate, and more expensive.

There are a lot of options available when buying OCR programs. Some of the more interesting ones can do the following things:

■ Read both mono and proportional spaced fonts

■ Read dot-matrix output

■ Learn new fonts

■ Mix text and graphics

■ Define frames of text to read

■ Retain character formatting attributes

■ Retain columns (tables)

■ Save in various word processing formats

■ Incorporate spell checking into the conversion process

Be aware, however, that character recognition systems rarely achieve more than 95% accuracy on anything but the cleanest of text. Even at 99% accuracy, there could be 20 mistakes on a typical 2,000-character page. So, budget time for spell checking and proofreading.

There are almost infinite combinations of specific scanners, computers, and software packages. If you have printed pages numbering in the hundreds, OCR may work for you. If you have massive amounts of printed text, you should consider hiring a data entry service to have it re-keyed.

Converting Text

Once you have the text files in electronic format, make sure they exist in a format usable by Windows with Multimedia. Electronic files exist in many different formats and these differences often complicate the conversion process.

For example, word processing software can provide great control over the appearance of printed output. This control is made possible through the special codes added to the text file by the word processor. Full-featured word processors such as Microsoft Word for Windows even show on the screen exactly what the printed output will look like—a feature often known as WYSIWYG (pronounced, "wizzywig"), which stands for "What You See Is What You Get."

Typesetting systems use even more extensive codes to control how text gets printed. You can add character formatting, such as bold or italic; paragraph formatting, such as hanging indents and justification; and other formatting, such as margins and page numbering, that applies to whole blocks of text.

If you are fortunate, there will be a relatively painless conversion method available for your particular set of formats. Many of the more powerful word processing programs can read and write files in a variety of formats. And even if none of the available formats is exactly what you want, one of them, such as RTF, may be easier to work with than the original format.

The Benefits of Using SGML Formatting

Individual differences among the internal tags used to structure documents can cause conversion problems. For example, one typist may define paragraphs one way (double spacing, 1.5 lines after); another typist may define paragraphs differently (single spacing, 2 lines after). Such differences can increase the time required to make the text consistent throughout an application.

One approach used to solve this problem is to format text according to the guidelines of the Standard Generalized Markup Language (SGML). The SGML standard helps to enforce consistency of tagging between texts. SGML tags define the structure of a document and the purpose of the various elements of the document, rather than the appearance of those elements.

For example, in a typical typesetting file, a chapter title might be coded as bold 24-point text centered on the page. The tagged title might look like this:

```
<FB><CP24>Taming the Wild Sloth<CP1><FS><QC><WR1><QL>
```

This tag set will produce the output desired for presentation on paper, but it may not be appropriate for other media. The same chapter title tagged in SGML might look like this:

```
<Chapter>Taming the Wild Sloth</Chapter>
```

This tag set simply says that this group of words is a chapter title. If the file is sent to a typesetting machine, an accompanying file, called a Document Type Definition (DTD), specifies that chapter titles are to be printed centered, in bold 24-point text. If the file is to be displayed on a computer screen by a program incapable of displaying 24-point type, a different DTD can be attached that specifies that chapter titles be displayed bold, centered, and underlined.

SGML can help simplify the conversion process. Nevertheless, the final electronic stage of most books is a typesetting format, not a word processing format or SGML. Whenever you convert text, make sure to examine your requirements first.

Analyze the Destination File

You should look at what you want to produce before you start to convert the text. There are a variety of elements that may require tagging in the text portion of a multimedia application:

- **Character attributes**. These are the codes that indicate bold or italic type styles, character fonts, color, inverse video, etc.

- **Hierarchy**. The document hierarchy is its basic structure. This is usually expressed in book terms, and includes such hierarchical elements as title; chapter heads; and first, second and third level heads.

- **Links**. These are the hypermedia elements that you click to initiate some action, such as jumping to another location, displaying a picture, or playing audio. Links are the most difficult element to automatically add to a file.

Define these and other elements of your target text before beginning the conversion process.

Analyze the Source File

Once you know where you want to end up, look at the source file to find out what format you are starting with. The worst, and fortunately least likely, case would be to have a file created by some obscure WYSIWYG word processor that stored text and formatting separately. More likely, you will have a file created by a type-setting system or a desktop publishing program that creates files in plain ASCII with embedded tags.

Ideally, you will have complete documentation on the system used, with a list of all tags and their precise meaning. If you don't have this information, extract a list of the tags from the source file, and then figure out the meaning of each by comparing its use in the source file to its effect in the printed document.

Once familiar with all the tags used in your source file, you can indicate on the tag list which to convert and which to delete. Your analysis should let you be able to directly convert character attributes and hierarchical elements. However, cross references, footnotes, and various kinds of other links will be more difficult.

Note The most difficult type of automatic tagging is that of cross references and other links because these often aren't tagged in the source file. The more obvious ones, such as "see Chapter 6," or "see Section 3.7.2," or "as shown in Figure 5-2," can probably be done, because they refer to an element that should already be tagged. References to something "earlier in this chapter" or "shown previously" are more difficult.

Convert the Text

Once you have the text tagged, you then must convert it to your target delivery format (e.g., ASCII or RTF).

The many different word processing file formats has generated many different conversion programs. For example, Word for Windows supports the conversion of many different word processing formats into RTF and ASCII. Many word processors also provide utilities to either convert text to RTF or they let you save text in ASCII format. (Understand, however, that you lose all formatting when you save to ASCII.)

All methods of text format conversion involve pattern recognition of some sort. The source file is scanned until a significant pattern is spotted, and then some appropriate action is performed—typically deleting the pattern or replacing all or some portion of it with another pattern. You should investigate the following types of conversion programs:

- Specific purpose—these programs automatically convert from one specific format to another. An example would be a WordStar to Word conversion utility. To run one of these, you simply provide the name of the input and output files and let the software run. If you can find or write one of these programs that matches your needs, it will probably be the fastest way to make your conversions.

- General purpose—these programs use some sort of look-up table to make conversions. By editing the look-up table, you can control the pattern searched for and what its replacement will be. These programs can support extremely elaborate patterns, but are only as good as your ability to initially recognize and uniquely define those patterns.

■ Word processors with Search and Replace—a powerful word processor with a strong macro language can often be useful during some stages of text conversion. But it can also be slow and cumbersome if you are working with megabytes of text. Microsoft Word for Windows is an especially powerful example of this category.

Tracking the Converted Files

One of your most important tasks is to track the flow of documents through the data preparation process. A large job, such as a 20 to 30-volume encyclopedia, might consist of 20 MB of data broken into thousands of individual files. You may have to pass each file through a dozen or more conversion stages.

There is no need to save every stage forever—you could have 100,000 files—but you shouldn't start deleting until certain the last stage is error free. If an error does pop up, you'll want to be able to retrace the path and spot the cause.

Proofing and Correction

Proofing is a tedious but essential step of text conversion. Two types of tools that take some of the pain out of the process are syntax checkers, and viewers that expand the tags.

Syntax checkers examine a file for such things as begin-end tag sets that aren't balanced and structural or nesting tags that aren't in an acceptable order. Most data preparation houses can write such programs for specific jobs.

A viewer capable of expanding the tags—hiding them from view and performing their function, such as bolding a string of text—makes it far easier to visually proof a document than if it is cluttered with tags. The availability of this feature alone is a compelling reason for converting source files to RTF. They can then be loaded into Microsoft Word for Windows for proofing and additional editing or tagging. The resulting file can be saved in RTF format, for input into the next stage of the document processing cycle.

You may discover that existing electronic files don't match the current printed material you want incorporated into the application. This can happen because corrections are typically made manually near print time, and sometimes those changes don't get made in the source text files as well. If you find discrepancies, you'll need to add another step to collect all the changes and incorporate them into the electronic files.

Text Preparation Hardware and Software

Since text can come from a variety of different sources and different formats, it's difficult to propose one single hardware/software solution for text preparation. Therefore, when preparing text for multimedia applications, the hardware and software identified below should provide a starting point for your own research:

- 80286 or 80386 based DOS compatible PC (if you plan to re-key the text, you'll need several PCs)

- RTF text editor such as Microsoft's Word for Windows

- Laser printer to output pages for proofreading

- VGA quality display

- 100 megabyte hard disk

- OCR scanner and software

- Tools to convert text tagged with word processor or typesetting codes to RTF

Chapter 9
Animation

Quality images add tremendous value to a multimedia title. You can increase this value, however, by making these images move. The Multimedia Development Kit provides the *Multimedia Movie Player* (known simply as the Movie Player) which plays animation files created with MacroMind Director. MacroMind Director is a multimedia authoring tool that runs on the Macintosh.

You can create animations (also referred to as *movie files*) using MacroMind Director and then convert them to Microsoft's Movie Player format. The MDK provides the Movie Convertor, a Macintosh-based file conversion utility, for this purpose.

This chapter discusses general authoring guidelines for creating animation files for the Multimedia Movie Player. The material assumes you already know how to author Director animations or are at least familiar with its terminology. This chapter also contains technical information about the programming functions associated with the Movie Player—for more information, see the MDK's *Programmer's Workbook* and *Programmer's Reference*.

Note   The Movie Player is the only animation player included with the Microsoft Multimedia Development Kit. However, other animation-tool vendors provide Windows-based animation players as well.

Making Movies with Director

There are two basic kinds of computer animations: *cast-based animation* and *frame animation*. Frame animation is created by designing a separate frame for each screen view, much like a film strip or video. Cast-based animation is created by individually designing all of the moving objects, assigning to each object its own character traits (such as position pattern, size, and ink), and then forming a complete picture frame composed of the individual objects. Both types of animations are played by flipping through the frames in quick succession.

MacroMind Director is a tool for creating cast-based animations, providing a number of features to support the authoring process. The end result is referred to as *movie*. Each frame can contain multiple unique *cast members* that can change position and appearance independently in each subsequent frame. Cast members can be graphics, sounds, text, and palettes. Collectively, the group of cast members for a movie is called the *cast*. The script that controls the cast members is called the *score*. The score is a grid that controls the appearance and behavior of the movie at each frame. Cast members must be referenced in the score to play a part in the animation.

When you play a Director movie, the individual cast members appear to move within a stage window. You can examine these cast members from Director in the *cast window*.

Building Director animations is direct and efficient, but still requires time and creativity. The following procedure outlines the basic process.

▶ **To create a movie file for the Windows environment:**

1. Create a movie for MacroMind Director on the Macintosh.

2. Once you have something you want to try on the PC, convert the file to Movie Player format by using the Microsoft Movie Convertor utility as described later in this chapter.

3. Run the movie file on the Multimedia PC, noting any problems with appearance that need to be fixed. Remember to test on a variety of machines to catch problems in performance and synchronization.

4. Go back to the Macintosh and integrate these changes.

5. Repeat steps 2 through 4 until the movie runs acceptably on the PC.

Playing Movies On a Multimedia PC

Once you've created a Director movie, you display it on any Multimedia PC that has the Multimedia Movie Player dynamic link library (MMP.DLL) loaded on its system. If your movie uses the Media Control Interface (MCI) to control audio or an external device, then the MCIMMP.DRV device driver must also be installed. The MDK's *Getting Started* book describes how to include these files with your application.

There are three ways for Windows with Multimedia to play your movie:

■ You can use the application programming interface (API) supported by the Movie Player DLL. To use the Movie Player API, you must write a custom movie-player program. The MDK includes a sample application called MMPLAY that uses the Movie Player functions (it does not use the MCI animation commands). MMPLAY is supplied in C source-code format; if you have Microsoft C and the Microsoft Windows SDK, you can build it and use it to test your movies. It also serves as an example from which you can build your own player.

■ You can run animations from the Multimedia Windows Media Player applet. Windows with Multimedia includes the Media Player, an application that you can use when testing your movie. Media Player (MPLAYER.EXE) is a general-purpose MCI player that allows you to control MCI devices installed on your system. Use the MCI "animation" device to play movies. Refer to the Media Player help file for instructions.

■ Finally, any authoring environment that supports the use of MCI (such as Asymetrix ToolBook) can play movie files using the MCI animation device.

The *Programmer's Workbook* discusses the methods of playing movie files, and the *Programmer's Reference* describes the MCI command messages, MCI command strings, and Movie Player functions that an application can use to play movie files.

The remainder of this chapter discusses the capabilities of the Movie Player and discusses guidelines for authoring Director files for playback under Windows with Multimedia.

Building Movies for Movie Player

When you author a movie to run on a Multimedia PC, you must consider the wide range of potential delivery platforms. Your product might run on PCs ranging from the base Multimedia PC (with an 80286, 10-MHz processor and 16-color VGA video adapter) to more powerful machines (equipped with 80386 or 80486 processors and 256-color VGA video adapters). These differences in CPU speed and palette handling can cause unexpected results when you play your movies.

The following guidelines summarize authoring tips for the Movie Player:

- To play movies well across varied platforms, limit the complexity of the animation, especially if the movies include synchronized sound. Complicated animations are computation-intensive and can cause gaps and skips in concurrent sound playback. Avoid palette effects and limit those inks used for matte, copy, and white transparent.

- To display complex, 256-color animations, limit your delivery platform to systems with 256-color VGA adapters. Play the movie in full-screen mode; don't try to share the screen with other applications. Your movie player application should take over the static colors, as described later in this chapter.

Finally, it's important to note that the Movie Player supports a subset of the MacroMind Director features and has changed others slightly. A movie that runs on the Macintosh may not appear exactly the same on a Multimedia PC. Before you design the animation sequences for your presentation, create test files to exercise the various Director features you wish to include. In particular, test transitions, inks, and tempo commands. Run the files on a range of delivery machines to see how CPU speed and data streaming rates affect performance of the Director feature.

When you test your movies, look for timing or synchronization problems. Note any color changes that occur. Record your comments and make the necessary adjustments to the original file.

Movie Player Capabilities

The Movie Player does a pretty good job at reproducing MacroMind Director animations on the PC, considering the differences between the authoring and delivery platforms. The Movie Player supports the following capabilities:

Feature	Movie Player Support
Transitions	All transition types are supported.
Inks	The following inks are supported: Copy Matte White Transparent The following inks are supported with restrictions: Ghost and Not Ghost Reverse and Not Reverse Transparent and Not Transparent Not Copy The following inks are supported in altered form: Mask
Cast members	All cast-member types are supported, except for QuickDraw PICT cast members.
Lingo	Lingo is not supported. The Movie Player supports the use of MCI commands in the script channel.
Tempo	All Tempo commands are supported including "wait for audio" on both streamed and embedded audio.
Palette Effects	Everything within the limits set in the next section.
Audio	The Movie Player supports embedded audio cast members. Using the MCI script-channel commands, a movie can also play audio compact-disc tracks, MIDI files, and waveform audio files.

Using Palettes and Bitmaps

When you author movies for the Multimedia PC, you always have to consider the differences between how the Macintosh handles color palettes and how Windows handles palettes. Hardware differences also factor into this. The Multimedia PC provides two standard types of video displays:

- A 16-color display that doesn't allow changes to the system palette.

- A 256-color display that does let you change up to 236 colors in the system palette.

You can get the system to let you change more colors, however, the appearance of your display under Windows will be altered. If you decide this is acceptable, you can do this by using through the **mmpLoadFile** function, which loads a movie file for playback. (See the *Programmer's Reference* for more information.) When loading a movie file with **mmpLoadFile**, specify the MMPLOAD_NOSTATIC option. This changes the system capabilities to this:

- 16-color display—you can now change 14 colors in the system palette.

- 256-color display—you can now change up to 254 colors in the system palette.

As you author movie files, you need to consider the restrictions associated with bitmaps and palettes. For example, with 1-bit movies, all features will work across both systems. With 4-bit and 8-bit movies, some additional restrictions apply.

The following tables show how movies authored with different inks and palette effects finally appear once ported to the Multimedia PC environment. The tables cover these scenarios:

- How colors appear when using inks that don't modify colors

- How colors appear when using inks that do modify colors

- How colors appear when using palette effects

Using Inks That Don't Modify Colors

The following table shows how colors in movies appear when using inks that do not modify colors (copy, matte, mask, and white transparent).

Display	8-Bit Movie	4-Bit Movie
16-color display	All colors are mapped to the nearest VGA system color.	All colors are mapped to the nearest VGA system color. If the Macintosh palette has the same colors as the VGA system palette, then the movies will appear the same.
16-color display with NOSTATIC option (requires VGAPAL driver)	All colors are mapped to the nearest VGA system color.	Colors will be correct.
256-color display	Last 237 colors and white in the Macintosh palette will be correct. The remaining colors will map to the nearest color in the system colors.	Colors will be correct.
256-color display with NOSTATIC option	Colors will be correct.	Colors will be correct.

Using Inks That Do Modify Colors

The following table shows how colors in movies appear when using inks that do modify colors (transparent, reverse, ghost, not copy, not transparent, not reverse, and not ghost).

Display	8-Bit Movie	4-Bit Movie
16-color display	Random colors.	Random colors unless the Macintosh palette is the exact reverse of the VGA system palette.
16-color display with NOSTATIC option (requires VGAPAL driver)	Random colors.	Colors will be correct.
256-color display	Random colors.	Random colors.
256-color display with NOSTATIC option	Colors will be correct.	Random colors.

Using Palette Effects

The following table shows how colors in movies appear that use palette effects (change, fade, and cycle).

Display	8-Bit Movie	4-Bit Movie
16-color display	No color changes.	No color changes.
16-color display with NOSTATIC option (requires VGAPAL driver)	Last 15 colors except for black will work.	Will work as in Director.
256-color display	Last 237 colors except for black will work.	Will work as in Director.
256-color display with NOSTATIC option	Will work as in Director.	Will work as in Director.

Using MCI Within Movies

One way to include sound in your movies is by using sound cast members embedded in the movie sound channel. These sound cast members are converted to waveforms by the Movie Convertor and built into the movie itself (adding to the size of the movie). Then, when it plays the movie, the Movie Player routes the sound to the waveform audio outputs.

Another way to add sound is by using the Media Control Interface (MCI) to play streamed audio from a waveform file, MIDI file, or compact disc. With streamed audio, the audio data is stored outside the movie file, thus reducing the size of the movie file. Since all of the movie is loaded into memory and audio data is often much larger than the rest of the movie file, the can provide large savings in memory. However, streamed audio can be more difficult to synchronize than embedded audio. Since MCI is not supported on the Macintosh, you'll need to transfer the movie file to the PC to test the synchronization.

Note   Detailed discussions of MCI and the MCI string interface appear in the MDK's *Programmer's Workbook* and *Programmer's Reference*.

The Movie Player recognizes two script-channel commands that allow you to control MCI devices from a movie. The commands are not case sensitive. You can use these commands to control any MCI device, including an audio compact disc, MIDI sequencer, and waveform-audio device.

Command	Description

mci <*MCI command string*>

> Sends the specified command string to MCI for processing. The <*MCI command string*> consists of an MCI command string, optionally enclosed in single or double quotation marks.

mciWait <*MCI device name*>

> Pauses frame advancement until the specified MCI device has completed the last command it received. The <*MCI device name*> consists of an MCI device name, optionally enclosed in single or double quotation marks.

Generally, streamed audio is useful for synchronizing audio with a block of frames; it's difficult to try to synchronize at a more detailed level. Embedded audio has the same problem. This more due to playing across different platforms than anything else.

Some Synchronization Tips

It can be very difficult to completely synchronize sound with specific image movements, like synchronizing the beat of a drum with a dancing figure. The task becomes more complex when you use streamed audio (such as CD audio or MCI waveform playback) due to the time it takes to open or seek in the audio file. If opens and seeks are minimized, then streamed audio can work as well as embedded audio.

One way to minimize synchronization problems is to loosely tie the audio to the action on the screen. Don't try to synchronize facial expressions or lip movements to voice narration. Instead, coordinate sounds with a series of frames. See the MCI script channel command example later in this chapter for a good model of how to do this.

Make sure you consider synchronization during design and you test your product on a range of delivery platforms.

Using MCI Script-Channel Commands

The Movie Player ignores any commands it cannot recognize. The Movie Player performs no error checking or error reporting on script-channel text. For example, the following script-channel command opens a waveform audio file called DING.WAV:

```
mci open ding.wav type WaveAudio
```

The following script-channel command pauses frame advancement until MCI finishes performing the last command sent for the DING.WAV file:

```
mciWait ding.wav
```

You can put multiple MCI commands in a single script-channel command; just separate each command with a semicolon. The commands are not guaranteed to be processed in left-to-right order, so if you need the commands to occur in a particular sequence, place them in different frames. For example, the following script-channel command opens two waveform files:

```
mci open yaz.wav type waveaudio; mci open node.wav type waveaudio
```

How MCI Commands are Processed

The Movie Player processes the script-channel text after it has finished drawing the current frame to the playback window and displayed the frame the required amount of time. The script-text processing is the last thing the Movie Player handles before moving to the next movie frame. With the following exceptions, you can use any MCI commands and options in the script channel:

- You cannot use the **notify** flag in any MCI command. If you need to pause playback until a certain command completes, you can use the **mciWait** script-channel command. The Movie Player uses the **notify** flag to implement the **mciWait** feature.

- You cannot use auto-opened MCI devices in the movie script channel. All MCI devices used by a movie must be explicitly opened.

- The Movie Player provides limited support for the "all" device name. You cannot use commands such as "play all," but you can use the "close all" command. If you use the "close all" command, the Movie Player closes all MCI devices opened by the movie (*not* all MCI devices opened by the application).

Your movie should include commands to close any MCI devices it opens. In any case, when the movie file is closed, the Movie Player closes all MCI devices the movie opened. It must close the devices, because it's possible that playback will be stopped before the movie reaches the frame containing the **close** command.

Tips for Using MCI Commands in the Script Channel

Before entering the MCI commands in the script channel of your movie, test them using the MCITEST application included with the MDK. You can simulate the **mciWait** command by appending the **wait** flag to the end of each command for which you plan to pause playback. (Be sure to remove the **wait** flags from the commands before entering them in the script channel.)

About Device Filenames

Since there's no automatic way to update script-channel text when a multimedia application is installed, you should avoid specifying absolute directory paths for multimedia data files you open using MCI. For example, the following **open** command depends on the CD-ROM drive being mapped to drive Q:

```
mci "open Q:\NABIRDS\MOCKBIRD.WAV type waveaudio alias mbird"
```

At author time, you have no way of knowing which drive letter will be mapped as the user's CD-ROM drive. Also, the installation program for your title will probably allow the user to specify the directory name for the title files.

By omitting the directory and drive name and using only the filename (for example, MOCKING.WAV) or a relative path name (for example, BIRDCALLS\MOCKING.WAV), your MCI **open** commands will be correct regardless of drive mappings or installation directories. Your multimedia application just needs to change directories to the appropriate base directory before starting the movie.

For example, you might store all Waveform audio files in a BIRDCALL directory located off the base directory (for example, D:\NABIRDS) for your application files. In this case, the following MCI **open** command succeeds, assuming your application changes to directory D:\NABIRDS before starting the movie:

```
mci "open BIRDCALL\MOCKBIRD.WAV type waveaudio alias mbird"
```

Examples of MCI Script-Channel Commands

The following example shows script-channel commands in a movie that plays compact-disc audio segments through MCI:

Frame	Script Text
2	`mci open cdaudio alias janes`
3	`mci set janes time format tmsf; mci stop janes`
4	`mci seek janes to 4:1:20`
9	`mciWait janes`
10	`mci play janes from 4:1:20 to 4:1:23`
12	`mciWait janes`
20	`mci play janes from 4:1:52 to 4:2:06`
22	`mciWait janes`
30	`mci play janes from 4:2:22 to 4:2:34`
31	`mciWait janes`
35	`mci play janes from 4:2:36 to 4:2:51`
39	`mciWait janes`
45	`mci play janes from 4:3:53 to 4:4:07`
46	`mciWait janes`
60	`mci seek janes to 11:1:22`
64	`mciWait janes`
65	`mci play janes from 11:1:22 to 11:1:32`
67	`mciWait janes`
75	`mci play janes from 11:1:32 to 11:2:12`
77	`mciWait janes`
90	`mci play janes from 11:3:12 to 11:3:24`
92	`mciWait janes`
97	`mci close janes`

The next example uses MCI to play a waveform audio file. It uses multiple MCI **play** commands and **mciWait** commands to synchronize sections of waveform audio with the appropriate movie frames.

Frame	Script Text
2	mci open narrat\fer.wav type WaveAudio alias fer
4	mci play fer from 0 to 20404
8	mciwait fer
25	mci play fer from 21426 to 31579
121	mciwait fer
123	mci play fer from 32700 to 37185
198	mciwait fer
200	mci play fer from 38231 to 41139
208	mciwait fer
210	mci play fer from 42300 to 50327
226	mciwait fer
228	mci play fer from 51455 to 56923
261	mciwait fer
262	mci play fer from 57631 to 62055
268	mciwait fer
269	mci play fer from 63285 to 70784

Since this movie file does not explicitly close the "fer" device before finishing, the Movie Player will close the device when the movie file is closed.

Using Custom Script-Channel Commands

The Movie Player can pass script commands to a movie player application for processing. This allows you to write a custom movie player that recognizes your own set of script commands. The *Programmer's Workbook* describes this capability and reviews a simple command processor included in the MMPLAY sample application on your MDK disc.

Improving Animation Performance

This section discusses assorted tips for improving the performance of your movie under the Multimedia extensions.

Limiting Movie Size

The standard that defines a Multimedia PC includes only 2 MB of RAM. Since the image portion of Director files must be loaded into memory to play, try to keep your movie files as small as possible (preferably under 500K). This will ensure, in most cases, that the entire sequence will fit in memory on the end-user's computer. Here are some ways to reduce the size of your movie files:

- Create a small number of bitmap cast members and reuse these. Use QuickDraw objects from Director's tools window whenever possible.

- Delete unused cast members; cast members not referenced in the score are still loaded into memory, thus wasting RAM and adding unnecessary load time. Use the Delete Unused Cast command.

  The Movie Player includes an option to exclude unused cast members at load time, but you need to write a custom movie player application to take advantage of this feature. Refer to the *Programmer's Workbook* for more information on limiting Movie Player memory usage.

- Clean up the cast. The Clean Up Cast command eliminates empty cast member positions, slightly reducing the size of the movie file.

- Use monochrome cast members where possible—change the color depth to one bit and set the foreground and background colors appropriately.

- Rather than include sound cast members in the movie file, use MCI to play the audio where possible. This is particularly useful if several movies in your presentation use the same audio sequences.

- It's a good idea to test your product on a Multimedia PC, and try running it alongside one or two other Windows applications. Assume that other programs will share the system memory. This will help you determine whether you've authored too large a movie.

The matte, white transparent, and mask inks require the creation of a monochrome version of the bitmap being drawn to the screen. This monochrome bitmap takes up additional memory space. The Not Transparent, Not Ghost, and Not Reverse inks can also require an extra monochrome bitmap.

Determining Movie Size   The movie file size is not a good indicator of the amount of space the movie will occupy when loaded into memory. The bitmaps in the movie file are compressed; when they are expanded, they occupy a great deal more space.

You can get a rough estimate of the movie memory size by looking at the "About MM Director" dialog box. Add the following values to estimate the memory size of the movie:

■ Screen buffer

■ Cast + score

■ Mattes

Using Cast Members Efficiently

Cast members that move on stage require more CPU calculations than do stationary cast members. Each time a cast member changes position, the Movie Player calculates the new location of the cast member, restores the stage appearance from the prior position of the cast member, and creates the correct depth perception when a cast member passes behind or in front of another cast member or background visual.

To minimize processing requirements, move as small an object as possible. For example, if a door on a house opens and closes, don't define a series of house cast members with different door positions; instead, define the door as a cast member. The house can be a QuickDraw image or another cast member.

Working with Graphics and Fonts

Instead of using a paint program to edit the images in your animation file, you may prefer to use the paint tool included with Director. Even though it has very few features, it is integrated into Director and any changes made get automatically adjusted in his work-in-progress. Using Director's graphics tools can save you the effort of transferring graphics between different software packages.

Fonts installed on the Macintosh may not supported on the Multimedia PC. MacroMind Director lets you use bitmaps and vector graphics to represent images and text in movies. By converting these elements to bitmaps, you can improve animation performance and avoid possible compatibility problems. Use Director's Convert to Bitmap command to change text and vector graphics to bitmaps.

Selecting Appropriate Transitions

Transitions define changes occurring between frames. Transitions are most effective when new cast members enter the stage or when movie scenes change. The Movie Player supports all MacroMind transitions. Some transitions play quickly and are appropriate for general use; others play more slowly and are better suited for infrequent use.

The following transitions play quickly; consider these for general use in your movies:

- Venetian blinds, vertical blinds
- Center out horizontal, center out square, center out vertical
- Checkerboard
- Cover down left, cover down right, cover up left, cover up right
- Dissolve boxy rectangles, dissolve boxy squares, dissolve patterns
- Edges in horizontal, edges in square, edges in vertical
- Random rows, random columns
- Strips (all)
- Wipes (all)

The following transitions play slowly; consider these for limited use in your movies:

- Cover down, cover left, cover right, cover up
- Dissolve bits, dissolve bits fast, dissolve pixels, dissolve pixels fast
- Push down, push left, push right, push up
- Reveal (all)
- Zoom close, zoom open

Converting MacroMind Director Files

The files produced by Director are stored in PICS format and can't be played directly by Windows with Multimedia. You must first convert the movie file to a MS-DOS file usable by Windows with Multimedia.

The Multimedia Movie Convertor, located on the Macintosh disk included in your MDK package, is a Macintosh utility that converts MacroMind Director movie files to the Multimedia Movie File format. To install the Movie Convertor, just copy it from the Macintosh disk to any folder on your Macintosh (for example, the folder in which MacroMind Director is installed). The Movie Convertor uses an interface similar to Apple File Exchange and supports single or batch conversions.

The Movie Convertor converts all elements of the Director movie file. By default, Multimedia Movie files are assigned filename extension .MMM. The convertor will suggest an MS-DOS compatible filename for the movies, which you may modify. After converting the movie file, you'll need to transfer the Movie Player version to the PC.

▶ **To convert a MacroMind Director file:**

1. Start the Movie Convertor.

2. To select the folder containing the MacroMind Director files you want to convert, choose the Select Folder button under the Source Folder box and select the source folder.

3. To select the destination folder for the converted files, choose the Select Folder button under the Destination Folder box and select the destination folder.

4. In the Source Folder box, select one or more movie files to convert.

5. Choose Convert.

   If you selected one movie file, a filename dialog box appears allowing you to change the destination filename.

   If you selected multiple movies files, the files are automatically converted. The Movie Convertor shortens the filename to eight characters and appends an .MMM filename extension.

   If the conversion will overwrite an existing file, the Movie Convertor displays a message and allows you to change the filename or cancel the conversion.

Part 2
Data Preparation
Tools User's Guide

Part 2, Data Preparation Tools User's Guide, describes the five data-preparation tools included with the Microsoft Multimedia Development Kit (MDK). The chapters in Part 2 describe the purpose of each tool, explain how to use the tool, and offer some practical examples of common usage. You will also learn about the common types of procedures necessary to prepare data for use in a multimedia title.

Part 1, Multimedia Authoring Guide, discussed the overall process of building a multimedia application.

Data Preparation Tools User's Guide

Chapters

10   Introduction

11   Understanding Data Preparation

12   Using Convert

13   Editing Bitmaps Using BitEdit

14   Editing Color Palettes Using PalEdit

15   Editing Waveform Files Using WaveEdit

16   Editing Files Using FileWalker

17   Questions and Answers About Preparing
          Bitmaps, Palettes, and Sound Files

Chapter 10
Introduction

Microsoft Windows graphical environment with Multimedia Extensions 1.0 extends the capabilities of Windows by adding support for new types of data: audio, lifelike images, and animation. Preparing this data for multimedia applications requires knowledge, skill, and the right tools.

This guide describes the data-preparation tools included with the Multimedia Development Kit (MDK). The MDK provides tools to manipulate and optimize the data used by multimedia applications. This guide explains different ways to obtain data for your application, and it describes the tools you use to prepare data. You will learn about the following topics:

- Data preparation

- Converting data using Convert

- Editing bitmaps using BitEdit

- Editing color palettes using PalEdit

- Editing waveform files using WaveEdit

- Editing files using FileWalker

Intended Audience   This guide is intended for anyone who collects and prepares the various data elements used by a multimedia application. Even though you don't need programming or engineering expertise, you should know how to use Microsoft Windows and be familiar with MS-DOS and personal computers.

Part 1 of this guide describes the role of each tool in preparing data for your multimedia applications.

The MDK Data-Preparation Tools

You'll find many different ways to use the data-preparation tools. For example, you might need to edit bitmap images and merge their color palettes. Or you might need to convert different file formats. Each activity involves different tools.

The MDK provides tools for a variety of tasks:

- Convert, used to convert data files into formats compatible with Windows with Multimedia.

- BitEdit, used to display and edit bitmapped image files.

- PalEdit, used to display and edit the colors associated with the palette file of a bitmap.

- WaveEdit, used to display, play, edit, and record audio waveform files.

- FileWalker, used to edit data files.

In some cases, certain MDK tools can exchange data with other tools. For example, you use the BitEdit tool to display and edit bitmap images. You use the PalEdit tool to edit the color palette associated with a bitmap. Using BitEdit and PalEdit simultaneously, you can edit different aspects of the same bitmap.

The following sections briefly describe the MDK data-preparation tools.

The Convert Tool

The main purpose of Convert is to convert data files from one format into another. Convert reads specified source files and creates new copies of those files in a specified destination format. It lets you work on a data file using your preferred tool, and then allows you to convert the data file to a format supported by Windows with Multimedia.

The Convert window looks like this:

For complete information on using Convert, see Chapter 12, "Using Convert."

The BitEdit Tool

BitEdit lets you import and enhance scanned bitmaps and images from paint programs. BitEdit has two basic purposes: to perform simple edits to a bitmap image and to act as a launching pad for the PalEdit tool. Once started, the BitEdit window looks like this:

BitEdit supplements rather than replaces full-featured paint programs. You should use a more sophisticated paint program to make extensive changes to an existing bitmap. For complete information on using BitEdit, see Chapter 13, "Editing Bitmaps Using BitEdit."

The PalEdit Tool

PalEdit lets you edit the color palette associated with a bitmap image. You can use PalEdit for the following tasks:

- To modify specific colors in a palette. For example, you can change a color in a bitmap from blue to green or to a more vibrant or deeper shade of blue.

- To reduce the number of colors in a palette. For example, reducing the number of colors can make it easier to develop a common palette for use with multiple images.

- To merge colors from several palettes. For example, you can establish a uniform palette to display several images simultaneously.

The PalEdit window looks like this:

For complete information on using PalEdit, see Chapter 14, "Editing Color Palettes Using PalEdit."

The WaveEdit Tool

WaveEdit lets you edit audio files that are in the Microsoft waveform format. It displays a graphic representation of a waveform file. You can use WaveEdit to play all or part of a given file, or use it to remove extraneous segments from an audio file. WaveEdit lets you cut and paste specific segments between files, create simple special effects, and even record waveform files.

The WaveEdit window looks like this:

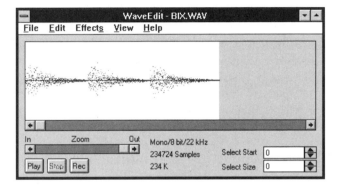

For complete information on using WaveEdit, see Chapter 15, "Editing Waveform Files Using WaveEdit."

The FileWalker Tool

The Filewalker tool lets you view and edit the contents of data files. The main purpose of FileWalker is to correct problems that arise when you create file formats. FileWalker is a developer's tool, and it is recommended only for developers already familiar with file formats and hexadecimal editing.

The FileWalker window looks like this:

```
┌─────────────────────────────────────────────┐
│ ▭   FileWalker - C:\IMAGES\EMPEROR.DIB  ▼ ▲ │
│ File  Edit  View  Help                        │
│          Win3DIBFile                           │
│            BitmapFileHeader                    │
│              Type       19778                  │
│              Size       36934                  │
│              Reserved1  0                      │
│              Reserved2  0                      │
│              OffsetBits 1078                   │
│            BitmapInfoHeader                     │
│            Win3ColorTable                       │
│            Filler                               │
│            Image                                │
│                                                 │
│ ◄ ◄                                        ► │
└─────────────────────────────────────────────┘
```

You can also use FileWalker as a hexadecimal editor to display and edit files. For complete information on using FileWalker, see Chapter 16, "Editing Files Using FileWalker."

Starting a Data-Preparation Tool

You start a tool just as you would any other Windows application. You can start the tool from the Program Manager menu, or you can double-click the tool icon. (For more information on either of these procedures, see the *Microsoft Windows User's Guide*.)

▶ **To start a tool from Program Manager:**

1. From the Program Manager File menu, choose Run.

   The Run dialog box appears.

2. In the Command Line box, type the name of the tool.

   You can include the data file to be edited in the command line. For example, type **bitedit pinnacle.pcx** to start BitEdit with the "PINNACLE.PCX" bitmap already open.

3. Choose OK.

   The tool starts and its window appears.

▶ **To start a tool from a program group:**

■ Double-click the icon for the tool you want to start.

   The tool starts and its window appears.

Required Hardware and Software

This guide assumes your data-preparation system has the following hardware and software capabilities. This is the minimum configuration capable of providing acceptable performance while manipulating large amounts of data.

- An IBM PC/AT or compatible personal computer (we recommend a personal computer with an 80386 processor or better)

- 40 megabytes of hard-disk storage (minimum)

- 2 megabytes of RAM (minimum)

- A Microsoft-compatible mouse

- A waveform audio device

- VGA+ (256 colors) color-graphics capability

- Microsoft Windows 3.0 or later

You must also install and set up Windows with Multimedia along with the core data preparation tools—BitEdit, PalEdit, Convert, WaveEdit, and FileWalker.

Related Documentation

The Microsoft Multimedia Development Kit (MDK) includes Multimedia Extensions 1.0, along with the following documentation:

- *Getting Started.* This guide describes the MDK and shows how to install its software.

- *Programmer's Workbook.* This workbook explains the enhancements provided by Windows with Multimedia and explains how to write programs that take advantage of these enhancements.

- *Programmer's Reference.* This reference details the application programming interface (API) to Windows with Multimedia. It covers all functions, messages, data types, file formats, and commands.

- *Multimedia Viewer Developer's Guide.* This guide describes how to build titles for the Multimedia Viewer software.

Conventions

The following sections explain conventions and basic terms used in this guide.

Document Conventions

Type Style	Used For
bold	A specific term intended to be used literally; for example, typing bitedit pinnacle.pcx starts BitEdit with the "PINNACLE.PCX" bitmap already open. You must type these terms exactly as shown.
italic	Indicates terms defined in text.
ALL CAPITALS	Directory names, filenames, and acronyms.
SMALL CAPITALS	Names of keyboard keys; for example, CTRL or ENTER.

Terms

This guide uses these basic Windows terms:

Active
Describes the window that is selected and to which the next keystroke or command will apply.

Choose
Perform an action on an object. For example, to choose a menu command means to click the command you want.

Run
Start an application.

Save
Store a file or changes to a file.

Select
Indicate the item that the next command you use will affect. This typically causes an item to become highlighted on a menu.

Key combinations and key sequences appear in the following format:

KEY+KEY

A plus sign (+) between key names means you must press the keys at the same time. For example, "Press ALT+ESC" means that you press the ALT key and hold it down while you press the ESC key.

Arrow keys

Keys on your computer keypad that indicate a direction. The names refer to the direction in which the arrow on the key points: UP ARROW, DOWN ARROW, RIGHT ARROW, or LEFT ARROW.

The following mouse actions are used in this guide:

Point

Move the mouse pointer until the tip rests on a specific object or area of your screen.

Click

Press and release the mouse button. "To click an object" means to point to that object (for example, an icon or a menu name), and then press and release the mouse button.

Double-click

Press and release the mouse button twice in rapid succession.

Drag

Press the mouse button and hold it down while moving the mouse pointer.

Chapter 11
Understanding Data Preparation

Adding multimedia support to applications adds data preparation to the traditional software development process of specification, design, and coding.

For example, a multimedia application presenting music history might include biographical information, musical scores, soundtracks, photographs of composers, and animated graphics showing the correct placement of the fingers and hands on a piano keyboard. This information can come from a variety of sources—encyclopedia entries, black-and-white photographs, phonograph recordings, and so on. All of this information must be converted to the application format used by Windows with Multimedia. Also, this information must be prepared before you can use it in your application. Tools included with the MDK help you prepare data for use in multimedia applications.

This chapter provides an overview of the data-preparation process and discusses the following topics:

- The types of data used in a multimedia application

- The role of CD-ROM

- The data formats supported by Windows with Multimedia

- The value of establishing design standards

- An introduction to the data-preparation process

- The role of data management

Note Be sure you obtain written permission for using professional materials in your application before bringing it to market. Most works, including reference texts, images, and sound recordings are copyrighted.

Data Makes Multimedia

Multimedia applications present large amounts of information in an interactive computing environment. Through the course of an application, a user can view and hear text, images, animation, and audio information. The ability to access large amounts of data is essential to a multimedia application.

Using Rich-Text Capabilities

A major feature of the Windows environment is its rich-text capabilities. The computer screen is no longer limited to fuzzy green patterns that scarcely resemble characters. Windows supports and displays characters in multiple typefaces of nearly any size. The improved appearance of text also makes the display much easier to read.

Using Images and Animation

Windows with Multimedia can display high-quality photographs and animation. This visual richness significantly enhances traditional computer displays. Adding lifelike images and animation to an application can also simplify complex ideas, making them easier to understand.

Using Audio

A multimedia computer includes specialized hardware to render quality sound. The audio component of multimedia makes it possible to add a greater richness of presentation in your applications. In place of transistorized beeps and robotic voices, multimedia applications can include high-fidelity music and sound effects, as well as the human voice.

The Use of CD-ROM

CD-ROM stands for compact disc–read only memory. The information used by a multimedia application is stored on a compact disc identical in size and appearance to an audio CD. You can only read data from a CD-ROM disc; you can't write information to it. The information contained on a CD-ROM disc is defined before the disc is manufactured. Once created, the CD-ROM disc remains unalterable.

The CD-ROM disc uses the same basic technology as an audio CD. An audio CD contains music translated into digital sound and pressed into the plastic as a sequence of pits. A laser beam from the CD player scans the CD surface, translates this information back into digital signals, and sends it for processing and amplification, which results in music from your speaker.

A CD-ROM disc is based on the same principle. But along with audio, it can also hold other types of digitized information, such as text and graphics. A single CD-ROM disc can hold up to 540 megabytes of information. You could conceivably store 150,000 printed pages or about 250 large books on one disc. Obviously, with this kind of capacity, a lot of information can fit into a small package.

Supported Data Types

Hardware and software vendors offer various products to create and enhance the images, sounds, and text used by a multimedia application. These diverse products generate many different file formats.

The sources for text, sounds, and images are universal. Books, newspapers, libraries, compact discs, phonograph records, movies—all provide potential material for use in a multimedia application. Data can come in many styles and formats. The key to preparing data for Windows with Multimedia is to identify the information you want to include and then convert it into a supported format.

Windows with Multimedia can use data files of the following formats:

Data	Description	Extension
Text	Rich-text format	.RTF
	Microsoft Word format	.DOC
	ASCII text format	.TXT
Images	Microsoft device-independent bitmap	.DIB
	RIFF device-independent bitmap	.RDI
Audio	Microsoft waveform audio	.WAV
MIDI	Musical instrument digital interface	.MID
	RIFF MIDI file	.RMI
Animation	MacroMind Director movie-file format	.MMM

The Elements of Data Presentation

Printed books have a certain look, an underlying graphic design that helps to promote consistency and clarity. Make sure your multimedia applications also adhere to a consistent internal design—screens look alike, typefaces are consistent, and multimedia elements such as audio, graphics, and animation integrate cleanly into the overall look and feel of your application. Establishing design standards before development takes time, but adhering to those standards will not only make your application look better, it will help make it easier to use. And easier to market.

Choosing Fonts

The fonts you choose for your text ensure the readability and aesthetic qualities of your application. Some typefaces are easier to read online than others. For example, some research indicates sans-serif fonts work better online than serif fonts. Windows with Multimedia provides flexibility in your choice of fonts, font size, and font colors. Inconsistency and poor design in the use of typefaces can detract from the content of your title.

Using Audio

Audio samples can substantially enhance your application. You must, however, make sure that any audio used is easy to understand, neither too loud nor too soft, and of a quality consistent with other sound samples used by your application.

Various factors affect audio samples: the number of bits used to store the sample (samples are typically 8-bit or 16-bit), the quality of the equipment used to obtain the sample, and the sampling rate at which the original sound was digitized (for example, 11.025 kHz, 22.05 kHz or 44.1 kHz). The higher the sampling rate, the better the quality. Of course, the better the quality, the more disk space required for storage.

Using Images and Animation

Images and animation add value to any application. The use of graphics and animation can help clarify relatively obscure information. Good graphics also communicate efficiently. If you choose to use graphics in your application, make sure to include their use in your design process.

Establish guidelines for all aspects of how your title will display graphics: their placement, the use of borders, number of colors, and graphics size.

Preparing Data

Animation, images, text, and sound must be captured from various sources, edited, and eventually converted into the final storage and presentation formats compatible with Windows with Multimedia.

Preparing Text

Text files form one of the largest segments of your base of information. Many multimedia applications will be composed mainly of text—often created by converting a book into an online multimedia product.

The original format of the text determines how much work is necessary. For example, if you start with text stored in Microsoft Word format, no conversion is necessary. If your existing text is formatted using typesetting codes, such as TROFF, you must first convert the text before incorporating it into your application.

Incorporating existing text into an application involves many challenges. Scanning or retyping both involve time and error correction. Formatting, indexing, and creating cross-references must be done manually and requires more time.

Preparing Images and Animation

Multimedia applications can use animation, photographs, clip art, and line drawings to add variety. Images can be scanned, digitized, or created using a combination of software and hardware. Animation is created using MacroMind Director and later transferred to the Windows with Multimedia environment. Animation created using MacroMind Director can then be played back using Windows with Multimedia.

You must convert all images into the Microsoft device-independent bitmap (.DIB) format. Microsoft provides the BitEdit and Convert tools to enhance images and translate them into .DIB format. Microsoft also provides the Movie Converter to convert MacroMind Director files into a format usable by Windows with Multimedia.

Preparing Audio

Text provides detailed information. Images offer visual metaphors and stimulation that can reinforce the text. Audio rounds out your multimedia application with music, sound effects, and speech. Each audio element has its role in a multimedia application. Music sets the mood and provides emphasis. Sound effects add variety. Speech offers yet another way to present information.

Narration, sound effects, and music often originate as studio-recorded analog data, although they can originate as digital recordings. All analog audio must be digitally sampled and stored in digital format.

The fidelity level of the audio portion of your application requires consideration. Better sound quality results from higher digital sampling rates; however, higher sampling rates require larger storage areas to hold numerous sound samples. You must balance the audio fidelity level of your application with its storage requirements.

Managing Multimedia Data

When creating multimedia applications, it's important that you manage the many data elements—text files, audio files, images—used by your application. Data resources are expensive in the following ways:

- Acquiring copyright for text, images, audio, and animation

- Preparing resources—converting from analog sources, translating different file formats, editing resources, as well as the time involved in each step

- Hardware needed to store, maintain, and back up the resources

You can control your costs by making your application as simple as possible. Only choose data that provides the most value for your application. One way to help control the costs of these resources is through effective data management. You can acquire a database-management application to track the data used during development so that you don't lose data already processed and to help you access specific items quickly.

You should now have a general understanding of the data types supported by Windows with Multimedia. The remaining chapters of this guide describe how to use the tools included with the MDK.

Chapter 12
Using Convert

The Convert tool lets you convert data files from one format to another. It reads specified source files and creates copies of those files in the format you want.

You'll find Convert extremely useful when building a multimedia application. Often a variety of tools must be used, each one involving a different file format. Convert lets you use the tools you're most comfortable with. When you finish creating your data files, you can use Convert to convert them to formats supported by Windows with Multimedia.

This chapter lists the types of file formats Convert can read and produce, and it describes how to start and use Convert. Convert is also *extensible*, which means that as new file-format converters become available, Convert will use them.

Valid File Formats

Convert works with audio files, bitmap files, palette files, and MIDI files. The following tables list the supported file formats. A file listed as "source" can supply data to Convert for conversion to another format. A file listed as "destination" can be generated by Convert through the conversion process.

Audio Formats

Convert works with audio files of the following formats:

Format	Extension	File Usage
Apple AIFF	.AIF	Source
Microsoft PCM Waveform	.PCM	Source
Microsoft Waveform	.WAV	Source, Destination

Bitmap Formats

Convert works with bitmap files of the following formats:

Format	Extension	File Usage
Apple Macintosh PICT	.PIC	Source, Destination
AutoCAD Import	.PLT	Source
CompuServe GIF	.GIF	Source
Computer Graphics Metafile	.CGM	Source
Encapsulated PostScript	.EPS	Source
Hewlett-Packard Graphic Language	.HGL	Source
Lotus 1-2-3 Graphics	.PIC	Source
Micrografx Designer/Draw Plus	.DRW	Source
Microsoft RIFF DIB	.RDI	Source, Destination
Microsoft RIFF RLE DIB	.RDI	Source, Destination
Microsoft RLE DIB	.DIB	Source, Destination
Microsoft Windows DIB	.DIB	Source, Destination
Microsoft Windows Metafile	.WMF	Source
PC Paintbrush	.PCX	Source, Destination
Tagged Image File Format (TIFF)	.TIF	Source
Truevision TGA	.TGA	Source, Destination

Palette Formats

Convert works with palette files of the following formats:

Format	Extension	File Usage
Microsoft DIB Palette	.DIB	Source
Microsoft Palette	.PAL	Source, Destination
Microsoft RIFF DIB Palette	.RDI	Source

Note   For Microsoft DIB Palette and RIFF DIB Palette files, Convert extracts information from the bitmaps.

MIDI Formats

Convert works with MIDI files of the following formats:

Format	Extension	File Usage
Microsoft RIFF MIDI	.RMI	Source, Destination
MIDI	.MID	Source, Destination

Starting Convert

You start Convert just as you would any Microsoft Windows application. The following procedure explains how to start Convert from Program Manager.

▶ **To start Convert:**

1. From the Program Manager File menu, choose Run.

   The Run dialog box appears.

2. In the Command Line box, type **convert**.

3. Choose OK.

You can also start Convert by double-clicking its icon (if it has been installed through the Program Manager).

The Convert window is divided into two areas: Source and Destination, as shown in the following illustration:

Source area

Destination area

The different parts of the Convert window have the following purposes:

Item	Purpose
Source Type box	Specifies the format of the source file(s).
Source File(s) box	Lists files you want to convert.
Add or Remove button	Adds or removes files displayed in the Source File(s) box.
Destination Type box	Specifies format of the destination file(s).
Destination Extension box	Specifies the extension added to the converted files.
Set Dest Dir button	Selects the destination directory for the converted file(s).
Convert button	Carries out the conversion.

Converting a File

Converting a file from one format to another involves the following steps:

- Specifying the source file format

- Specifying the source file(s)

- Specifying the destination file type

- Specifying the destination directory

- Converting the file(s)

Follow these steps whether you are converting a bitmap or a sound file. The following sections explain each of these steps.

Specifying the Source File Format

You must specify the format of the source file(s) used. Convert can read any of the formats listed in "Valid File Formats," earlier in this chapter.

▶ **To specify the source file format:**

1. Locate the Source Type box near the top of the Convert window.

2. Click the down arrow to display the list of valid source formats.

Valid formats

Source
Type:

Microsoft Windows DIB
Microsoft RIFF DIB
Microsoft Palette
Microsoft DIB Palette
Microsoft RIFF DIB Palette
PC Paintbrush

Add...

Remove

3. Scroll through the list and select the format you want.

   For example, if you select Microsoft Windows DIB format, Microsoft Windows DIB appears in the Source Type box.

Specifying the Source File(s)

After you identify the format of the files you want to convert, you must specify which files to convert. You can convert one file or a group of files simultaneously. You can add and remove files from the Source File(s) box in the Source area of the Convert window.

▶ **To specify the source file(s):**

1. In the Source area of the Convert window, click the Add button.

   The Add dialog box appears.

   The edit box displays the default file extension for the specified source format. For example, if you specified Microsoft Windows DIB format, the list box displays the appropriate file extensions.

2. Move to the directory that contains the file(s) you want to convert.

   • To select the directory you want, you can double-click the directories in the directory/device box.

   • Or, in the edit box, you can type the full path to the file(s) you want. For example, you might type **\images*.dib** and press ENTER.

   A list of files in that directory appears in the list box to the left of the directory/device box. This list is based on the wildcard character and default extension in the edit box; for example, *.DIB.

3. Scroll through the list and select the source file(s) you want.

   - Click each filename to select it. Click the filename again to cancel the selection.

   - Or, to select all listed files, choose the Select All button.

4. To put the selected file(s) into the Source File(s) box in the Convert window, choose the Add button.

5. Repeat steps 2, 3, and 4 to identify additional files in other directories that you want to convert.

6. When you finish selecting all the files you want to convert, choose the Done button.

   The Add dialog box closes and the filenames you selected appear in the Source File(s) box, as shown in the following illustration:

The Source File(s) box is dynamic. With it, you can review files selected for conversion, add new entries to the list, and delete existing entries as needed.

▶ **To delete files from the Source File(s) box:**

1. Scroll through the Source File(s) box and display the file(s) you want removed.

2. Click each filename to select it for removal; click it again to cancel the selection.

3. Choose the Remove button to remove the filename(s) from the Source File(s) box.

Specifying the Destination File Format and Extension

After you identify the file(s) you want to convert, you must specify the file formats you want them written to. You do this in the lower half of the Convert window.

▶ **To specify the destination file format:**

1. In the Destination Type box, click the down arrow to display the list box and scroll through the valid options. Convert lists appropriate destination formats based on the specified source format.

Convert can convert files into the following formats:

- Microsoft Windows DIB (with or without run-length encoding compression)
- Microsoft Windows RIFF DIB (with or without run-length encoding compression)
- PC Paintbrush
- Apple Macintosh PICT
- Microsoft Palette
- Microsoft Waveform
- MIDI
- RIFF MIDI

2. Scroll through the list and select the format you want. The format name appears in the Destination Type box. The default extension for that file type appears in the Extension box. You can use the extension that Convert supplies, or you can enter a different extension.

Note The significance of RIFF file formats will increase as enhancements are made to media-element files. However, for the current release of Windows with Multimedia, use file formats supported by your application.

▶ **To enter a new extension for destination files:**

1. Move to the Extension box.

2. Type the extension you want.

Now you can specify the location where you want Convert to put the converted files.

Specifying the Destination Location

You must specify the directory where you want Convert to put the new file(s). Convert can put the converted file(s) in the same directory as the source file(s) or in a different directory.

▶ **To specify a directory for the destination file(s):**

1. Choose the Set Dest Dir button.

   The Set Directory dialog box appears.

```
┌─────────────────────────────────────────┐
│ ━     Set Directory                      │
├─────────────────────────────────────────┤
│ Directory:[                    ]         │
│ Directories:                             │
│ C:\WIN3                                  │
│ ┌──────────────┐ ┌──────────┐            │
│ │[..]        ↑ │ │  Open    │            │
│ │[old]         │ └──────────┘            │
│ │[resource]    │                         │
│ │[save]        │ ┌──────────┐            │
│ │[system]      │ │  Set Dir │            │
│ │[-a-]         │ └──────────┘            │
│ │[-b-]       ↓ │ ┌──────────┐            │
│ └──────────────┘ │  Cancel  │            │
│                  └──────────┘            │
└─────────────────────────────────────────┘
```

The Set Directory dialog box allows you to specify a path for storing converted files. The Open button adds the selected subdirectory from the list or adds the subdirectory specified in the edit box to the current path specification. The Set Dir button sets the destination directory to the current path.

2. Search the directory structure until you locate the directory in which you want to place the converted files. You can change directories in one of the following ways:

- By typing the full path to the directory in the edit box near the top of the dialog box and pressing ENTER.

- By selecting the directory name in the directory/device list and choosing the Open button to move to the directory.

- By double-clicking the directory name.

3. Choose the Set Dir button to select the directory.

   The directory appears after Dir in the Destination area of the Convert window.

Once you specify the directory for converted files, you can convert the file(s).

Converting the File

Before you continue, examine the Convert window to be sure you have identified the source and destination formats, source files, destination extension, and destination directory. If the settings are correct, you can convert the file(s).

▶ **To convert the file(s):**

- Click the Convert button.

  Convert creates a version of the source file with the specified filename and format. A status dialog box appears, as in the following example:

```
┌─────────────────────────────────────┐
│              Convert                 │
├─────────────────────────────────────┤
│ Converting:                          │
│ PARROT.DIB to PARROT.PIC.            │
│ Writing Bits                         │
│                                      │
│ ┌─────────────────────────────┐     │
│ │███████████87%███████████     │     │
│ └─────────────────────────────┘     │
│                       ┌────────┐     │
│                       │ Cancel │     │
│                       └────────┘     │
└─────────────────────────────────────┘
```

Messages appear, describing the various stages of the conversion. As long as the status dialog box remains displayed, you can cancel the conversion by choosing the Cancel button. When the progress bar reaches 100%, conversion is complete. You can convert more files, or you can quit Convert.

When reading certain file formats, additional dialog boxes might appear. These dialog boxes are explained later in this chapter.

Using the Select Bitmap Size Dialog Box

The Select Bitmap Size dialog box appears when you convert files of the following formats:

- AutoCAD Import (.PLT)

- Computer Graphics Metafile (.CGM)

- Encapsulated PostScript (.EPS)

- Hewlett-Packard Graphic Language (.HGL)

- Lotus 1-2-3 (.PIC)

- Micrografx Designer/ Draw Plus (.DRW)

- Tagged Image File Format (.TIF)

The Select Bitmap Size dialog box has the following settings:

Default Size
   When this check box is selected, you can create a destination image file of approximately the same size and proportions as the source image file.

Maximum Width and Maximum Height
   You can set the image size (in pixels) using these spin boxes (if you don't want the default size).

Retain Proportions
   When this check box is selected, the destination image retains the same proportions as the original source file.

Using the CGM Import Filter Dialog Box

The CGM Import Filter dialog box appears when you convert files from Computer Graphics Metafile (.CGM) format.

```
┌──────────────────────────────────────────────┐
│ ▬              CGM Import Filter               │
├──────────────────────────────────────────────┤
│  ⊠ Ignore background         ┌──────────┐      │
│                              │    OK    │      │
│  ☐ Force vector fonts        └──────────┘      │
│                              ┌──────────┐      │
│  ☐ Dot lines                 │  Cancel  │      │
│                              └──────────┘      │
│  ☐ Default Color Table       ┌──────────┐      │
│                              │   Help   │      │
│  % COMPLETE  [            ]   └──────────┘      │
│                                                │
│              0%.....................100%       │
│  ────────────────────────────────             │
│              (c) Copyright 1990                │
│        Access Softek & Microsoft Corp.         │
│             All Rights Reserved                │
│                                    V 22        │
└──────────────────────────────────────────────┘
```

The CGM Import Filter dialog box includes the following settings:

Ignore Background
   When this check box is selected, Convert makes the output picture transparent by discarding the background rectangle on which the original image was drawn.

Force Vector Fonts
   When this check box is selected, Convert converts fonts into vector fonts before translating them into bitmap fonts. Use this option when converting bitmaps that contain rotated or skewed text.

Dot Lines
   When this check box is selected, Convert changes dotted lines in the image into solid lines. When this option is cleared, Convert displays dotted lines at the width of one pixel, which might not be visible on some monitors.

Default Color Table
   When this check box is selected, Convert translates colors for .CGM files from Harvard Graphics.

Using the DRW Import Filter Dialog Box

The DRW Import Filter dialog box appears when you convert files from Micrografx Draw Plus or Micrografx Designer (.DRW) format.

```
┌─────────────────────────────────────────────┐
│ ─        DRW Import Filter                    │
│                                               │
│  ☒ Ignore background       ┌──────────┐      │
│                            │    OK    │      │
│                            └──────────┘      │
│  ☐ Force vector fonts      ┌──────────┐      │
│                            │  Cancel  │      │
│                            └──────────┘      │
│  % COMPLETE   ┌───────────────────────┐     │
│               └───────────────────────┘     │
│               0%..............................100%  │
│  ─────────────────────────────────────────   │
│              (c) Copyright 1990               │
│        Access Softek & Microsoft Corp.        │
│           All Rights Reserved                 │
│                                      V 08     │
└─────────────────────────────────────────────┘
```

The DRW Import Filter dialog box includes the following settings:

Ignore Background
    When this check box is selected, Convert makes the output picture transparent by discarding the background rectangle on which the original image was drawn.

Force Vector Fonts
    When this check box is selected, Convert converts fonts to vector fonts before translating them into bitmap fonts. Use this option when converting bitmaps that contain rotated or skewed text.

Using the Color Reduction Options Dialog Box

The Color Reduction Options dialog box appears when you convert files from Truevision (.TGA) format or 24-bit nonpalette images.

```
┌─────────────────────────────────────────────────────┐
│                 Color Reduction Options               │
│ ┌─Palette───────────────────────────────────────────┐ │
│ │  ● Optimal Colors                                 │ │
│ │                     Number of colors: │236│        │ │
│ │  ○ Greyscale                                      │ │
│ │                                                   │ │
│ │  ○ Palette File: │vga.pal        │  │ Browse... │  │ │
│ └───────────────────────────────────────────────────┘ │
│   ☐ Enable Dithering        │  OK  │   │ Cancel │      │
└─────────────────────────────────────────────────────┘
```

The Color Reduction Options dialog box includes the following settings:

Optimal Colors
   When this option is selected, Convert uses those colors from the original image that most closely re-create the original image. You can specify up to 256 colors.

Greyscale
   When this option is selected, Convert re-creates the image in black-and-white with levels of grey. You can specify up to 256 levels of grey.

Palette File
   When this option is selected, Convert creates the image using the specified palette file as the source for its colors. The VGA.PAL file is the default conversion palette consisting of 16 system-defined colors. You can select the default palette, enter the name of the palette file in the edit box, or choose the Browse button to display a file/directory box and select the file you want.

Enable Dithering
   When this check box is selected, Convert turns dithering on.

Using the Input Data Format Dialog Box

Convert writes only to sound files in Microsoft Waveform format. However, not every format contains the information required to translate the file into the Microsoft Waveform format. If you convert a file from a format that does not supply this information, such as a .PCM file, the Input DATA Format dialog box appears.

```
┌─────────────────────────────────┐
│        Input DATA format        │
├─────────────────────────────────┤
│ ┌─Channels───────┐  ┌─────────┐  │
│ │ ⦿ Mono         │  │   Ok    │  │
│ │ ○ Stereo       │  └─────────┘  │
│ └────────────────┘  ┌─────────┐  │
│                     │ Cancel  │  │
│ ┌─Sample Size────┐  └─────────┘  │
│ │ ⦿ 8 Bits       │               │
│ │ ○ 16 Bits      │               │
│ └────────────────┘               │
│ ┌─Frequency──────┐               │
│ │ ○ 44.1 kHz     │               │
│ │ ⦿ 22.05 kHz    │               │
│ │ ○ 11.025 kHz   │               │
│ └────────────────┘               │
└─────────────────────────────────┘
```

You can use the options in the Input DATA Format dialog box to specify the format of the sample data in your input file, which includes the following settings:

Channels
  This option specifies whether the audio file stores mono or stereo sound.
  Select Mono for single-channel audio; select Stereo for dual-channel audio.

Sample Size
  This option specifies the number of bits used for the sample size. Select either 8 Bits or 16 Bits.

Frequency
  This option specifies the frequency used for the audio sample. Select 44.1 kHz, 22.05 kHz, or 11.025 kHz.

Quitting Convert

You quit Convert the same way you quit any Microsoft Windows application.

▶ **To quit Convert:**

1. Click the Control menu box to display its menu.

2. Choose Close (or double-click the Control menu box).

Editing Bitmaps Using BitEdit

A multimedia application can require a large number of different bitmap images. You can get these images from various sources—for example, from scanners, paint programs, or clip art. All bitmaps must eventually be in a format supported by Windows. For bitmaps other than .DIB, the Convert tool includes translators that convert bitmap files into supported formats.

Once in the right format, a bitmap might still require enhancement before it's suitable for a multimedia application; for example, scanning can introduce streaks or other irregularities that must be corrected. You might adjust the color for a more natural or pleasing display. Or an image might have superfluous elements that must be eliminated. These types of procedures require a tool to edit and enhance the bitmap file.

This chapter introduces BitEdit, a tool you use to manipulate bitmap images. BitEdit has two basic purposes:

- To perform simple edits and color changes to bitmap images
- To work with PalEdit (a tool that edits color palettes associated with bitmap images)

With BitEdit, you can edit scanned bitmaps or you can import and enhance images from other paint programs. Note that BitEdit supplements, rather than replaces, full-featured paint programs. Although BitEdit offers some image-editing capabilities, it is usually best to use a more sophisticated paint program to create bitmaps or to make extensive changes to existing bitmaps.

This chapter describes the basic BitEdit features. For information on how to edit the color palettes associated with bitmaps, see Chapter 14, "Editing Color Palettes Using PalEdit."

Valid File Formats

BitEdit can edit bitmap files of the following formats:

Format	Extension	File Usage
Apple Macintosh PICT	.PIC	Source, Destination
AutoCAD Import	.PLT	Source
CompuServe GIF	.GIF	Source
Computer Graphics Metafile	.CGM	Source
Encapsulated PostScript	.EPS	Source
HP Graphic Language	.HGL	Source
Lotus 1-2-3 Graphics	.PIC	Source
Micrografx Designer/Draw	.DRW	Source
Microsoft RIFF DIB	.RDI	Source, Destination
Microsoft RLE DIB	.DIB	Source, Destination
Microsoft RLE RIFF DIB	.RDI	Source, Destination
Microsoft Windows BMP	.BMP	Source
Microsoft Windows DIB	.DIB	Source, Destination
Microsoft Windows Metafile	.WMF	Source
PC Paintbrush	.PCX	Source, Destination
Tagged Image File Format (TIFF)	.TIF	Source
Truevision TGA	.TGA	Source, Destination

Note   All PC Paintbrush files generated with BitEdit use an 8-bit (256 color) palette.

Starting BitEdit

You can start BitEdit just as you do any other Windows application. The following procedure explains how to start BitEdit from Program Manager. You can also start BitEdit from File Manager or by double-clicking the BitEdit icon.

▶ **To start BitEdit:**

1. From the Program Manager File menu, choose Run.

   The Run dialog box appears.

2. In the Command Line box, type **bitedit**.

   You can include an initial bitmap in the command line. For example, type **bitedit pinnacle.dib** to start BitEdit with the bitmap "PINNACLE.DIB" already open.

   Note If the bitmap you want to load is not in the current directory, you must include its complete path.

3. Choose OK.

   The BitEdit window appears.

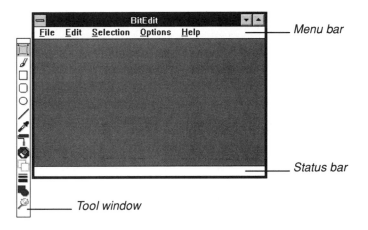

A series of menu names appear in the menu bar at the top of the work area. The *tool window*, a second, separate window to the left of the BitEdit window contains several icons representing each BitEdit tool.

Scroll bars along the right and bottom edges of the window let you scroll the display area. Scroll bars appear only when a bitmap is larger than the BitEdit window.

The status bar at the bottom of the BitEdit window displays a single line of informational text. When the cursor is in the work area, the status bar displays the coordinates of the cursor.

The BitEdit Menus

BitEdit displays five main menus: File, Edit, Selection, Options, and Help.

The File Menu

Use the commands on the File menu to load and save bitmap files to disk. You can also use these commands to close the current bitmap without leaving BitEdit, start another BitEdit window, and quit BitEdit.

Command	Description
New	Creates an empty bitmap file.
Open	Opens an existing bitmap file.
Close	Closes the current bitmap file without quitting BitEdit.
Save	Saves changes made to a bitmap file.
Save As	Saves the bitmap with a new filename.
Revert	Restores the version of the bitmap file last saved on disk.
Run BitEdit	Opens a new BitEdit window.
Exit	Quits BitEdit.

The Edit Menu

Use the commands on the Edit menu to change the contents of a particular bitmap.

Command	Description
Undo	Undoes the last edit operation.
Cut	Removes a selected area from a bitmap and places it on the Clipboard.
Copy	Copies a selected area from a bitmap to the Clipboard.
Paste	Pastes the contents of the Clipboard into a bitmap.
Paste Without Color	Pastes the contents of the Clipboard into a bitmap, ignoring the Clipboard palette. Colors in a pasted bitmap use the closest matching colors from the current palette.

Command	Description
Paste Palette	Replaces the palette of the current bitmap with the palette on the Clipboard.
Delete	Deletes a selected area of a bitmap. The area deleted is *not* placed on the Clipboard.
Select All	Selects the entire bitmap.
Preferences	Sets conversion and sizing preferences.

The Selection Menu

You can use the commands on the Selection menu to change the way a selected area of a bitmap is displayed.

Command	Description
Crop	Deletes the portion of the bitmap outside the selected area.
Flip Horizontal	Creates a mirror image of a selected area.
Flip Vertical	Inverts a selected area.
Rotate	Rotates a selected area by a specified number of degrees.
Selected Colors First	Reorders the palette so that the colors in a selected area appear first in the palette.
Select in PalEdit	Identifies color entries in the palette that are within the selected area of the bitmap.

The Options Menu

You can use the commands on the Options menu to start the PalEdit tool, to reduce the number of colors in the associated color palette of a bitmap, to resize a bitmap, and to specify edit operations that involve a transparent background.

Command	Description
Show Palette	Runs the PalEdit tool that shows the associated color palette for a displayed bitmap. A check mark appears next to the command name when PalEdit is running.

Command	Description
Color Reduction	Reduces the number of colors in the image palette. You can select the number of colors and view the image before any changes are made.
Resize Image	Changes the size of a bitmap and lets you adjust image depth.
Use Transparency	Controls transparency mode, which ignores background-colored pixels when drawing and pasting objects into a bitmap.

The BitEdit Tools

The tool window appears at the left edge of the BitEdit window or where you last placed it.

▶ **To use a BitEdit tool:**

- Click the tool you want.

The following tools are provided with BitEdit:

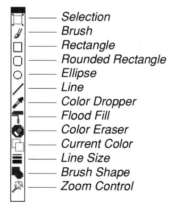

Selection
Brush
Rectangle
Rounded Rectangle
Ellipse
Line
Color Dropper
Flood Fill
Color Eraser
Current Color
Line Size
Brush Shape
Zoom Control

You can use these tools to perform the following tasks:

Tool	Use
Selection	Selects an area of a bitmap, deletes, or performs other operations on the selection.
Brush	Paints the selected color on a bitmap.
Rectangle	Draws filled and hollow rectangles.
Rounded Rectangle	Draws filled and hollow rounded rectangles.
Ellipse	Draws filled and hollow ellipses.
Line	Draws lines.
Color Dropper	Sets foreground and background colors based on a selected color in the bitmap.
Flood Fill	Fills an area with a selected color.
Color Eraser	Changes areas from a foreground color to a background color, or vice versa.
Current Color	Sets foreground and background colors based on colors you select from a color palette.
Line Size	Sets the line width for the other tools.
Brush Shape	Sets the shape of the Brush tool.
Zoom Control	Magnifies a bitmap image.

Opening a Bitmap File

Before you can edit a bitmap, you must first open it in BitEdit. BitEdit can open bitmaps in many standard formats (for more information, see "Valid File Formats," earlier in this chapter).

When you load a bitmap into the BitEdit window, BitEdit creates a copy of the bitmap in memory. You edit and make changes to the copy in memory. When you save your changes, the Save command writes all changes to the disk version of the bitmap file.

▶ **To open a bitmap file:**

1. From the File menu, choose Open.

   The Open Bitmap dialog box appears.

2. Scroll through the List Files of Type box and select the file format you want.

```
┌─────────────────────────────────────────────────────────┐
│ ▬                    Open Bitmap                          │
├─────────────────────────────────────────────────────────┤
│ File Name:                Directories:                    │
│ [*.dib;*.bmp        ]     c:\win3         ┌─────────────┐ │
│  ┌──────────────────┐    ┌──────────────┐ │     OK      │ │
│  │ ant75.dib      ▲ │    │ 📂 c:\        │ └─────────────┘ │
│  │ bixlake.dib      │    │ 📂 win3       │ ┌─────────────┐ │
│  │ boxes.bmp        │    │ 📁 old        │ │   Cancel    │ │
│  │ chess.bmp        │    │ 📁 resource   │ └─────────────┘ │
│  │ chess2.bmp       │    │ 📁 save       │                 │
│  │ critter.dib      │    │ 📁 system     │                 │
│  │ hallowen.bmp   ▼ │    └──────────────┘                 │
│  └──────────────────┘                                     │
│ List Files of Type:        Drives:                        │
│ [Microsoft Windows DIB ▼]  [💻 c: richbix          ▼]    │
└─────────────────────────────────────────────────────────┘
```

3. Scroll through the drives, directories, and filename lists to find the file you want to edit, and then select the filename.

4. Choose OK.

BitEdit opens the bitmap file, converts it to .DIB format if necessary, and displays it. The bitmap might be smaller or larger than the BitEdit window. If it exceeds window boundaries, use the scroll bars to change the way the bitmap is displayed. Resizing the window doesn't affect the bitmap size.

Note   When reading certain file formats, additional dialog boxes might appear as described in Chapter 12, "Using Convert."

Setting Preferences

You can use the Preferences command on the Edit menu to change the way BitEdit opens files, manages memory, and displays the tool window.

▶ **To set file preferences:**

1. From the Edit menu, choose Preferences.

The BitEdit Preferences dialog box appears.

```
┌─────────────────────────────────────────────┐
│ ⊟            BitEdit Preferences              │
├─────────────────────────────────────────────┤
│  ┌──────────────────────────────┐  ┌──────┐  │
│  │ ☒ Resize Window to Bitmap on Open│  │  OK  │  │
│  │ ☐ Disable Undo               │  ├──────┤  │
│  │ ☒ Detached Tools Window      │  │Cancel│  │
│  └──────────────────────────────┘  └──────┘  │
└─────────────────────────────────────────────┘
```

2. Set the preferences you want using the following settings:

Resize Window to Bitmap on Open
When this check box is selected, the BitEdit window changes size to match the size of the open bitmap file. If the bitmap is too large to fit on your screen, BitEdit displays as much of the bitmap as will fit.

When cleared, the BitEdit window remains the same size when you open a bitmap file. If the bitmap is smaller than the window, the rest of the window remains empty. If the bitmap is larger than the window, only a portion of the bitmap appears, although you can use the scroll bars to view the entire bitmap.

Disable Undo
When this check box is selected, you cannot undo your most recent change made to the bitmap. This feature is useful when your system is low on memory, for example, when working with very large bitmaps.

When cleared, you can undo the most recent edit made to the bitmap.

Detached Tools Window
When this check box is selected, BitEdit displays the tool icons in a second window, separate from the BitEdit window. Using the detached tool window, you can move the BitEdit tool icons to a more convenient place on your screen while you work.

When cleared, BitEdit displays its tool icons at the left of the BitEdit window; the tools cannot be moved.

3. When you have selected the preferences you want, choose OK.

Using the Editing Tools

Use the BitEdit tools to fine-tune and enhance your bitmaps. You choose a tool by clicking one of the icons in the tool window. If you prefer having the tool window separate from the BitEdit window, you can detach and move tool window to another area on your screen.

▶ **To detach and move the tool window:**

1. From the Edit menu, choose Preferences.

2. Select the Detached Tools Window check box.

3. Choose OK.

4. Drag the tool window to its new location.

Changing Background and Foreground Colors

Several of the BitEdit editing tools focus on two colors: the *foreground* color and the *background* color. The foreground color is the color placed by any painting operation. The background color is the color displayed when part of a bitmap is moved or altered.

You can select the foreground and background colors in one of two ways: from a palette displaying all bitmap colors or directly from the bitmap.

▶ **To choose the foreground color from a palette:**

1. Point to the Current Color tool icon (two overlapping squares).

2. Hold down the left mouse button to display the colors in the open bitmap palette.

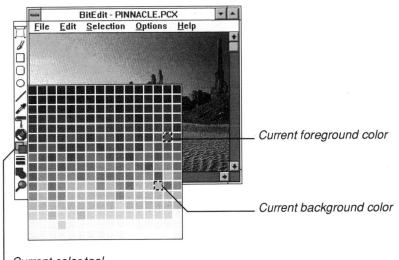

Current foreground color

Current background color

Current color tool

3. With the color palette displayed, drag the mouse pointer into the color palette.

   As the mouse pointer enters the palette region, it changes into a red-and-white frame that surrounds the palette-color entry.

4. Continue to drag the mouse to the color you want to use, then release the mouse button to select the highlighted color as the current foreground color.

   The Current Color tool provides visual confirmation of the new foreground color by changing its foreground rectangle to the new color.

▶ **To select the background color from a palette:**

1. Point to the Current Color tool icon (two overlapping squares).

2. Hold down the right mouse button to display the colors in the open bitmap palette.

3. With the color palette displayed, drag the mouse pointer into the color palette. As the mouse pointer enters the palette region, it changes into a blue-and-white frame that surrounds the palette-color entry.

4. Continue to drag the mouse pointer to the color you want to use, then release the mouse button to select the highlighted color as the current background color.

   The Current Color tool provides visual confirmation of the new background color by changing its background rectangle to the new color.

▶   **To choose colors directly from a bitmap:**

1. Click the Color Dropper tool icon (a medicine dropper).

2. Click anywhere in the bitmap to select a color.

   • To select the foreground color, click the left mouse button.

   • To select the background color, click the right mouse button (or press SHIFT + the left mouse button).

   The color you select becomes the foreground or background color. The foreground or background box in the Current Color tool icon changes to the selected color.

Drawing Freehand on a Bitmap

With the BitEdit Brush tool, you can draw lines and arcs of different shapes, widths, and colors on any displayed bitmap. You can use the Brush Shape tool to adjust the brush shape to a circle or a square. Use the Line Size tool to adjust the width of the lines produced by the Brush tool.

▶   **To use the Brush tool:**

1. Click the Brush tool icon (a paintbrush).

2. To begin drawing, point to the place on the bitmap where you want to begin drawing.

   • To begin drawing using the foreground color, hold down the left mouse button and drag the mouse.

   • To begin drawing using the background color, hold down the right mouse button (or press SHIFT + the left mouse button) and drag the mouse.

The color you select as the foreground (or background) color appears on the bitmap. To change colors, use the Current Color tool or the Color Dropper tool.

▶   **To change the brush width:**

1. Click the Line Size tool icon (a stack of lines of varying thicknesses) and hold down the mouse button.

   A group of available line widths appears.

2. Drag the selection to the line width you want.

▶ **To change the brush shape:**

1. Click the Brush Shape tool icon (an overlapping circle and square) and hold down the mouse button.

   A group of available brush shapes appears.

2. Drag the selection to the brush shape you want.

Drawing Rectangles, Circles, and Lines on a Bitmap

Using the BitEdit geometric drawing tools, you can draw a variety of shapes in different sizes, line widths, and colors on any displayed bitmap. You can draw two kinds of rectangles (square-cornered and round-cornered), as well as circles, ellipses, and line segments.

Controls for foreground color, background color, and line width for the geometric drawing tools and the Brush tool are identical. You use the Current Color tool or the Color Dropper tool to set the foreground and background colors, and the Line Size tool to set line width.

▶ **To use the rectangle tools:**

1. Click the Rectangle or Rounded Rectangle tool icon.

2. Point to the place on the bitmap where you want one corner of the rectangle.

   • To begin drawing a rectangle with the foreground color forming the edge of the rectangle and the background color filling inside the border, hold down the left mouse button and drag the mouse.

   • To begin drawing a rectangle with the background color forming the edge of the rectangle and the foreground color filling inside the border, hold down the right mouse button (or press SHIFT + the left mouse button) and drag the mouse.

   The rectangle expands or shrinks as you move the mouse around the work area.

3. When you reach the location where you want the opposite corner of the rectangle, release the mouse button.

▶ **To use the Ellipse tool:**

1. Click the Ellipse tool icon.

2. Point to the place on the bitmap where you want the left or right edge of the ellipse.

   • To begin drawing an ellipse with the foreground color forming the edge of the ellipse and the background color filling inside the border, hold down the left mouse button and drag the mouse.

   • To begin drawing an ellipse with the background color forming the edge of the ellipse and the foreground color filling inside the border, hold down the right mouse button (or press SHIFT + the left mouse button) and drag the mouse.

     The ellipse expands or shrinks as you move the mouse around the work area.

3. When the ellipse is the size and shape you want, release the mouse button.

▶ **To use the Line tool:**

1. Click the Line tool icon.

2. Point to the place on the bitmap where you want one end of the line segment.

   • To begin drawing a line segment using the foreground color, hold down the left mouse button and drag the mouse.

   • To begin drawing a line segment using the background color, hold down the right mouse button (or press SHIFT + the left mouse button) and drag the mouse.

     The line segment rotates, expands, or shrinks as you move the mouse around the work area.

3. When the line segment is the length and orientation you want, release the mouse button.

Filling in a Bitmap Area

You can use the BitEdit Flood Fill tool to replace a section of a bitmap that is one color with another color. The Flood Fill tool changes all adjoining pixels that are one color to the foreground or background color.

▶ **To fill in a section of a bitmap:**

1. Click the Flood Fill tool icon (a paint roller).

2. Point to the part of the bitmap you want to fill.

   • To fill the section with the foreground color, click the left mouse button.

   • To fill the section with the background color, click the right mouse button (or press SHIFT + the left mouse button).

The pixel you click and all adjoining pixels of the same color change to the foreground or the background color. To change colors, use the Current Color tool or the Color Dropper tool.

Using the Color Eraser

You can use the Color Eraser tool to change foreground-colored pixels in a bitmap to the background color, or vice versa. By coordinating the Color Eraser tool with the Current Color tool, you can change part or all of any color in a bitmap to any available color.

▶ **To use the Color Eraser tool:**

1. Click the Color Eraser tool icon (a pencil eraser).

2. Adjust the width of the Color Eraser by clicking the Line Size tool icon and dragging the selection to the appropriate line width. Release the mouse button to select the highlighted line width.

3. Point to the place in the bitmap where you want to begin erasing.

   • To change foreground-colored pixels to the background color, hold down the left mouse button and drag the mouse.

   • To change background-colored pixels to the foreground color, hold down the right mouse button (or press SHIFT + the left mouse button) and drag the mouse.

Using the Zoom Control Tool

You can use the Zoom Control tool to make it easier to edit a bitmap by magnifying a portion of a bitmap two, four, or eight times its original size. Magnifying a bitmap displays each pixel in a larger size, which makes the Zoom Control tool particularly useful for highly detailed, pixel-by-pixel editing.

▶ **To enlarge a portion of a bitmap:**

1. Point to the Zoom Control tool icon (a magnifying glass).

2. Click and hold down either mouse button.

    A display of available magnifications appears.

3. Drag the selection to the magnification you want.

    A box appears in the bitmap.

4. Move the box to the area of the bitmap you want to magnify.

5. Click either mouse button.

    A magnified section of the bitmap appears. In the upper-right corner, a *zoom box* shows the section in its original size. This box shows you the effects of changes you make.

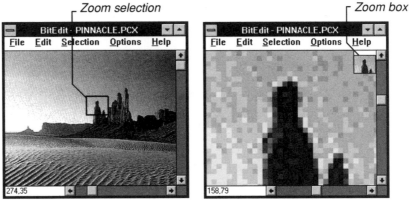

Before   *After*

6. To move the zoom box to a different location on your screen, drag it to the new location.

Undoing Your Changes

You can undo your most recent edit to a bitmap by using the Undo command.

▶ **To undo a change:**

■ From the Edit menu, choose Undo.

Note   If the change can't be undone, the Undo command won't be available on the Edit menu.

Selecting Parts of a Bitmap

You can use the Selection tool to select areas of the bitmap. You might select a bitmap area for several reasons: to move it, to delete it, to copy it to the Clipboard, or to paste the contents of the Clipboard into a selected area. All editing commands apply to the current selection. In fact, many edit and selection commands are not available until you select an area.

Using the Selection Tool

Use the Selection tool to select a bitmap area before choosing the edit command you want.

▶ **To select an area of a bitmap:**

1. Click the Selection tool icon (a dashed rectangle at the top of the tool window).

2. Point to one corner of the area you want to select.

3. Hold down the left mouse button and drag the mouse to the opposite corner of the area.

   A flashing red selection box appears around the selected area, as shown in the following illustration:

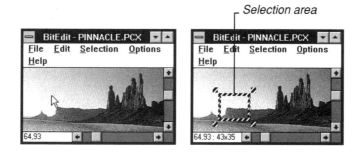

4. Adjust the location of the box until it frames the area you want, and then release the mouse button.

The *x* and *y* coordinates associated with the selected area appear in the lower-left corner of the BitEdit window. The first two numbers identify the *x*- and *y*-value of the upper-left corner of the selected area; the last two numbers identify the number of pixels (horizontally and vertically) enclosed by the selection.

For example, the numbers 64,93 and 43x35 in the previous illustration mean the upper-left corner is at a position 64 pixels from the left edge of the bitmap and 93 pixels from the top edge of the bitmap, and the selection encloses a rectangle 43 pixels wide and 35 pixels high.

The selection stays in effect until you click outside the selected area or until you select a different BitEdit tool. When you cancel your selection, the selection box disappears. If your selection covers the entire BitEdit window, click the status bar to cancel the selection.

▶ **To move a selection box:**

1. Point to one of the sides of the selection box (be sure the tip of the mouse pointer is touching the selection box).

2. Hold down either mouse button.

   • If the selection box turns blue, release the mouse button, click outside the selected area, and try again.

   • If the selection box remains red, drag the box to the new location.

3. Release the mouse button.

▶ **To resize a selection box:**

   ▪ Point to one of the handles at the corners of the selection box and drag the handle in any direction.

Using the Select All Command

The Select All command on the Edit menu provides a quick way to select an entire bitmap. Once selected, you can cut or copy an entire bitmap to the Clipboard by using commands on the Edit menu. The Clipboard can be used to transfer images into other bitmaps and applications.

Detaching and Moving a Selected Bitmap Area

You can move a selected bitmap area, or you can copy a selected bitmap area and move the copy to another location in a bitmap.

▶ **To detach and move a selected bitmap area:**

1. Place the mouse pointer anywhere inside the selection box.

2. Hold down the left mouse button.

   The flashing highlight around the selection box turns blue, freezing the boundaries of the selected area (the blue boundary indicates the selection is detached).

3. Drag the selection box to the new position.

   The selected area pulls free from the bitmap and moves where it is dragged. The hole in the bitmap changes to the background color, as shown in the following illustration:

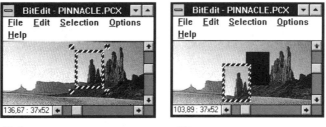

Before   *After*

4. To move the selected area again, drag the area to the new position.

5. Move the mouse pointer outside the selection box and click the left mouse button.

   The selection box disappears and the selected area is attached to the bitmap in its new position. The portion of the bitmap under the selection box disappears.

6. If you inadvertently attach a selection to the wrong place and want to restore it to its previous position, from the Edit menu, choose Undo.

7. If you save or close the file without attaching a detached selection, a dialog box appears asking you if you want to attach the selection at its current location.

   • To attach the selection, choose Yes.

   • To save or close the file without attaching the selection, choose No.

▶ **To detach a copy of a selected bitmap area:**

1. Place the mouse pointer anywhere inside the selection box.

2. Hold down the right mouse button (or press SHIFT + the left mouse button).

   The flashing selection box turns blue, freezing the boundaries of the selected area (the blue boundary indicates the selection is detached).

3. Drag the selection box to the new position.

   A copy of the selected area pulls free from the bitmap and moves, as shown in the following illustration:

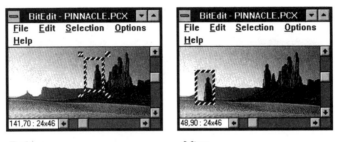

Before   *After*

4. To move the copied area again, drag the area to the new position.

5. Move the mouse pointer outside the selection box and click either mouse button.

   The selection box disappears and the copied area is attached to the bitmap in its new position. The portion of the bitmap under the selection box disappears.

6. If you inadvertently attach a selection to the wrong place and want to restore it to its previous position, from the Edit menu, choose Undo.

7. If you save or close the file without attaching a detached selection, a dialog box appears asking you if you want to attach the selection at its current location.

   • To attach the selection, choose Yes.

   • To save or close the file without attaching the selection, choose No.

Editing an Image Using Edit Commands

Several of the Edit menu commands work directly with the Windows Clipboard. The Clipboard is an area of memory used for the short-term storage of different objects, such as text and bitmaps. You can use the following commands to edit bitmaps, moving information to and from the Clipboard.

Cut

Removes a selected area from a bitmap and places it on the Clipboard, along with a copy of the bitmap color palette. The deleted area of the bitmap changes to the current background color.

Copy

Places a copy of the selected area from a bitmap on the Clipboard, along with a copy of the bitmap color palette. The selected area remains part of the bitmap and is unchanged.

Paste

Places the contents of the Clipboard into a bitmap. Colors in the Clipboard palette are added to any available positions at the end of the bitmap palette. If the pasted palette contains more colors than available spaces, BitEdit uses as many colors as it can and discards the rest. Pixels in the pasted bitmap that use discarded colors are mapped to available colors.

Delete

Deletes an object from the bitmap. The deleted area of the bitmap changes to the current background color.

Paste Without Color

Places the contents of the Clipboard into a bitmap, ignoring the pasted-area color palette. BitEdit maps the colors in the pasted area to the closest colors in the bitmap palette.

Paste Palette

Replaces the palette of the current bitmap with the current palette of the Clipboard. Colors in the bitmap are mapped to the closest matching colors in the new palette. If the Clipboard doesn't have a current palette, this command cannot be used.

Note   Unlike other Edit menu commands, Delete does not use or affect the Clipboard; this means an object removed by the Delete command is not placed on the Clipboard.

Many Windows applications use the Clipboard as a temporary storage area. An object remains on the Clipboard until it is either pasted into the application or replaced by a different object.

Pasting from the Clipboard

You can use the Paste command to place the contents of the Clipboard into a BitEdit window. For example, use the Paste command to overlay a selected area of an existing bitmap, or to paste several objects together to create new bitmaps.

Paste also pastes colors on the Clipboard into the bitmap palette in the BitEdit window. If there isn't enough room in the bitmap palette for the additional colors, BitEdit displays a dialog box asking you to map the colors from the Clipboard to the bitmap palette. If you choose Yes, the Clipboard colors are added to the bitmap palette until the palette is full. Any colors in the Clipboard image not pasted are remapped to colors in the palette.

Pasting Without a Selected Area

How Paste works depends on whether you have selected an area in the BitEdit window. If you haven't selected an area, BitEdit places the contents of the Clipboard as a *detached selection* in the window. You can position a detached selection just as you would any selection. The following illustration shows how the Paste command works when no area is selected:

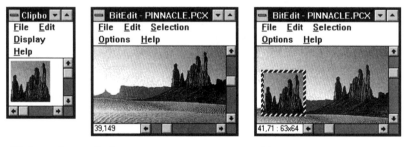

Clipboard   Before   After

Pasting into a Selected Area

If a selected area exists when you choose Paste, BitEdit expands or shrinks the Clipboard contents to fit into the current selection. After the command is complete, the selected area is detached, and you can position it just as you would any detached selection. The following illustration shows how the Paste command works when an area is selected.

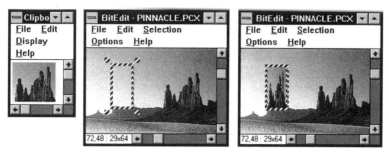

Clipboard   *Before*   *After*

Pasting Without Clipboard Colors

If you don't want the colors in the Clipboard palette to be added to the palette of the bitmap in the BitEdit window, use the Paste Without Color command on the Edit menu. This command pastes the image from the Clipboard into the BitEdit window, but it doesn't paste any colors from the Clipboard palette. The colors in the pasted image are mapped to the bitmap palette in the BitEdit window.

Pasting into a New BitEdit Window

You might want to edit the contents of the Clipboard before pasting it into your bitmap. The image might need cropping or other edits. To do this, you can copy the contents of the Clipboard to a new BitEdit window, edit the image, and then insert the edited image into your bitmap.

▶ **To paste the contents of the Clipboard into a new BitEdit window:**

1. From the File menu, choose Run BitEdit.

2. From the Edit menu in the new BitEdit window, choose Paste.

   Edit the image as needed. When you finish editing, you can save the image or copy the new image back to the Clipboard for transfer to another bitmap.

Editing an Image Using Selection Commands

The Selection menu commands apply to the current selection. Most of these commands manipulate the contents of the selection in some way, leaving the rest of the bitmap intact. The Crop command uses a reverse strategy, however, leaving the selection intact while deleting the rest of the bitmap.

Note   Unlike the Edit menu commands, the commands discussed in this section do not affect the contents of the Clipboard.

Cropping a Bitmap Image

You can use the Crop command to cut away unnecessary portions of a bitmap, removing all parts of a bitmap outside the selected area.

▶ **To crop a bitmap image:**

1. Select the area of the bitmap you want to keep.

2. From the Selection menu, choose Crop.

Flipping a Selection

You can use the Flip Horizontal and Flip Vertical commands to transpose the orientation of part of the bitmap.

The Flip Horizontal command transposes the left and right sides of a selected bitmap area, producing a mirror image of the selection area, as shown in the following illustration:

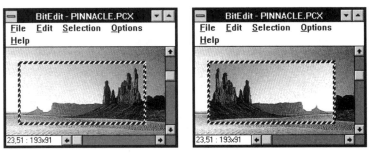

Before   **After**

The Flip Vertical command transposes the top and bottom of a selected bitmap area, inverting the selection area, as shown in the following illustration.

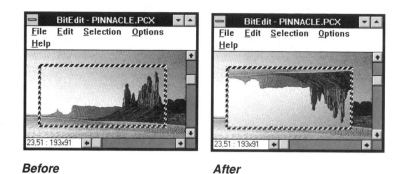

Before   *After*

▶ **To flip a selected bitmap area:**

1. Select the area of the bitmap you want to transpose.

2. From the Selection menu, choose either Flip Horizontal or Flip Vertical.

Rotating a Selection

You can use the Rotate command to turn a selected bitmap area any number of degrees, up to one revolution. The following illustration shows how Rotate affects a pasted object (for information on pasting objects using a transparent background, see "Using Transparent Color," later in this chapter):

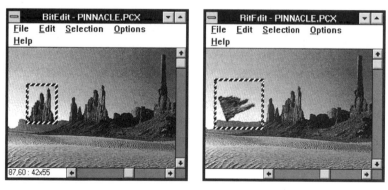

Before   *After*

▶ **To rotate a selected bitmap area:**

1. Select the area of the bitmap you want to turn.

2. From the Selection menu, choose Rotate.

   The Rotate Selection dialog box appears.

```
┌─────────────────────────────────┐
│ ━  │   Rotate Selection   │      │
├─────────────────────────────────┤
│  Rotate by:  [0   ]  degrees     │
│  ☐ Use Transparency              │
│  [Rotate]   [Done]   [Cancel]    │
└─────────────────────────────────┘
```

3. Enter the number of degrees you want to rotate the selection.

   Positive values turn the selection clockwise. Negative values turn the selection counterclockwise. The zero-degree position is the original orientation of the selection.

4. Select the Use Transparency check box to change the current background color into a transparent color during rotation. Transparent color is a special effect described in detail in "Using Transparent Color," later in this chapter.

5. Choose the Rotate button.

6. Choose Done to include the rotated selection in your bitmap.

   To cancel the Rotate command without turning the selection, choose Cancel. The bitmap is unchanged and the area remains selected.

Working with a Bitmap Palette

With several BitEdit commands, you can change and select the colors in a bitmap. You can replace one color palette with another, reduce the number of colors in a palette, reorder the color entries in a palette, select color entries in a palette that are used within a selection, or change the color palette directly using PalEdit. The following illustration shows a bitmap in BitEdit and the palette for the bitmap in PalEdit.

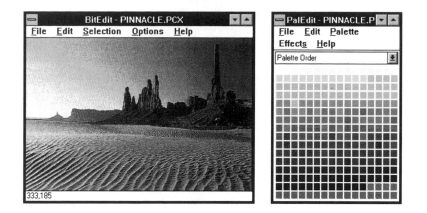

The PalEdit tool is the most powerful and comprehensive way to modify bitmap colors. You can display a color palette and use PalEdit by using the Show Palette command on the Options menu. For more information on using PalEdit, see Chapter 14, "Editing Color Palettes Using PalEdit."

Pasting a Palette

You can replace the palette of the current bitmap with the palette from the Clipboard by using the Paste Palette command on the Edit menu. The Clipboard palette can be a palette cut or copied from another bitmap file or from a palette file.

▶ **To replace a bitmap palette with another palette:**

1. From the File menu, choose Open to open the bitmap that contains the palette you want.

2. Select any part of the bitmap, or, from the Edit menu, choose Select All.

3. From the Edit menu, choose Copy.

   The current bitmap palette is copied to the Clipboard.

4. From the File menu, choose Open to open the bitmap that contains the palette you want to replace.

5. From the Edit menu, choose Paste Palette.

   The palette on the Clipboard replaces the bitmap palette. The bitmap changes, using the colors in the new palette.

Reducing Bitmap Colors

To paste colors from diverse sources into a single palette (such as building a palette that works with several bitmaps) or to use a bitmap on several types of monitors (such as 16- and 256-color monitors), you can reduce the number of colors in the bitmap. Reducing the number of colors needed to display a bitmap simplifies the task of building a composite palette and increases its versatility. You can reduce the number of colors a bitmap uses by using the Color Reduction command on the Options menu.

The Color Reduction command provides the following settings:

Optimal Palette
   This option is the best color-reduction method. It locates a palette of a specified size that best represents the image. Entries in the new palette are median values that result from grouping related entries.

Optimal Palette for Selection
   This option works similar to the Optimal Palette option, but it places a higher priority on the colors in the selected area of the bitmap. Use this option to ensure the color quality of the selected portion of a bitmap. The Optimal Palette for Selection option is available only when the selection area (indicated by a red-and-white or blue-and-white box) appears on the bitmap.

Truncated Palette
   This option keeps the top palette entries and discards lower palette entries. This reduction method maps each discarded color to the closest color retained in the palette. Truncating the palette is useful when building new palettes from composite palettes or removing unused colors from scanned images.

Palette From File
   This option replaces the current bitmap palette with another palette that you specify. This option is useful when linking a bitmap to a composite palette or a special-effects palette.

In addition to reducing color choices, you can dither a bitmap using the new palette to further enhance the image.

▶ **To reduce the number of colors used in a bitmap:**

1. From the Options menu, choose Color Reduction.

   The Color Reduction dialog box appears.

   ```
   ┌─────────────────────────────────────┐
   │ ▭        Color Reduction            │
   ├─────────────────────────────────────┤
   │ Reduce to │256│  ▲▼  Colors          │
   │  ◉ Optimal Palette                   │
   │  ○ Optimal Palette for Selection     │
   │  ○ Truncated Palette                 │
   │  ○ Palette From File                 │
   │  ┌────────┐ ┌────────┐ ┌────────┐   │
   │  │ Accept │ │ Dither │ │ Cancel │   │
   │  └────────┘ └────────┘ └────────┘   │
   └─────────────────────────────────────┘
   ```

2. Enter the number of colors you want to retain.

3. Choose one of the four color-reduction methods.

4. Choose Accept, Dither, or Cancel.

Accept
: This button reduces the number of colors, and then redraws the bitmap and displays the new palette (if PalEdit is active).

Dither
: This button reduces the number of colors using dithering, and then redraws the bitmap and displays the new palette (if PalEdit is active). *Dithering* is a method of blending colors together by interspersing different colors in the region where blending occurs.

Cancel
: This button closes the Color Reduction dialog box without changing the bitmap or palette.

Reordering a Color Palette

You can move the colors in a selected bitmap area to the top of the associated color palette. Placing the most important colors in a bitmap at the beginning of a palette is beneficial. Windows considers colors at the beginning of a palette to be more important than colors further down in the palette.

Reordering the palette is also useful in palette animation—the process of cycling through colors in a palette to give the impression of motion. For example, falling water in rain and waterfalls can be simulated by cycling through the color palette. For more information on palette cycling, see Chapter 14, "Editing Color Palettes Using PalEdit."

▶ **To move colors in a selection to the top of a color palette:**

1. Select the bitmap area that contains the colors you want to move.

2. From the Selection menu, choose Selected Colors First.

Selecting Palette Colors

You can identify color entries in PalEdit in a selected area of a bitmap. This is useful for performing several editing tasks. For example, to modify all of the colors in a particular area of a bitmap, you can select that area and cause the colors in the area to be selected in PalEdit. Then you can move to PalEdit and edit each color, or you can merge the colors and edit the resulting color.

▶ **To select colors in PalEdit from a bitmap:**

1. Select the bitmap area that contains the colors you want selected in PalEdit.

2. From the Selection menu, choose Select In PalEdit.

   You can now move to PalEdit and work with the selected colors.

Note   If you use a mouse to activate the PalEdit window after you select colors using BitEdit, be sure you don't click inside the color grid because this cancels the color selection. Instead, click the PalEdit title bar or menu bar.

Using Transparent Color

The Use Transparency command on the Options menu turns the current background color into a transparent color for the Paste command, the rectangle drawing tools, and the Ellipse drawing tool. This command is useful when framing an object or pasting an object into a bitmap. The following illustration shows how the Use Transparency command affects the Paste command.

Clipboard   ***Before***   ***After*** *(with transparent background)*

The following procedure explains how to copy an object to a bitmap without extraneous background detail. This procedure assumes the following:

- A color common to both bitmaps that serves as background color already exists in both bitmap palettes. (In some situations, you might need to copy a color from one palette to another. For information on copying colors among palettes, see Chapter 14, "Editing Color Palettes Using PalEdit.")

- One instance of BitEdit is necessary to perform this procedure.

▶ **To copy an object without background detail:**

1. Open the bitmap containing the object you want to copy.

2. Identify the object you want to copy.

3. Use the Selection tool to select the object.

4. Crop the bitmap, leaving the selected area containing the object you want to copy.

5. Click the Current Color tool icon and hold down the right mouse button to display the palette. From the colors in the palette, select a background color.

   You should select a color from the palette that highly contrasts with the object you're copying.

6. Using the Brush tool, click background pixels around the selected object with the right mouse button to change unwanted pixels to the current background color.

   The following tools can help you with this process:

   - For detailed work, click the Zoom Control tool icon and drag the mouse to an appropriate magnification level. Then move the box to the area of the bitmap you want to magnify. Zoom Control lets you magnify the pixel size of a portion of a bitmap, simplifying the process of painting individual pixels.

   - For painting large areas, click the Line Size tool icon and drag the mouse to a larger line width. Using a large line width increases the number of pixels you can paint in a single stroke.

7. From the Edit menu, choose Select All, then choose Copy to copy the object to the Clipboard.

   You should make a backup copy of the object on the Clipboard. To save the object, use the Save As command on the File menu.

8. Open the bitmap file you're constructing.

9. From the Options menu, choose Use Transparency (if Use Transparency is already active, a check mark appears next to the command name).

10. Use the Current Color tool to select the background color. Choose the same color that you selected in step 5.

11. From the Edit menu, choose Paste to copy the object from the Clipboard into the bitmap.

    During the paste operation, BitEdit might display a dialog box requesting confirmation to map colors from the object on the Clipboard into the bitmap palette. To continue the paste and map the object to the bitmap palette, choose OK; to cancel the paste, choose Cancel.

Now you can move the object to the appropriate place in the bitmap.

▶ **To draw hollow rectangles, circles, and ellipses:**

1. From the Options menu, choose Use Transparency (a check mark next to the command name indicates this command is active).

2. Select the Rectangle or the Ellipse tool.

3. Draw the rectangle, circle, or ellipse. Use the left mouse button to draw the framc in the foreground color. Use the right mouse button to draw the frame in the background color.

Resizing a Bitmap

You can alter the height, width, and color depth for any bitmap. The best image sizes are between 3-by-5 inches and 8-by-10 inches. If an image is outside this range, the end-user might experience difficulty obtaining the intended information from the image. It is also important to track the amount of storage used for each image as you manage the storage needs for all media elements used in your application.

▶ **To resize a bitmap:**

1. From the Edit menu, choose Resize Image.

   The Resize Bitmap dialog box appears.

Resize Bitmap
Width: 468
Height: 198
Ok   Cancel
Resize Options
☒ Scaling Resize
☒ Retain Proportions
Colors
○ 1 bit per pixel
○ 4 bits per pixel
⊙ 8 bits per pixel

2. The Scaling Resize check box performs the following:

   • Select the Scaling Resize check box to scale the image to the specified bitmap dimensions.

- Clear the Scaling Resize check box to adjust the bitmap frame size while maintaining the image resolution. If you enlarge the bitmap dimensions, BitEdit displays the original image unchanged and fills the new area of the bitmap with the background color. If you reduce the dimensions, BitEdit crops the image to fit the smaller area. This cropping function defines the upper-left corner of the bitmap as its origin and crops the right and lower edges to the specified dimensions.

3. The Retain Proportions check box performs the following:

- Select the Retain Proportions check box to maintain the current aspect ratio (width-to-height proportion) of the image. Retaining proportions prevents distortion during resizing.

- Clear the Retain Proportions check box to adjust the horizontal and vertical dimensions independently. Adjusting individual image dimensions introduces distortion into an image.

4. To change the number of colors available to the bitmap, select the value you want in the Colors area. A 1-bit bitmap has two colors, a 4-bit bitmap has 16 colors, and an 8-bit bitmap has 256 colors. Changing this value does the following:

- Increasing the number of bits allows the image to support a larger color palette, but doesn't cause any immediate visual changes.

- Decreasing the number of bits limits the size of the bitmap color palette. If the current number of colors in the palette is larger than the number supported by the selected bit size, some colors will be lost. BitEdit rebuilds the bitmap using the remaining colors.

5. To change the size of the bitmap, change the values in the Width or Height spin boxes. You can enter new values or use the arrows to the right of the boxes.

   If the Retain Proportions check box is selected, the values in Width and Height automatically adjust to maintain the aspect ratio.

6. Choose OK.

Creating a New Bitmap File

You can use BitEdit to create new bitmaps, as well as to edit existing bitmaps. For example, you can draw using the Brush tool or fill areas with color using the Flood Fill tool. You can create a new bitmap by integrating pieces of several bitmaps. Or you can take areas from existing bitmaps to create new bitmaps, as shown in the following illustration.

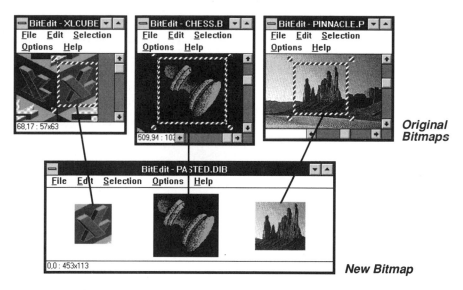

Original Bitmaps

New Bitmap

▶ **To create a new bitmap file:**

1. From the File menu, choose New.

   The New Bitmap dialog box appears.

2. Enter the Width and Height (in pixels) of the new bitmap you want to create.

3. In the Colors area, select the value to control the maximum number of colors available to the bitmap. A 1-bit bitmap supports two colors, a 4-bit bitmap supports 16 colors, and an 8-bit bitmap supports 256 colors.

4. Choose OK.

5. Add objects to the bitmap by cutting or copying areas from other bitmaps, then pasting them from the Clipboard. You can start multiple copies of BitEdit to open, edit, and copy images or selections using the Clipboard.

Note   To use the BitEdit editing tools to add to an empty bitmap, the bitmap must have a color palette. You can create a palette yourself in PalEdit, or you can paste a palette from the Clipboard using the Paste Palette command on the Edit menu. For more information on working with palettes in BitEdit, see "Working with a Bitmap Palette," earlier in this chapter.

Saving Your Changes

After you finish editing a bitmap file, you must save your changes before you quit BitEdit. You can use one of the following commands:

- The Save command on the File menu saves your changes using the same filename and the same format.

- The Save As command on the File menu saves your changes using a different filename or different format.

▶   **To save a bitmap using a new filename or format:**

1. From the File menu, choose Save As.

   The Save Bitmap dialog box appears (this dialog box also appears the first time you save a bitmap file, or when you attempt to save changes to a bitmap that is currently in a file format that BitEdit can't write to).

2. Enter the filename under which you want to save the bitmap file.

   If you don't type an extension, BitEdit adds ".DIB" to indicate it is a .DIB file.

3. To save the file using a different format, in the Save File as Type box, enter the format you want or select one from the list.

4. Choose OK.

Note   Once you specify a filename, you should use the Save command regularly to ensure that your changes are made to the disk file.

Quitting BitEdit

When you finish your editing, you can quit BitEdit.

▶ **To quit BitEdit:**

1. From the File menu, choose Exit.

   If you haven't saved your latest changes, a dialog box similar to the following appears, asking if you want to save them.

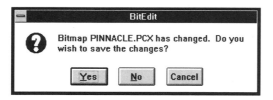

2. To save your changes, choose Yes; to exit without saving your changes, choose No; or to continue working with BitEdit, choose Cancel.

Note   If you haven't completed particular BitEdit actions (such as attaching a detached selection or reducing colors) and then choose the Exit command, dialog boxes appear asking you to complete the tasks before quitting BitEdit.

Chapter 14
Editing Color Palettes Using PalEdit

When you open a bitmap using BitEdit, BitEdit uses the *color palette* associated with the bitmap to determine which colors to use. Color palette files can also exist independently of a bitmap. This chapter describes color palettes and explains how to display and edit palettes using the PalEdit tool.

PalEdit provides color touch-up capabilities for digital images—improving image quality, preparing images for display on different types of hardware, and preparing multiple images for simultaneous display. You can use PalEdit for the following:

- Modifying any color in a palette.

- Modifying the entire palette for brightness, contrast, or color tint. Scanned images often require touch-up for brightness or contrast. Tinting and other special effects are also available.

- Reducing the number of colors in a palette. Managing the number of colors in a palette can save memory or improve consistency among a group of pictures. PalEdit lets you control the way colors are reduced, so you can preserve the quality of a bitmap even though its palette is smaller.

- Copying colors from one palette to another. When combining bitmap images or creating special effects, you can copy colors from one palette to another. PalEdit allows you to use the Clipboard to copy and transfer one or more colors among palettes.

- Building a palette that works with multiple bitmaps. Using the color-reduction and color-copying features of PalEdit, you can build a composite palette that contains the most important colors for a group of bitmaps. You can also use PalEdit to link a composite palette back to each bitmap providing the colors.

About Color Palettes

The bitmaps used by a multimedia application can come from different sources, and many will come from photographs. A photograph uses continuous tones and shades—colors that blend smoothly from one to another. By using a scanner or special digitizing equipment, you can transform photographs into bitmap images.

As the tones in the photograph are sampled to create a bitmap, a color palette—a table of distinct color values—is also created. Each color in a palette is identified by components of the colors red, green, and blue (RGB). The digitizing software assigns an entry in this palette to each pixel in the bitmap. The number of colors in the palette depends on the *image depth* (the number of bits used to define each pixel in the bitmap). Windows with Multimedia uses these image depths:

- 1-bit bitmaps can display two colors (typically black and white)

- 4-bit bitmaps can display 16 colors

- 8-bit bitmaps can display 256 colors

Many scanners offer several image-depth settings. Because Windows with Multimedia supports 1-bit, 4-bit, and 8-bit bitmaps, any palette can contain up to 256 unique colors. The quality of a scanned bitmap depends on how well a system can re-create the effect of a continuous-tone image using these 256 colors.

Some bitmaps use 8-bit palettes called *identity palettes*. These palettes provide a performance boost when you open bitmaps and store system-defined colors in the first 10 and last 10 colors of a palette. For information on identity palettes, see "Creating an Identity Palette," later in this chapter.

Note   Windows with Multimedia also supports nonpalette images, dividing the 24-bits comprising each pixel into thirds to store red, green, and blue color components.

Starting PalEdit

You can start PalEdit from within BitEdit to edit a color palette associated with a particular bitmap image. You can also start PalEdit as an independent application to edit palette files apart from associated bitmaps.

▶ **To start PalEdit from BitEdit:**

1. Activate the BitEdit window that contains the bitmap and bitmap palette you want to edit.

2. From the Options menu, choose Show Palette.

    PalEdit starts, and displays the bitmap palette.

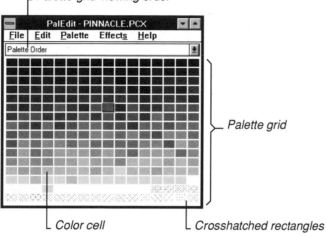

Palette-grid viewing order

Palette grid

Color cell   *Crosshatched rectangles*

To edit a palette stored as a separate file, rather than as a palette associated with a particular bitmap, you must start PalEdit as an independent application.

▶ **To start PalEdit as a stand-alone application:**

1. From the Program Manager File menu, choose Run.

    The Run dialog box appears.

2. In the Command Line box, type **paledit**.

The PalEdit window contains a grid of all the colors used by the bitmap. Each palette color appears as a separate color cell in the grid. Crosshatched rectangles indicate the palette has more than 236 colors. When you first start PalEdit, it displays the palette colors in *palette order*—the actual order in which colors are arranged in the palette. You can change the order of colors in the palette by selecting a different view from the list box above the grid. This box contains all of the available views.

If you open PalEdit from BitEdit, the title bar at the top of the PalEdit window contains the name of the bitmap file associated with the palette. If you open an independent palette file, the title bar contains the name of the palette file.

The PalEdit Menus

PalEdit displays five main menus: File, Edit, Palette, Effects, and Help. You can control the appearance and content of a color palette by using commands on these menus.

The File Menu

You can use the commands on the File menu to load and save palettes. The commands available depend on whether you start PalEdit from BitEdit or start PalEdit alone to work on an independent palette file.

Command	Description
New	Creates a new palette file.
Open	Opens an existing palette file.
Close	Closes an existing palette file.
Save	Saves changes to a palette file.
Save As	Specifies a palette file and saves changes to that file.
Apply From File	Attaches a new palette to the current bitmap in BitEdit.
Save To File	Saves the current palette in a separate palette file.
Exit	Quits PalEdit.

The Edit Menu

You can use the commands on the Edit menu to change the content of individual cells in a palette, select groups of cells in a palette, and specify viewing preferences.

Command	Description
Undo	Undoes the last change to a palette.
Cut	Cuts a selected cell or group of cells from a palette and places the contents of the selection on the Clipboard.
Copy	Copies a selected cell or group of cells from a palette and places the contents of the selection on the Clipboard.

Command	Description
Paste	Pastes the contents of the Clipboard into a palette.
Delete	Deletes a selected cell or group of cells from a palette. The deleted selection is *not* placed on the Clipboard.
Select All	Selects all of the cells in a palette.
Select Similar Colors	Selects the color cells that have similar color components based on a specified color.
Select Unused Colors	Selects the color cells that are unused in an associated bitmap.
Flash Selected Colors	Causes the currently selected colors to blink in the palette and in the associated bitmap image.
Merge Selected Colors	Merges a set of selected colors into one color entry, which is an average of all selected colors.
Preferences	Sets the palette-viewing mode and update method.

The Palette Menu

You can use the commands on the Palette menu to change color-cell definitions, define new color cells, rearrange color-cell sequence in a palette, and transform a palette into an identity palette.

Command	Description
Edit Color	Changes the color of a selected cell.
Add Color	Adds a new color to the end of the palette.
Reorder Palette as View	Changes the palette order to match the order of a specific color sort. This command name changes to Copy View when PalEdit shows two views of a palette.
Make Identity Palette	Restructures the current palette into an identity palette.

The Effects Menu

You can use the commands on the Effects menu to globally adjust the color of all cells in a palette, as well as to set up a palette for simulating animation in associated bitmaps.

Command	Description
Adjust Brightness	Raises or lowers the brightness level of all colors in a palette.
Adjust Contrast	Raises or lowers the contrast level of all colors in a palette.
Add Selected Color	Adds RGB values of a selected color to all colors in a palette.
Fade to Selected Color	Causes all colors in a palette to converge to the RGB values of a selected color.
Fade to Palette	Adjusts all colors in the current palette to similar colors in a specified palette.
Cycle RGB	Adjusts the hues of all colors except white, grey, and black.
Cycle Palette	Swaps color assignments within a specified block of cells.

Using Palette Files

The most common use of PalEdit is to edit the palette associated with a bitmap file. If you start PalEdit as an independent application, you can open an existing palette file or create a new palette file.

PalEdit gives palette files the extension .PAL. Existing files might include the default palettes VGA.PAL and STANDARD.PAL, along with any palette files you create. You might want to create a new palette file to associate a specific set of colors with a bitmap or group of bitmaps.

You can work with palette files in the following ways:

- Open and edit new or existing palette files.

- Save a palette associated with a bitmap file as an independent palette file.

- Apply a palette file to a particular bitmap.

The ability to create, edit, and save palette files separate from bitmap files enables you to share a common palette among multiple bitmaps. This is particularly important if you plan to display several bitmaps on screen simultaneously (all bitmaps on the screen use the palette of the bitmap in the active window). If bitmaps use different color palettes, switching from one window to another can cause noticeable changes in bitmap appearance.

For example, if you display two bitmaps, one with 20 green tones and another with 20 red tones, when the green bitmap is the active window, both bitmaps become green because they both use the green palette. When the red bitmap is the active window, both bitmaps become red. By creating a common palette for a group of bitmaps, you can obtain a consistent appearance for the bitmaps when displaying them simultaneously.

▶   **To open an existing palette file:**

1. From the File menu, choose Open.

2. Scroll through the file, directory, and file-type lists and select the file you want.

3. To confirm the file type before you open it, select the Confirm File Type check box.

4. Choose Open.

▶   **To create a new palette file:**

1. From the File menu, choose New.

   The New Palette dialog box appears.

2. Enter the number of initial palette entries you want the new palette file to have (the default is 2).

3. Choose OK.

When the file opens, the initial color cells are black. You can change these colors, add new colors, and paste additional color cells from other palettes.

Setting Preferences

You can use the Preferences command on the Edit menu to see one or two concurrent views of a palette and to set the palette-update procedure used by PalEdit.

▶ **To set PalEdit preferences:**

1. From the Edit menu, choose Preferences.

   The PalEdit Preferences dialog box appears.

   ![PalEdit Preferences dialog box with Dual View and Delay Updates checkboxes, OK and Cancel buttons]

2. Select one or both of the following check boxes:

   • When the Dual View check box is selected, the PalEdit window displays two views of the palette. Each view has its own viewing order to organize palette color cells. The following illustration shows the PalEdit window in single-view and dual-view modes:

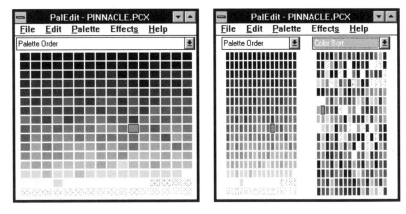

Single view   *Dual view*

You can change the viewing order for either or both views. For information on viewing orders, see the following section, "Changing the Palette View."

The color selection process is identical with single and dual views; however, when you select a color in dual view, the selection appears in both views.

- When the Delay Updates check box is selected, PalEdit doesn't update the PalEdit window when you change the associated bitmap using BitEdit. By omitting palette recalculations for each bitmap change, you avoid waiting for the palette view to update.

3. Choose OK.

Note   To update the palette view when the Delay Updates check box is selected, reselect the viewing order, as described in the following section.

Changing the Palette View

You can view a palette in a variety of color arrangements without affecting the structure of the palette. PalEdit supports the following views:

- The Palette Order view lists colors in the order in which they are stored in a palette.

- The Brightness view sorts colors by brightness, with the lightest colors in the upper-left corner and the darkest colors in the lower-right corner.

- The Darkness view sorts colors by brightness, with the darkest colors in the upper-left corner and the lightest colors in the lower-right corner.

- The Color Sort view sorts by color, placing colors with similar RGB values together.

- The Bitmap Occurrence view sorts a palette in order of color frequency, with the colors used most frequently in the associated bitmap in the upper-left corner and the least common colors in the lower-right corner. When you start PalEdit independently, without an associated bitmap, this view is not available.

For information on changing the order of colors, see "Changing Palette Structure," later in this chapter.

▶ **To change to a different viewing order:**

1. Click the arrow next to the current viewing order (just above the color grid).

A list of the available viewing orders appears.

Current viewing order

2. Select the viewing order you want.

Selecting Color Cells

All PalEdit editing functions require that you first select a single color cell or several cells. After you make your selection, you can cut, move, or copy the selection (for placement in the current palette or in another palette), as well as change the color values associated with the selection.

▶ **To select a single cell:**

1. Display the PalEdit window.

2. Click the cell you want to select.

   When a cell is selected, its border changes color.

▶ **To select multiple cells:**

■ Drag the mouse over the cells you want to select.

▶ **To select a row of cells:**

■ Click in the margin of the color grid, just left of the row you want to select.

▶ **To select all cells in a palette:**

▪ From the Edit menu, choose Select All.

▶ **To cancel a single-cell selection:**

▪ Point to the cell and click the right mouse button (or press SHIFT + the left mouse button).

▶ **To cancel a multiple-cell selection:**

▪ Using the right mouse button, drag the mouse across the selection (or press SHIFT and drag the mouse using the left mouse button).

▶ **To cancel all selected cells:**

▪ Click in the area between the color grid and the palette-view box.

Selecting Similar Colors

For any selected color cell, you can identify and select a group of cells that resemble the selected color by using the Select Similar Colors command on the Edit menu.

▶ **To select a group of similar colors:**

1. Select a color cell. The other colors in the palette will be compared to the RGB values of the color you select. If you select two or more cells, PalEdit uses the first selected cell.

2. From the Edit menu, choose Select Similar Colors.

   The Select Similar Colors dialog box appears.

3. Enter the number of cells in the group. If needed, adjust the group size using the scroll bar. Or, use the scroll bar until you've included all the appropriate cells in the group. As you adjust the group size, PalEdit selects or cancels the selection of those palette entries that have the closest RGB component values to the selected color.

4. Choose OK.

Selecting Unused Palette Colors

The Select Unused Colors command on the Edit menu identifies color cells used by the associated bitmap opened in BitEdit. By displaying unused color cells, this command identifies color cells you can delete without affecting your bitmaps when you merge palettes and create identity palettes.

▶ **To select unused palette cells:**

■ From the Edit menu, choose Select Unused Colors.

Selecting Colors from BitEdit

You can cause the colors in an area of a bitmap displayed in BitEdit to be selected in PalEdit. This is useful if you want to see which colors appear in a particular part of a bitmap, or if you want to change these colors.

For example, to modify the colors of a bird that appears in an image, you can select the bird in BitEdit, and then move to PalEdit to see which colors are used.

▶ **To select colors in a palette from BitEdit:**

1. Activate the BitEdit window.

2. Select the portion of the bitmap that contains colors you want to select.

3. From the Edit menu, choose Select In PalEdit.

4. Activate the PalEdit window by clicking in the PalEdit title bar.

The colors in the BitEdit selection are selected.

Flashing Selected Colors

You can cause the colors you select in PalEdit to flash in the associated bitmap. This helps you see the areas of a bitmap that use particular colors. Flashing selected colors also helps you determine the effect of deleting or modifying the colors.

▶   **To flash selected colors:**

1. Make sure you can see the associated BitEdit window.

2. Select the colors you want to flash.

3. From the Edit menu, choose Flash Selected Colors.

The selected colors flash once in the palette *and* in the associated bitmap.

Changing Color Definitions

Changing palette colors can be simple—you can adjust the RGB values of one color cell to match a desired color. However, changing colors can also be more complex—you can fade the entire palette to a single color or adjust the contrast of the entire palette. Using PalEdit, you can edit individual palette colors, introduce new colors into a palette, and touch up bitmaps by adjusting a palette for brightness, contrast, and tint. You can also test the compatibility of bitmaps with other palettes.

Editing Color Cells

You can modify any color in a palette by using the Edit Color command on the Edit menu. When you use the Edit Color command to change a specific color, areas in the bitmap displayed by BitEdit that use that color change on screen. You might want to edit a color for the following reasons:

■   To fine-tune the appearance of a bitmap. You can brighten or darken large areas of a bitmap or make colors more vibrant.

■   To see how important a particular color is to the bitmap. If you change a color and it doesn't visibly affect the bitmap, you can reduce the palette size by eliminating that color from the palette.

▶ **To edit cell color:**

1. Select the cell that contains color you want to edit.

2. From the Edit menu, choose Edit Color (or double-click the color cell). The Edit Color dialog box appears.

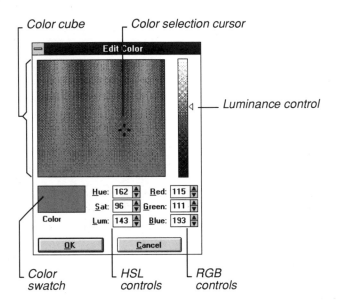

3. Enter the settings you want (each setting is explained in the following section).

4. Choose OK.

Using the Edit Color Dialog Box

The Edit Color dialog box contains a color swatch that shows you a sample of the selected cell, along with a set of numeric fields and a color cube you can use to define colors. The color cube shows the available colors. The color selection cursor in the cube shows the current color setting for the selected cell. Each color is defined in values for red, green, blue (RGB), and hue, saturation, and luminance (HSL). RGB and HSL each completely define a given color—they are simply different perspectives.

You use the Edit Color dialog box to manipulate the values for these components, changing and creating colors as necessary. When you change color values, the updated color appears in the color swatch below the color cube. If there is an associated bitmap displayed in the BitEdit window, the color in the bitmap also changes.

▶ **To set colors using RGB components:**

- In the Red, Green, and Blue spin boxes, enter the values you want (each color in a palette can be described by a combination of red, green, and blue components, each of which can range from 0 through 255).

▶ **To set colors using HSL components:**

1. In the Hue spin box, enter the value you want (hue is defined by its position along the color spectrum, which can range from 0 through 239).

2. In the Sat spin box, enter the value you want (saturation defines the purity of hue, ranging from grey to pure color, which can range from 0 through 240).

3. In the Lum spin box, enter the value you want (luminance refers to brightness, which can range from 0, pure black, through 240, pure white).

A quick, but somewhat less precise way to edit a color is by using the color selection cursor in the color cube.

▶ **To set colors using the color selection cursor:**

- Move the color selection cursor to set the values for red, green, blue, hue, and saturation. The hue value increases as you move within the color cube along its x-axis (from left to right). The saturation value increases as you move within the color cube along its y-axis (from bottom to top). You can adjust luminance by positioning the control at the right of the cube.

After you change one or more color values using the Edit Color dialog box, you must save your changes to the current palette in memory. These changes aren't saved to disk until you save the bitmap file in BitEdit (or save the palette file in PalEdit).

▶ **To save your color changes:**

- Choose OK.

Adding a Color to a Palette

You can add a color to a palette using the Add Color command on the Palette menu. This is useful when you must use a specific color for a portion of a bitmap. For example, if a bitmap includes a logo that must be a certain color not currently in its palette, you can use the Add Color command to create the color you need.

▶ **To add a color to a palette:**

1. Make sure the palette has room for the new color (a palette can contain up to 256 colors).

2. From the Palette menu, choose Add Color.

   The Add Color dialog box appears.

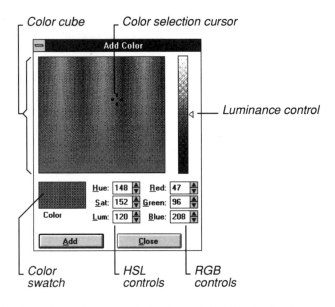

3. Use the color controls in the Add Color dialog box to create the color you want (these controls work the same as those for the Edit Color dialog box—for more information, see the previous section, "Using the Edit Color Dialog Box").

4. Choose Add to add the color to the palette.

5. Choose Close.

Adjusting Palette Brightness

Brightness adjustment allows you to touch up or compensate for overexposed or underexposed bitmaps. The Adjust Brightness command on the Effects menu raises or lowers the RGB color components of all color cells uniformly. The following illustration shows how increasing brightness affects a palette:

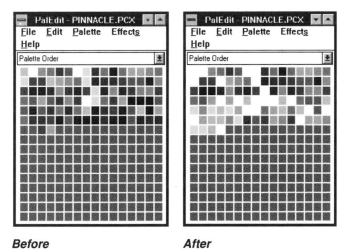

Before   *After*

▶ **To adjust palette brightness:**

1. From the Effects menu, choose Adjust Brightness.

   The Adjust Brightness dialog box appears.

2. In the Adjustment box, enter the level of brightness to increase or decrease brightness (or use the scroll bar until you reach an appropriate brightness level).

3. Choose OK.

Adjusting Palette Contrast

You can also touch up a bitmap by adjusting the palette contrast; this allows you to increase or decrease the distinction between light and dark areas in your bitmaps. Increasing the contrast lightens colors that are lighter than a median grey and darkens remaining colors. Decreasing the contrast fades all colors to a median grey. The following illustration shows how increasing contrast affects a palette:

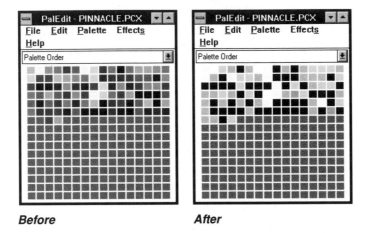

Before   *After*

▶   **To adjust the palette contrast:**

1. From the Effects menu, choose Adjust Contrast.

    The Adjust Contrast dialog box appears.

2. In the Percentage box, enter the level of contrast you want (or use the scroll bar to set the appropriate contrast).

3. Choose OK.

Tinting, Filtering, and Fading a Palette

You can edit any palette by tinting, filtering, and fading color cells in a palette. Tinting a palette adds a specified color to all cells of the palette, causing one color to dominate your bitmap. Filtering a palette is the inverse of tinting—filtering removes a specified color from a palette. Fading a palette transforms palette cells into one or more specified colors. PalEdit provides three commands for tinting, filtering, and fading your palettes.

Adding and Removing a Specific Palette Color

You can tint and filter a palette using a specified color by using the Add Selected Color command on the Effects menu. As you adjust the amount of color, BitEdit shows the effects of the color change in the associated bitmap.

▶   **To add or remove a selected color from a palette:**

1. Select one or more colors from the palette. If you select one color, PalEdit uses the RGB values of the selected color to adjust the palette entries. If you select more than one color, PalEdit uses average RGB values of the selected colors.

2. From the Effects menu, choose Add Selected Color.

   The Add Selected Color dialog box appears.

3. In the Percent Added box, enter the amount of the selected color you want to add or subtract from the other colors (or use the scroll bar to set the appropriate percentage of color).

4. Choose OK.

Fading a Palette to a Specific Palette Color

You can converge a palette to a single color or several shades of one color by using the Fade to Selected Color command on the Effects menu. Fade to Selected Color takes a specified color (target color) and standardizes each palette color cell on the selected color. As you adjust the amount of fading, BitEdit shows the effects of the color change in the associated bitmap.

▶   **To fade a palette to a selected color:**

1. Select one or more colors from the palette. If you select one color, PalEdit uses the RGB values of the selected color as its target color. If you select more than one color, PalEdit uses the average of RGB values of the selected colors as its target color.

2. From the Effects menu, choose Fade to Selected Color.

    The Fade to Selected Color dialog box appears.

3. In the Percentage box, enter the amount of fading you want on the palette (or use the scroll bar to set the appropriate color). As the percentage increases, the RGB components of each color cell in the palette converge to target RGB values. At 100% fade, color cells in the palette converge completely to the target RGB values.

4. Choose OK.

Fading Palette Colors to a Second Palette

You can fade the contents of the current palette in PalEdit to the colors of a second palette by using the Fade to Palette command on the Effects menu. For each color cell of the current palette, Fade to Palette selects a target color—the closest matching color—from the second palette and transforms the color cell to the target color. As you adjust the amount of fading, BitEdit shows the effects of the color change in the associated bitmap.

▶ **To fade a palette to a second palette:**

1. From the Effects menu, choose Fade to Palette.

   The Load Palette From dialog box appears.

```
┌──────────────────────────────────────────────────────┐
│ ▬                    Load palette from...              │
├──────────────────────────────────────────────────────┤
│  File Name:              Directories:                  │
│  ┌──────────────┐        c:\dib          ┌─────────┐   │
│  │ *.pal        │        ┌────────────┐  │   OK    │   │
│  ├──────────────┤        │ ☞ c:\      │  └─────────┘   │
│  │ pin.pal      │        │ ☞ dib      │  ┌─────────┐   │
│  │ pinnacle.pal │        │            │  │ Cancel  │   │
│  │ squirrel.pal │        │            │  └─────────┘   │
│  │              │        │            │                │
│  └──────────────┘        └────────────┘                │
│                                                        │
│  List Files of Type:     Drives:                       │
│  ┌───────────────────┐▼  ┌──────────────────┐▼         │
│  │ Microsoft Palette │   │ ▣ c: [richbix]   │          │
│  └───────────────────┘   └──────────────────┘          │
│  ☐ Confirm File Type                                   │
└──────────────────────────────────────────────────────┘
```

2. Select a bitmap or palette file (PalEdit selects its target colors from that file).

   The Fade to Palette dialog box appears.

```
┌──────────────────────────────┐
│        Fade to Palette        │
├──────────────────────────────┤
│   0                    100%   │
│  ┌─┬──────────────────────┬─┐ │
│  │◄│                      │►│ │
│  └─┴──────────────────────┴─┘ │
│  Percentage:  ┌──────────┐    │
│               │ 0        │    │
│               └──────────┘    │
│    ┌────────┐   ┌────────┐    │
│    │   OK   │   │ Cancel │    │
│    └────────┘   └────────┘    │
└──────────────────────────────┘
```

3. In the Percentage box, enter the amount of fading you want (or use the scroll bar to set the appropriate color). As the percentage increases, the RGB components of each color cell in the palette converge to target RGB values. At 100% fade, color cells in the original palette converge completely to the closest colors in the new palette.

4. Choose OK.

Cycling Hue Sequences in a Palette

Using the Cycle RGB command on the Effects menu, you can change colors in a bitmap by shifting all color definitions in the palette according to a pair of color-shift sequences: red-green-blue-red and cyan-yellow-magenta-cyan. White, grey, and black are unaffected by this command.

▶ **To cycle RGB values in a palette:**

1. From the Effects menu, choose Cycle RGB.

   The Cycle RGB dialog box appears.

2. In the Percentage box, enter the amount of hue shift you want (or use the scroll bar to set the appropriate set of hues).

   The values 0 and 100 produce the same results—they leave the palette unchanged.

   A value of 33 shifts each cell one color in the sequence. For example, primary colors change shades of red to shades of green, greens to blues, and blues to reds; secondary colors change shades of cyan to shades of yellow, yellows to magentas, and magentas to cyans.

   A value of 66 shifts each cell two colors in the sequence. For example, primary colors change shades of red to shades of blue, greens to reds, and blues to greens; secondary colors change shades of cyan to shades of magenta, yellows to cyans, and magentas to yellows.

   Other percentages produce colors located between adjacent colors in the sequence. For example, a value of 50 changes red to blue-green.

3. Choose OK.

Changing Palette Structure

The palette-order view shows the actual order of colors in a color palette. This order is defined when the bitmap is created and has nothing to do with the frequency or importance of the colors in the bitmap. You can reorder and edit the sequence of color cells in a palette in the following ways:

- Reorder the entire palette according to the current palette view or by placing selected colors at the beginning of the palette.

- Move individual cells in a palette.

- Cut, copy, and paste cells from one palette to another.

- Merge colors from several cells into one color cell.

- Swap color definitions among a set of color cells.

- Consolidate colors from BitEdit.

- Transform the palette into an identity palette.

Reordering an Entire Palette

The simplest way to preserve important colors when you reduce the number of colors in a bitmap is by reordering the entire palette so that it matches a particular viewing order. For example, if you reorder a palette by bitmap occurrence, the most frequently used colors are placed at the beginning of the palette. You can also reorder a palette based on brightness, darkness, or color.

▶ **To reorder an entire palette:**

1. From the list box above the color grid, choose the viewing order you want.

   If you are using a dual view, display Palette Order on one side and the viewing order you want on the other side.

2. From the Palette menu, choose Reorder Palette as View (if you are displaying a single view).

   If you are displaying a dual view, choose Copy View.

Moving Individual Cells

If a bitmap contains colors that are important but not very common, you can move the important colors up on the color grid. This ensures that the important colors will be preserved if you truncate the palette or create an identity palette.

For example, if you have an image of a red rowboat on a green ocean and you sort the palette by bitmap occurrence, the red colors of the rowboat might appear near the bottom of the palette. If you reduce the colors by truncating the palette, the red rowboat might disappear. By moving the red colors toward the top of the palette, you can preserve them even if you truncate the palette.

▶   **To move one or more palette colors:**

1. Select the cell(s) containing the color(s) you want to move.

2. Click the selected cell(s) and hold down the left mouse button.

    An outline of the selected cell(s) appears.

3. Drag the group of cells to the new position in the palette.

    The flashing insertion point indicates the new position.

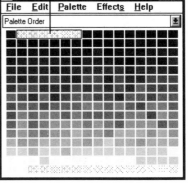

New position

Selected cells in the new position

Selected cells

Other cells shift right

You can also move colors between two views while in dual view. With Palette Order on one side, you can select colors from inside the other view and drag them to a new location in Palette Order.

Another way to select the colors in a particular area of a bitmap is by using BitEdit's Select In PalEdit command on the Selection menu.

Deleting Individual Cells

If a palette contains colors you don't want, you can delete them from the palette. Colors below the deleted colors shift up to fill empty grid positions; unused cells are placed at the end of the palette.

▶   **To delete color cells from a palette:**

1. Select the cells you want to delete.

2. From the Edit menu, choose Delete.

    All cells to the right of and below the deleted cells shift left and up to fill empty grid positions, as shown in the following illustration:

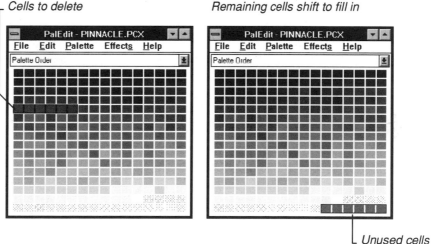

Cells to delete   *Remaining cells shift to fill in*

Unused cells

Note   BitEdit reassigns colors deleted from a palette using remaining colors of the nearest RGB values.

Pasting Color Cells

You can use the Paste command on the Edit menu to combine colors from different palettes into one palette. If a palette contains too many colors to hold the colors you want to paste, you can also replace selected colors.

▶ **To paste colors from one palette to another:**

1. Display the palette that contains the colors you want to incorporate.

2. Select the color cell(s) you want to paste.

3. From the Edit menu, choose Copy.

   PalEdit creates a new color palette that contains the selected colors and places the palette on the Clipboard.

4. Activate the PalEdit window that displays the color palette into which you want to paste the colors (make sure it displays Palette Order view).

5. From the Edit menu, choose Paste.

   PalEdit pastes the color palette from the Clipboard into the color palette associated with the active window. The pasted cells are added at the end of the palette.

   If the active-window palette doesn't have enough room for all the colors on the Clipboard palette, PalEdit displays a message telling you how many colors on the Clipboard palette cannot be added to the active-window palette.

6. Choose OK.

▶ **To replace cells in one palette with cells from another:**

1. Display the palette that contains the colors you want to add.

2. Select the color cell(s) you want to add.

3. From the Edit menu, choose Copy.

   PalEdit creates a color palette that contains only the selected colors and places the palette on the Clipboard.

4. Activate the PalEdit window that displays the color palette into which you want to paste the colors (be sure it displays Palette Order view).

5. Select the cells you want to replace.

6. From the Edit menu, choose Paste.

PalEdit pastes the color palette from the Clipboard into the color palette associated with the active window, replacing the selected cells. The palette changes as follows:

- If the number of cells pasted is greater than the number of cells selected, the palette increases in size. Selected cells are replaced first, then additional cells are addcd immcdiately afterward. If there is a bitmap associated with the palette, PalEdit updates the bitmap to incorporate the newly pasted colors.

- If the number of cells pasted is less than the number of cells selected, the palette decreases in size. Selected cells are replaced, and PalEdit updates the bitmap to incorporate the newly pasted colors.

If the active-window palette doesn't have enough room for all of the colors on the Clipboard palette, PalEdit displays a message telling you how many colors on the Clipboard palette cannot be added to the active-window palette.

7. Choose OK.

Merging Selected Color Cells

You can also use the Merge Selected Colors command on the Edit menu to reduce the number of colors in a palette by merging color cells. You can also select and combine similar colors into a single color, reducing the palette size.

▶ **To merge selected color cells:**

1. Select the color cells you want to merge.

2. From the Edit menu, choose Merge Selected Colors.

The newly combined color cell moves to the upper-left selected cell.

Cycling Palette Colors

Cycling colors in a palette lets you preview color animation by shifting color definitions from cell to cell through the palette. You can simulate light movements and effects by arranging color sequences in a palette, then cycling through the sequence. The Cycle Palette command on the Effects menu lets you test color sequencing and color animation. The following illustrations show palette cycling and how color shifts in a palette affect the associated image.

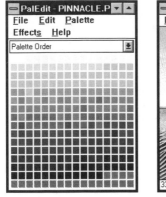

Before Cycle

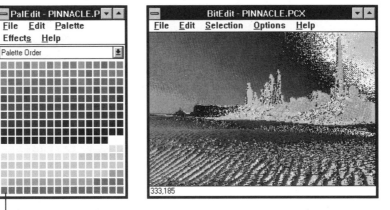

└ Shifted palette   **After Cycle**

▶ **To cycle palette colors:**

1. Organize the color cells in the palette to create the color sequence you want.

2. Identify the cycle color sequence by selecting the first and last color cells of the color sequence.

3. From the Effects menu, choose Cycle Palette.

   The Cycle Palette dialog box appears.

```
┌─────────────────────────────────────┐
│            Cycle Palette             │
│  ┌─Palette Index Range─────────────┐ │
│  │ Cycle Palette from  0    to  255│ │
│  └─────────────────────────────────┘ │
│    0                         100%     │
│   ┌──┬──────────────────────┬──┐      │
│   │◄ │▓▓▓▓▓▓▓▓▓▓▓▓▓▓▓▓▓▓▓▓▓▓│► │      │
│   └──┴──────────────────────┴──┘      │
│    Percentage:  │                     │
│                                       │
│       ┌──────────┐  ┌──────────┐      │
│       │    OK    │  │  Cancel  │      │
│       └──────────┘  └──────────┘      │
└─────────────────────────────────────┘
```

4. In the Percentage box, enter the amount of color cycling you want (or use the scroll bar to cycle back and forth through the specified color sequence).

5. Choose OK.

Consolidating Colors from BitEdit

You can use the Color Reduction command on the Options menu in BitEdit to specify the number of color entries in a palette and the method for reducing the number of colors in a palette. For more information, see Chapter 13, "Editing Bitmaps Using BitEdit."

Creating an Identity Palette

When you transform a palette into an identity palette, you restructure the palette to provide quicker bitmap loading while adding 20 system-defined colors to the palette. You can transform any palette into an identity palette by using the Make Identity Palette command on the Palette menu.

The Make Identity Palette command inserts system-defined colors into your palette, putting them in the first 10 and last 10 cells of a palette. While you can use the Make Identity Palette command with any palette view, the Palette Order viewing sequence provides the clearest view of the transformation. You can change the palette view by selecting a viewing sequence from the list box under the PalEdit menu bar.

If your palette contains more than 236 colors, this command truncates the palette to the first 236 cells, adds the system-defined colors to the palette, and remaps deleted colors to the closest remaining colors in the palette.

▶ **To create an identity palette:**

■ From the Palette menu, choose Make Identity Palette.

If your palette contains more than 236 colors, you should consider reducing the number of palette color cells by using one or more of the following methods:

- Remove unused cells from the palette by using the Select Unused Colors and the Cut commands both on the Edit menu.

- Merge similar colors in the palette by using the Select Similar Colors command on the Edit menu, and then use the Merge Selected Colors command also on the Edit menu to blend the colors into a single entry.

- Allow BitEdit to reduce the palette size. Start BitEdit using a bitmap that also uses the palette you're editing. Then use the BitEdit Color Reduction command on the Options menu, specifying 236 colors and Optimal Palette. BitEdit will reduce the palette to the 236 best colors for the bitmap.

Saving Palette Files

When you work with a palette associated with a bitmap, you can save the palette in a separate file. You can then apply the palette file to other bitmaps. When you work with a stand-alone palette, you can save the palette using the original palette filename or with another filename.

▶   **To save a palette associated with a bitmap:**

1. From the File menu, choose Save To File.

   The Save Palette dialog box appears.

```
┌─────────────────────────────────────────────────────────┐
│ ▬                    Save Palette                         │
├─────────────────────────────────────────────────────────┤
│  File Name:              Directories:        ┌─────────┐  │
│  *.pal                   c:\dib              │   OK    │  │
│  ┌──────────────┐        ┌─────────────┐     └─────────┘  │
│  │ squirrel.pal │        │ 🗁 c:\       │     ┌─────────┐  │
│  │              │        │ 🗀 dib       │     │ Cancel  │  │
│  │              │        │             │     └─────────┘  │
│  │              │        │             │                  │
│  │              │        │             │                  │
│  └──────────────┘        └─────────────┘                  │
│  Save File as Type       Drives:                          │
│  ┌──────────────────┐    ┌──────────────────┐            │
│  │ Microsoft Palette ▼│   │ 🖴 c: [richbix]  ▼│           │
│  └──────────────────┘    └──────────────────┘            │
└─────────────────────────────────────────────────────────┘
```

2. Enter a name and location for the new file.

3. Choose OK.

▶ **To save a stand-alone palette:**

- From the File menu, choose Save.

▶ **To save a stand-alone palette using another filename:**

1. From the File menu, choose Save As.

   The Save Palette dialog box appears.

2. Enter a new name and/or location for the new file.

3. Choose OK.

Applying a Palette File to a Bitmap

You can apply a palette file to a bitmap. For example, to use one palette for several bitmaps, you can open each bitmap, then apply the same palette file to each one. You can use the following palette files included with the MDK with a variety of bitmaps:

Palette File	Description
VGA.PAL	Standard VGA 16 color palette.
STANDARD.PAL	A 196-color palette that conforms to NTSC color standards.
BW.PAL	A 2-color black-and-white palette (useful for dithering images to black and white).
GRAY16.PAL	A 16-color grey-scale palette (useful for mapping images to grey-scale for display on VGA monitors).
GRAY236.PAL	A 236-color grey-scale palette (useful for mapping 16-bit and 24-bit images to grey-scale for display on 256-color monitors).
SEPIA236.PAL	A 236-color palette with sepia colors (useful for creating images with an antique look).
RGB8.PAL RGB64.PAL RGB216.PAL	A linear N-color palette created by traversing the color cube in N steps (useful for dithering images. The 8, 64, and 216 color sizes are based on the cubes of 2, 4, and 6. The 216-color RGB palette is commonly used on the Macintosh).

You can apply a palette used in one bitmap to another bitmap. When you apply a new palette to a bitmap, the new palette replaces the palette already associated with the bitmap. When the bitmap is displayed, it uses the new palette.

▶ **To apply a palette to a bitmap:**

1. Open the bitmap file in BitEdit.

2. Start PalEdit by choosing Show Palette from the Options menu.

3. From the File menu, choose Apply From File.

   The Open Palette dialog box appears.

4. Select the palette or bitmap file that has the palette you want to apply to the bitmap.

5. Choose Open to apply the new palette.

   A message appears, warning you that color information might be lost.

6. Choose OK.

   If applying another palette to an image produces undesirable results, you can recover the previous palette by using the Undo command on the PalEdit Edit menu.

Quitting PalEdit

When you finish editing a palette, you can quit PalEdit.

▶ **To quit PalEdit:**

1. From the File menu, choose Exit.

   If you are running PalEdit as an independent application, and you have made changes to a palette file, PalEdit asks you if you want to save changes to the file.

2. To save your changes, choose Yes; to exit without saving your changes, choose No; or to continue to work with PalEdit, choose Cancel.

Chapter 15

Editing Waveform Files Using WaveEdit

There are times when recorded sound can enhance an application. Because any recording can be converted into a waveform audio file, including sound in your application can be easy. The WaveEdit tool enables you to record and edit waveform files.

With WaveEdit, you can also cut unwanted or unnecessary sounds from a waveform file. Because waveform files can require large amounts of memory, you can use WaveEdit to shorten these files without removing important information. WaveEdit can also create simple sound effects by repeating various parts of a waveform file or by cutting segments from one file and pasting them into another.

This chapter describes how to use WaveEdit to accomplish the following tasks:

- Open waveform files of various formats

- Display and modify waveform files

- Play and record waveform files

- Save waveform files in Microsoft Waveform format

Valid File Formats

WaveEdit can edit waveform files of the following formats:

File Format	File Usage
AIF (Apple AIFF)	Source
Microsoft PCM	Source
WAVE (Microsoft Waveform)	Source, Destination

Starting WaveEdit

You can start WaveEdit just as you do any Windows application. The following procedure explains how to run WaveEdit from Program Manager; you can also start WaveEdit from File Manager or by double-clicking the WaveEdit icon.

▶ **To start WaveEdit:**

1. From the Program Manager File menu, choose Run.

   The Run dialog box appears.

2. In the Command Line box, type **waveedit**.

   You can include an initial waveform file in the command line. For example, type **waveedit voice.wav** to start WaveEdit with the "VOICE.WAV" waveform file already open. However, you must include the complete path of the waveform file you want to open.

3. Choose OK.

   The WaveEdit window appears.

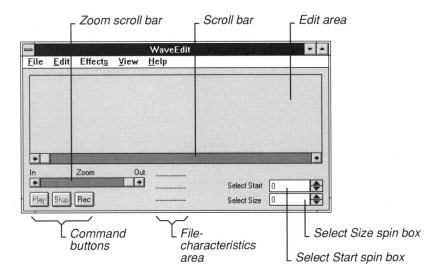

The major feature of the WaveEdit window is the Edit area where the contents of waveform files are displayed. The Edit area is where you select and edit part or all of a waveform. Using the scroll bar, you can view different sections of the waveform. The Zoom scroll bar is like a magnifying glass. With it you can determine the detail with which you view a waveform.

The waveform data is plotted along a horizontal bar in the Edit area. The time span of the waveform lies horizontally along the x-axis; the amplitude of the waveform at each point stretches vertically along the y-axis.

You use the Play, Stop, and Rec buttons to play, stop, and record a waveform file. The Select Start and Select Size spin boxes display the numeric position of a selected portion of a waveform. The File Characteristics area shows you information about the current waveform file.

The WaveEdit Menus

WaveEdit has five menus: File, Edit, Effects, View, and Help.

The File Menu

You can use the commands on the File menu to load waveform files into WaveEdit and save them to disk.

Command	Description
New	Creates an empty waveform file.
Open	Opens an existing waveform file.
Close	Closes an open waveform file without quitting WaveEdit.
Save	Saves changes made to a waveform file.
Save As	Saves the waveform with a new filename.
Run WaveEdit	Opens another WaveEdit window.
Exit	Quits WaveEdit.

The Edit Menu

You can use the commands on the Edit menu to cut and paste waveform data to and from the Clipboard.

Command	Description
Undo	Undoes the last edit operation.
Cut	Removes a selected area from a waveform and places it on the Clipboard.
Copy	Copies a selected area from a waveform to the Clipboard.
Paste	Pastes the contents of the Clipboard into the Edit area. If part of a waveform is selected in the Edit area, that area is replaced with the contents of the Clipboard. If no part of a waveform is selected, WaveEdit pastes the contents of the Clipboard at the cursor.
Mix Paste	Mixes the contents of the Clipboard with the contents of the waveform. If part of a waveform is selected in the Edit area, that selection is mixed with the contents of the Clipboard. If no part of a waveform is selected, WaveEdit pastes the contents of the Clipboard at the cursor.
Delete	Deletes a selected area of a waveform. The area deleted is *not* placed on the Clipboard.
Select All	Selects the entire waveform for editing. This can also be done by double-clicking anywhere in the Edit area.

The Effects Menu

You can use the commands on the Effects menu to make changes to the contents of a waveform.

Command	Description
Change Characteristics	Changes the mono/stereo characteristics, frequency, and number of bits used to represent each sample.
Insert Silence	Inserts silence into a waveform. When an area is selected, the command name changes to Silence.
Fade Down	Fades the current selection from 100% amplitude to silence (0% amplitude).
Fade Up	Fades the current selection from silence (0% amplitude) to 100% amplitude.
Amplify	Increases or decreases the amplitude of the file or the current selection by a specified percentage.

The View Menu

You can use the commands on the View menu to change the appearance of the WaveEdit screen.

Command	Description
Left Channel	Shows the left channel of a stereo waveform file.
Right Channel	Shows the right channel of a stereo waveform file.
Milliseconds	Changes WaveEdit to show all measurements in milliseconds.
Samples	Changes WaveEdit to show all measurements in number of samples.
Zoom	Adjusts the zoom control to magnify the currently selected portion of the waveform.

Opening Waveform Files

You can create waveform files using WaveEdit. You can also edit waveform files and work with many files concurrently, using multiple WaveEdit windows.

Opening a New Waveform File

▶ **To create a waveform file:**

1. From the File menu, choose New.

   The New File Data Format dialog box appears.

```
┌─────────────────────────────────────┐
│        New file data format          │
│ ┌─Channels──────┐   ┌──────────┐     │
│ │ ◉ Mono        │   │    OK    │     │
│ │ ○ Stereo      │   └──────────┘     │
│ └───────────────┘   ┌──────────┐     │
│ ┌─Sample Size───┐   │  Cancel  │     │
│ │ ◉ 8 Bits      │   └──────────┘     │
│ │ ○ 16 Bits     │                    │
│ └───────────────┘                    │
│ ┌─Frequency─────┐                    │
│ │ ○ 44.1 kHz    │                    │
│ │ ○ 22.05 kHz   │                    │
│ │ ◉ 11.025 kHz  │                    │
│ └───────────────┘                    │
└─────────────────────────────────────┘
```

2. Select the channel, sample size, and frequency settings you want.

   - Select the Mono channel option to specify one sound channel in the file. Select Stereo to include two sound channels (with added storage overhead).

   - Select the 8 Bits sample-size option to specify a dynamic range of 65000+ levels. Select 16 Bits for a dynamic range of 2,000,000+ levels.

   - Select the 11.025 kHz frequency option for a voice-grade sound sampling rate. Select 22.05 kHz for an AM-quality sampling rate. Select 44.1 kHz for an audio CD-quality sampling rate.

   Default settings of Mono channel, 8 Bits sample size, and 11.025 kHz frequency provide the most economical storage.

3. Choose OK.

   After the new file opens, you can paste or record a new waveform into the file.

For more information on the options in the New File Data Format dialog box, see "Changing Waveform Characteristics," later in this chapter.

Opening an Existing Waveform File

▶ **To open an existing waveform file:**

1. From the File menu, choose Open.

   The Open Wave File dialog box appears.

2. Scroll through the file-type list and select the file format you want.

└ *Selected file type*

3. Scroll through the drives, directories, and filename lists to find the file you want to edit, and then select the filename.

4. To confirm the file type when WaveEdit opens the waveform file, select the Confirm File Type check box.

5. Choose OK.

When opening Microsoft PCM Waveform files, WaveEdit converts the data into a Microsoft waveform and requests information not supplied in the file. You can set channels, sample size, and frequency from the Input DATA Format dialog box.

Opening Multiple WaveEdit Files

You can work with two or more WaveEdit files simultaneously. This is particularly useful when copying information between WaveEdit files.

▶   **To open two waveform files:**

1.   Open the first waveform file by choosing Open from the File menu.

2.   After you open the first file, from the File menu, choose Run WaveEdit. Another WaveEdit window appears.

3.   Click anywhere in the new WaveEdit window to make it the active window.

4.   From the File menu, choose Open to open the second waveform file.

Viewing a Waveform

Once you open a waveform file, WaveEdit displays the waveform in the Edit area of the WaveEdit window. You use this area to select parts of the waveform for editing. The waveform displayed in the Edit area is a graphical representation of the waveform data. The following illustration is a sample of a waveform:

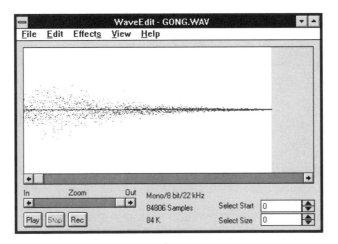

The horizontal axis represents the time span of the waveform—the amount of time that the sound actually plays. The vertical axis represents the amplitude of the waveform—the volume of the waveform at specific points.

Using the Zoom Scroll Bar

You can use the Zoom scroll bar to determine the amount of detail displayed by WaveEdit. Moving the scroll box to the right displays less detail. This gives the effect of zooming out, or away, from the waveform, as shown in the following illustration:

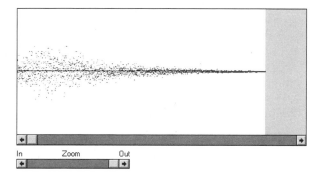

Moving the scroll box to the left zooms in on the waveform, showing it in more detail, as shown in the following illustration:

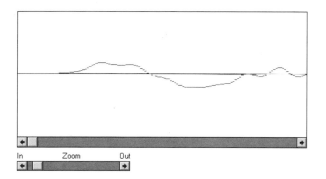

The Zoom scroll bar is especially useful when editing waveforms. Moving the scroll bar to the right displays the entire waveform at once, so you can edit larger portions of the waveform. Moving the scroll bar all the way to the left allows for very fine editing. Also, when you zoom in to display a portion of the waveform, you can use the scroll bar at the bottom of the Edit area to move through a waveform quickly.

Changing the Measurement Scale

The WaveEdit window displays waveform-size information based on one of two scales: either a time scale (in milliseconds) or a scale based on the number of digital samples in the waveform. For example, a file might contain 1328 sample points and take 620 milliseconds to play. You can switch back and forth between each unit of measurement.

▶ **To change the measurement scale for a waveform:**

- From the View menu, choose Milliseconds (or, from the View menu, choose Samples).

Viewing Channels of a Stereo Waveform

When you first open a stereo waveform, both the left and right channels are displayed. The left channel appears in red; the right channel appears in black. You can view either channel separately by turning off the display of the other channel.

When a channel is displayed, a check mark appears next to the corresponding Channel command on the View menu.

▶ **To display or hide the left or right channel of a stereo waveform file:**

- From the View menu, choose the command (Left Channel or Right Channel) for the channel you want to display or hide.

Selecting Parts of a Waveform

You can select any part of a waveform. You might want to select an area of the waveform for several reasons: to delete unwanted or unnecessary waveform data, to replace part of the waveform with another waveform, or to play a specific section without playing the entire waveform.

Using a Mouse

The most common way to select a portion of the waveform is by using a mouse.

▶ **To select an area of the waveform using a mouse:**

1. Position the mouse pointer anywhere along the waveform.
2. Click the left or right mouse button.

   A cursor appears at the position of the mouse pointer.
3. Drag the selection in either direction.

   As you drag the selection, the selected waveform area becomes highlighted. WaveEdit automatically scrolls the Edit area when you drag the selection beyond the left or right boundaries. You can also extend a selection by doing the following:

   • To extend a selection to current mouse-pointer position, press and hold down SHIFT and click the waveform. This extends the selection to the current mouse-pointer position.

   • To select from the current mouse-pointer position to the beginning of a file, drag up and out of the Edit area.

   • To select from the mouse-pointer position to the end of a file, drag down and out of the Edit area.

Using the Select Start and Select Size Spin Boxes

You can use the Select Start and Select Size spin boxes, in the lower-right corner of the WaveEdit window, to enter values that specify the beginning point and size of a selection. Depending on the scale used, these values relate to the number of sample points or to the number of milliseconds in a given waveform. (You can change from one measurement to another by using the commands on the View menu.) The total size of the waveform is displayed to the left of the spin boxes.

For example, if you're editing a waveform with 42018 sample points, entering 0 in the Select Start spin box places the cursor at the beginning of the waveform; 42017 places the cursor at the end of the waveform. (The range 0 through 42017 equals 42018 total sample points.) Any value greater than 0 and less than 42017 places the cursor between the beginning and end of the waveform.

Changing the Select Size value lets you select a specific number of sample points (or milliseconds) to the right of the cursor. For example, a value of 420 selects an area of 420 sample points (or milliseconds) to the right of the cursor.

▶ **To select an area using the Select Start and Select Size spin boxes:**

1. Double-click the Select Start spin box.

2. Enter a value for the starting location of the selection (or use the arrows to the right of the box to enter the value you want).

   The cursor appears in the Edit area at the location specified by the Select Start value. If the location is not displayed in the Edit area, you will not see the cursor. If you want to see where the cursor is, move the Zoom scroll box all the way to the right to see the entire waveform.

3. Double-click the Select Size spin box.

4. Enter a value for the size of the selection (or use the arrows to the right of the box to enter the value you want).

Selecting an Entire Waveform

You can select an entire waveform at once. This is useful when you want to modify, replace, or copy a complete waveform at one time.

▶ **To select an entire waveform:**

▪ From the Edit menu, choose Select All (or double-click anywhere in the Edit area).

Using the Zoom Command

To take a closer look at a selected area, you can use the Zoom command to view specific parts of a waveform. The Zoom command fills the Edit area with the current waveform selection, placing the left edge of the selection at the left edge of the Edit area and adjusting the detail level of the selection to fit in the Edit area. The Zoom scroll bar, however, is a more general feature that allows you to adjust the Edit area to any level of detail.

▶ **To zoom in on a waveform selection:**

1. Select the part of the waveform you want to view.

2. From the View menu, choose Zoom.

Editing a Waveform

You can use the commands on the Edit menu in WaveEdit to remove, insert, or rearrange sections of a waveform. In general, the following commands work like the equivalent commands in other Windows applications:

Cut
　Removes a selected area and places it on the Clipboard.

Copy
　Places a copy of the selected area on the Clipboard. The contents of the Edit area remain unchanged.

Paste
　Places the contents of the Clipboard into the Edit area. If an area is selected, that area is replaced by the contents of the Clipboard. If no area is selected, the contents of the Clipboard are inserted into the waveform at the cursor location.

Mix Paste
　Mixes the contents of the Clipboard with the waveform in the Edit area. Each sample in the Clipboard's waveform is added to the corresponding area in the waveform in the Edit area. Both sounds are played when you play the waveform.

　If no part of the waveform in the Edit area is selected, the selection on the Clipboard is mixed with the waveform in the Edit area, beginning at the cursor location. If the Clipboard contents are longer than the waveform in the Edit area (measured from the cursor location to the end), the excess length of the Clipboard contents is added to the end of the waveform in the Edit area.

　If part of the waveform in the Edit area is selected, mixing begins at the first sample of the Clipboard waveform. The two waveforms mix until the end of one is reached, at which point mixing ends. For example, if the Clipboard contains a waveform with 20000 samples, and the Edit area contains a selection of 5000 samples, when you choose the Mix Paste command, only the first 5000 samples are mixed with the selected area.

Delete
　Deletes the contents of a selected area; nothing is placed on the Clipboard.

Modifying a Waveform

You can make changes to waveform shape and characteristics by using the commands on the Effects menu: Change Characteristics, Insert Silence, Fade Down, Fade Up, and Amplify.

Changing Waveform Characteristics

You can change the number of channels, sample size, and frequency of a waveform file using the Change Characteristics command on the Effects menu.

▶ **To change file settings:**

1. From the Effects menu, choose Change Characteristics.

   The Change Characteristics dialog box appears.

   Change Characteristics

   Channels
   ● Mono
   ○ Stereo

   Ok
   Cancel

   Sample Size
   ● 8 Bits
   ○ 16 Bits

   Frequency
   ○ 44.1 kHz
   ● 22.05 kHz
   ○ 11.025 kHz

2. Select the Mono or Stereo option button to specify whether the file has one or dual channels (stereo provides better sound quality, but it requires more disk space than mono).

   Changing a file from mono to stereo doesn't affect sound quality. However, changing from stereo to mono degrades the quality.

3. Select the 8-Bits or 16-Bits option button to specify the number of bits used with the sample. The 16-Bits option provides better sound quality, but requires more disk space than the 8-Bits option.

   Changing a file from 8 Bits to 16 Bits doesn't affect sound quality. However, changing from 16 Bits to 8 Bits degrades the quality.

4. Select the frequency option for the sample. The 44.1 kHz option provides the best quality, but requires more disk space. Conversely, 11.025 kHz offers the lowest sound quality, but requires less disk space.

   Changing from 11.025 kHz to a higher value doesn't affect sound quality, but changing from 44.1 kHz to a lower value degrades sound quality.

5. Choose OK.

Inserting Silence

You can insert a specified length of silence (0 amplitude) into a waveform file or replace a selected portion of a file with silence.

▶ **To insert silence into a file:**

1. Position the cursor at the point in the file where you want to insert silence.

2. From the Effects menu, choose Insert Silence.

   The Insert Silence dialog box appears.

```
Insert Silence
                    OK
0        mSec
                  Cancel
```

3. Enter the number of samples (or milliseconds) of silence you want to insert.

4. Choose OK.

▶ **To replace a selection with silence:**

1. Select the portion of the file you want to replace with silence.

2. From the Effects menu, choose Silence.

Fading a Selection Up and Down

You can fade the current selection anywhere within a range of 100% amplitude to silence (0% amplitude), or from silence to 100% amplitude. The amplitude of each sample in the selected area is reduced according to the percentage you choose.

▶ **To fade a selection:**

1. Select the portion of the file you want to fade up or down.

2. From the Effects menu, choose Fade Up or Fade Down.

Changing the Amplitude of a Selection

You can also change the amplitude of a selection. Each sample in the selection is increased or reduced according to the percentage you choose.

▶ **To change the amplitude of a selection:**

1. Select the portion of the file you want to change.

2. From the Effects menu, choose Amplify.

   The Change Amplitude dialog box appears.

```
┌──────────────────────────────────────────┐
│            Change Amplitude                │
├──────────────────────────────────────────┤
│                          ┌──────────┐      │
│                          │    OK    │      │
│  Amplitude %   │100│ ◆   ├──────────┤      │
│                          │  Cancel  │      │
│                          └──────────┘      │
└──────────────────────────────────────────┘
```

3. Enter the percentage by which you want to increase or reduce the amplitude of the selection. For example, 50% reduces the amplitude by one half, 200% doubles the amplitude.

4. Choose OK.

Undoing Your Changes

The Undo command on the Edit menu always refers to the most recent action. For example, if you accidentally clear a section of a waveform that you want to keep, you can restore the selection by using the Undo command. Undo, however, does not work with commands on the View menu, such as Zoom.

▶ **To undo a change:**

■ From the Edit menu, choose Undo.

If the menu contains a Can't Undo command, either no changes have been made or it is not possible to undo the operation.

Playing Waveform Files

By choosing the Play button, you can play any open waveform file. If no area of the waveform is currently selected, WaveEdit plays the entire waveform. If you select an area of the waveform, WaveEdit plays only the selected area.

By choosing the Stop button, you can stop playing a waveform. When you choose Play again, playback resumes at the beginning of the waveform or selection.

Recording Waveform Files

The sound card in your computer supports input from a microphone or other device, allowing you to use WaveEdit as a recording control. By choosing the Rec button, you can do the following:

- Record a new waveform file

- Insert waveform samples into a existing waveform

- Replace a section within a waveform

Note You can improve system responsiveness during recording by using one or more of the following techniques: reduce the size of the WaveEdit window, compact your hard disk to consolidate free space, or record temporary waveform files onto a RAM disk.

To route temporary files to an existing RAM disk, add the following lines to the MMTOOLS.INI file in your Windows directory:

```
[MedWave]
TempFiles= <disk and directory specification for RAM disk>
```

▶ **To record a new waveform file:**

1. First, if a file is currently open, close it.

2. Choose the Rec button.

   WaveEdit creates a new file and the New File Data Format dialog box appears.

3. Select the settings you want the new file to have.

4. Choose OK to start recording.

   The Record dialog box appears.

5. Set the recording level on your input device or microphone and play one or more sounds to set the WaveEdit recording level.

6. Choose OK to accept the recording level and begin recording.

   The new waveform appears as you record.

7. When you finish recording, choose the Stop button.

8. From the Edit menu, choose Save or Save As to save the updated waveform file.

Note   Some hardware configurations don't support all of the options presented in the New File Data Format dialog box. If you select a format that is beyond the capabilities of your configuration, WaveEdit issues a warning when it first attempts to record the waveform.

▶ **To insert a recording into a waveform file:**

1. Position the cursor at the point where you want to insert the recording.

2. Choose the Rec button.

   The Record dialog box appears.

3. Set the recording level on your input device or microphone.

4. Choose OK to start recording.

   The waveform appears as you record.

5. When you finish recording, choose the Stop button.

6. From the Edit menu, choose Save or Save As to save the updated waveform file.

▶ **To replace a section of a waveform file with a new recording:**

1. Select the section of the waveform you want to replace.

2. Choose the Rec button.

    The Record dialog box appears.

3. Set the recording level on your input device or microphone.

4. Choose OK to start recording. Recording begins when redrawing of the Edit area is complete.

    The selected section of the waveform is replaced by the new recording.

5. When you finish recording, choose the Stop button.

6. From the Edit menu, choose Save or Save As to save the updated waveform file.

Note   You can configure the amount of memory reserved for playback and recording of audio waveforms. To do this, start the Drivers applet from the Multimedia Control Panel. Use the Setup option for MCI Waveform Audio. You can reset its default time of 4 seconds to a higher value. This is useful when working on slower computers or when playing several waveforms simultaneously in several WaveEdit windows.

Saving a Waveform File

WaveEdit can load and play files in Microsoft Waveform format, AIFF format, and PCM format. To save your edits, however, you must save them to a Microsoft Waveform file. You can do this by using either the Save or Save As command on the File menu. Note that you can't save edits to a file in AIFF or PCM format.

▶ **To save a waveform file:**

■ From the File menu, choose Save.

The Save command replaces the waveform on disk with the edited version of the waveform. WaveEdit writes this edited file to disk in the Microsoft Waveform format.

▶ **To save a waveform file using a different name or location:**

1. From the File menu, choose Save As.

   The Save Wave File dialog box appears.

```
┌─────────────────────────────────────────────────────────┐
│ ═                     Save Wave File                      │
├─────────────────────────────────────────────────────────┤
│  File Name:              Directories:                     │
│  ┌──────────────┐        c:\win3\resource    ┌─────────┐  │
│  │ bix.wav      │                             │   OK    │  │
│  ├──────────────┤        ┌──────────────┐     └─────────┘  │
│  │ bells.wav   ▲│        │ 📁 c:\        │     ┌─────────┐  │
│  │ blocks.wav   │        │  📂 win3      │     │ Cancel  │  │
│  │ chord.wav    │        │   📂 resource │     └─────────┘  │
│  │ clap.wav     │        │               │                 │
│  │ clock.wav    │        │               │                 │
│  │ door.wav     │        │               │                 │
│  │ drat.wav     │        │               │                 │
│  │ drum.wav    ▼│        │               │                 │
│  └──────────────┘        └──────────────┘                 │
│                                                            │
│  Save File as Type       Drives:                          │
│  ┌────────────────────┐  ┌────────────────────┐           │
│  │ Microsoft Waveform ▼│  │ ▣ c: [richbix]    ▼│           │
│  └────────────────────┘  └────────────────────┘           │
└─────────────────────────────────────────────────────────┘
```

2. Enter the name and location for the new file.

3. Choose OK.

Quitting WaveEdit

When your waveform files are ready to be incorporated into your application, you can quit WaveEdit.

▶ **To quit WaveEdit:**

1. From the File menu, choose Exit.

   If you haven't saved your latest changes, a dialog box appears asking if you want to save them.

```
┌─────────────────────────────────────────────┐
│ ═                  WaveEdit                   │
├─────────────────────────────────────────────┤
│   ┌─┐   File BELLS.WAV has changed.  Do you wish to │
│   │?│   save the changes?                     │
│   └─┘                                          │
│        ┌───────┐  ┌───────┐  ┌────────┐       │
│        │  Yes  │  │  No   │  │ Cancel │       │
│        └───────┘  └───────┘  └────────┘       │
└─────────────────────────────────────────────┘
```

2. To save your changes, choose Yes; to exit without saving your changes, choose No; or to continue working in WaveEdit, choose Cancel.

Chapter 16
Editing Files Using FileWalker

FileWalker is a file editor. For any file, FileWalker can serve as a hexadecimal editor, allowing you to view and edit individual bytes. For several file types, FileWalker outlines the file structure and presents information through a structural outline. This chapter explains how to use FileWalker to display and edit the contents of files. You'll learn how to perform the following tasks:

- View the outline and data structures of a file

- Edit file data

FileWalker displays structured format files, such as RIFF files, as a series of cascading levels, similar to the levels in an outline. Elements with the same indent are on the same level. Each level has a heading that you can expand to display a structured representation of the data under that level.

FileWalker is a developer's tool and is not recommended unless you are familiar with file formats and hexadecimal editing.

Caution   Using FileWalker requires a thorough understanding of file formats used in multimedia applications. You can damage or destroy a file by editing it incorrectly. For more information on the file formats you can use in Microsoft Windows with Multimedia applications, see the *Programmer's Reference*.

Valid File Formats

You can use FileWalker to display and edit the following formats:

- Microsoft RIFF DIB

- Microsoft RIFF MIDI

- Microsoft Waveform Audio File

- Microsoft Palette File

- Microsoft DIB

- Generic RIFF File

You can use also use the Hex Bytes format in FileWalker to edit any file as a hexadecimal array.

Starting FileWalker

You can start FileWalker just as you do any Windows Application. The following procedure explains how to run FileWalker from Program Manager. You can also start FileWalker from File Manager by double-clicking the FileWalker icon.

▶ **To start FileWalker:**

1. From the Program Manager File menu, choose Run.

   The Run dialog box appears.

2. In the Command Line box, type **filewalk**.

   You can also include an initial file in the command line (you must specify the complete path of the file). For example, type **filewalk pinnacle.rdi** to start FileWalker and open the "PINNACLE.RDI" bitmap file.

3. Choose OK.

The FileWalker window appears.

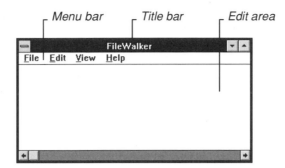

FileWalker works much the same as other Microsoft Windows applications. The title bar displays the name of the open file, if there is one. The menu bar contains a series of menus that contain the commands you use when editing data files.

The FileWalker Menus

FileWalker has four menus: File, Edit, View, and Help.

The File Menu

You can use the commands on the File menu to open and save files in FileWalker.

Command	Description
Open	Opens an existing file.
Save	Saves changes made to a file.
Save As	Specifies a file and saves changes to that file.
Exit	Quits FileWalker.

The Edit Menu

You can use the commands on the Edit menu to edit the contents of a file.

Command	Description
Cut	Removes the current selection from the file and places a copy of it on the Clipboard.
Copy	Copies the current selection onto the Clipboard.
Copy Text	Copies the file as currently displayed on the Clipboard.
Paste	Pastes the contents of the Clipboard in the file at the currently selected item.
Delete	Deletes the current selection from the file (the deleted selection is *not* placed on the Clipboard).
Edit Component	Activates edit mode so you can edit a selected item.
Insert Array Element	Inserts one or more new elements into a file.
Insert RIFF Chunk	Activates insert mode so you can add a RIFF chunk to a RIFF file.

The View Menu

You can use the commands on the View menu to change the way a file is displayed in FileWalker.

Command	Description
Display Offsets	Shows the file offset of each item in the file.
Expand	Displays the detail level of the selected heading.
Contract	Hides the detail level of the selected heading.
Contract Parent	Hides the detail level of the parent heading containing the current selection.
Next	Moves the selection from the current item to the next item of the same detail level.

Command	Description
Previous	Moves the selection from the current item to the previous item of the same detail level.
Goto Parent	Moves the selection from the current item to its parent heading.
Goto Offset	Moves the selection from the current item to the specified offset in the file.
Description	Displays a description of the selected item.

Opening Files

Before you can edit a file, you must first open it in FileWalker.

▶ **To open a file:**

1. From the File menu, choose Open.

   The Open File dialog box appears.

2. Specify the path and filename of the file you want to edit.

3. Confirm the file format. To select another file format, scroll through the Format box and select the file format you want.

   The default file type in the Format box is derived from the extension of the selected filename. If Hex Bytes is displayed initially, FileWalker doesn't recognize the file type and assumes the file is unstructured.

4. From the Options area, select the copy of the file that FileWalker uses directly; the default selection lets you edit the copy of the file in memory. You can choose one of the following options:

Edit File in Memory
   Loads the file into memory. Any edits you make affect the file in memory; you can choose whether to keep the changes when you save the file to disk. This option improves FileWalker performance.

Edit Backup Copy of File
   Creates a backup copy of the file. Any edits you make affect the backup copy. This option is useful if you don't want to make changes directly to the original file. You can use this option when you don't have enough available memory to use the Edit File in Memory option.

Edit File Directly (Modify While Editing)
   Allows you to edit the original file directly on disk. Any edits you make affect the original file. You can use this option if you don't have enough memory or sufficient disk space to load the file into memory or to make a backup copy on disk.

5. The Allow File Modification check box in the Options area lets you protect the integrity of the file. When this check box is selected, you can edit the file. To view the file as read-only, clear this check box.

6. Choose Open.

Viewing a File

You can control the way a file is displayed on your screen by using one of the following methods:

- Displaying it as an unstructured file

- Displaying it as a structured file

- Displaying its offsets

- Expanding the view

- Contracting the view

- Moving through the file

- Getting information about a file element

These different controls let you examine a file before you begin editing its contents.

Displaying an Unstructured File

When you open a file in Hex Bytes format, it appears as an array of hexadecimal bytes. The following illustration shows a bitmap file, PINNACLE.RDI, displayed in Hex Bytes format:

```
                    FileWalker - C:\DIB\PINNACLE.RDI
 File  Edit  View  Help
[00000000]    52 49 46 46    9E 50 01 00    52 44 49 42    64 61 74 61    RIFF
[00000010]    92 50 01 00    42 4D 92 50    01 00 00 00    00 00 36 04    'P..  E
[00000020]    00 00 28 00    00 00 63 01    00 00 EF 00    00 00 01 00    ..(.
[00000030]    08 00 00 00    00 00 5C 4C    01 00 00 00    00 00 00 00    .....
[00000040]    00 00 00 01    00 00 00 01    00 00 00 00    00 00 18 10    .....
[00000050]    18 00 40 18    10 00 18 10    38 00 40 18    28 00 48 10    ..@.
[00000060]    38 00 18 10    50 00 30 18    38 00 48 10    50 00 18 38    8... E
[00000070]    18 00 18 28    38 00 30 38    18 00 48 38    18 00 48 28    ...( 8
[00000080]    38 00 20 18    68 00 18 38    38 00 30 38    38 00 48 28    8..  h
[00000090]    50 00 38 38    38 00 50 38    38 00 50 20    68 00 18 38    P.88 8
[000000A0]    50 00 20 18    90 00 28 50    28 00 38 40    48 00 38 40    P..
[000000B0]    50 00 58 50    28 00 48 40    50 00 50 20    90 00 58 40    P.XP (
[000000C0]    50 00 20 40    68 00 78 40    50 00 50 40    68 00 58 60    P. @ H
[000000D0]    28 00 58 50    50 00 78 60    28 00 20 50    68 00 50 40    (.XP E
[000000E0]    78 00 58 50    58 00 20 40    90 00 88 50    50 00 20 80    x.XP X
[000000F0]    18 00 48 50    68 00 20 28    C8 00 58 50    68 00 78 58    ..HP h
[00000100]    50 00 A8 68    28 00 50 40    98 00 28 60    68 00 70 60    P.¨h (
[00000110]    50 00 58 28    C8 00 A0 58    50 00 78 60    50 00 78 58    P.X(
[00000120]    60 00 38 58    80 00 90 58    60 00 58 60    68 00 58 50    `.8X
```

An offset number appears to the left of each line. The ANSI character equivalents for the values in the line are displayed to the right of each line. You can scroll left and right to view the data.

Displaying a Structured File

When you first open a file in one of the formats FileWalker supports, the file is displayed in outline form. The following illustration shows a Windows RIFF DIB, PINNACLE.RDI, displayed in Windows RIFF DIB format:

```
┌─────────────────────────────────────────────────┐
│ ─    '      FileWalker - C:\DIB\PINNACLE.RDI   ▼ ▲│
│ File  Edit  View  Help                            │
│              RIFF                                 │
│                    FormHeader RDIB                │
│                    data                           │
│                                                   │
│                                                   │
│                                                   │
│ ◄ ▐                                             ► │
└─────────────────────────────────────────────────┘
```

Each heading (except the title at the top) can be expanded to display a group of fields, an array, a stream of hexadecimal values, or additional headings. You can edit values of fields, array elements, and hexadecimal bytes.

You can use the mouse or the commands on the View menu to change the way a file is displayed—by expanding and contracting file headings—to move through a file.

When you expand certain headings in some formats (such as file headers), you see a group or C structure of data fields associated with that heading, as shown in the following illustration:

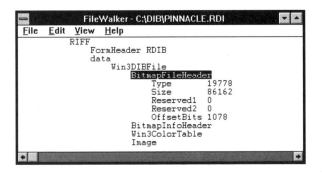

When you expand the heading for a data array (such as a color table in a bitmap or color-palette file), you see a table showing values for each color. Each color has a hexadecimal index number next to it, as shown in the following illustration.

```
┌─────────────────────────────────────────────────────────┐
│ ═    FileWalker - C:\DIB\PINNACLE.RDI           ▼ ▲      │
├─────────────────────────────────────────────────────────┤
│ File   Edit   View   Help                                │
│         RIFF                                         ↕    │
│              FormHeader RDIB                             │
│              data                                        │
│                   Win3DIBFile                            │
│                        BitmapFileHeader                  │
│                        BitmapInfoHeader                  │
│                        Win3ColorTable                    │
│                        Blue    Green   Red   Unused      │
│ [00000000]             0       0       0     0           │
│ [00000001]             24      16      24    0           │
│ [00000002]             64      24      16    0           │
│ [00000003]             24      16      56    0           │
│ [00000004]             64      24      40    0      ↓    │
├─────────────────────────────────────────────────────────┤
│ ◄ ▓                                                  ► │
└─────────────────────────────────────────────────────────┘
```

When you expand the heading of a stream of hexadecimal bytes in a file (for example, the pixel data in a bitmap or the sound samples in a waveform), you see block hexadecimal values, as shown in the following illustration:

```
┌─────────────────────────────────────────────────────────┐
│ ═         FileWalker - C:\DIB\PINNACLE.RDI        ▼ ▲    │
├─────────────────────────────────────────────────────────┤
│ File   Edit   View   Help                                │
│   RIFF                                               ↕    │
│        FormHeader RDIB                                   │
│        data                                              │
│             Win3DIBFile                                  │
│                  BitmapFileHeader                        │
│                  BitmapInfoHeader                        │
│                  Win3ColorTable                          │
│                  Image                                   │
│ 00]              D9 E3 D5 72  29 19 38 63  80 B2 D9 D2  D9 B3 59 6F   Üã│
│ 10]              89 85 85 A9  B9 D2 EB D2  4B 24 79 64  36 71 BF 71   ▮▮│
│ 20]              6D 98 8F 9A  C2 9A C2 D9  BD 72 30 44  5C 78 85 79   m.│
│ 30]              63 4C 60 6E  C1 C7 C2 8F  71 45 27 74  B2 C8 B9 99   cL│
│ 40]              71 64 51 36  22 3A 4F 95  8F A9 C1 D2  B9 74 4F 2A   qd↓│
├─────────────────────────────────────────────────────────┤
│ ◄          ▓                                         ► │
└─────────────────────────────────────────────────────────┘
```

An offset number appears to the left of each line. The ANSI character equivalents for values in the line are displayed to the right of each line. You can scroll left and right to view the data.

Displaying Offsets

When you first open a file and expand its element headings, offsets are displayed only in the array elements of the file (bitmaps, waveforms, and so on). This display makes it easy to keep track of your position in the section.

You can display offsets for all elements of a file, including element headings, data in file headings, and colors in color tables. Displaying offsets shows you the exact location of each byte in a particular file.

▶ **To display offsets:**

- From the View menu, choose Display Offsets.

Offsets into the file appear in the left margin, next to the headings in the outline, as shown in the following illustration:

Note   Choosing the Display Offsets command changes the offset numbers in the array elements of a file. For example, if there are 35 (hex) bytes of information in a file header, when the Display Offsets command is not in effect, the offset for the first line of a data array is 00000000. When you choose the Display Offsets command, numbering begins at the beginning of the file, and the offset for the first line of the data array changes to 00000436. Subsequent lines of the data element are also renumbered.

Expanding a File Heading

When you first open a file, you see only an outline of element headings and subheadings. To edit data, you must expand one or more file headings.

▶ **To expand a file heading:**

- Double-click the heading you want to expand (or select the heading and from the View menu, choose Expand).

▶ **To display data under a subheading:**

1. Double-click the heading to display the subheading.

2. Double-click the subheading to display the data.

Contracting a File Heading

You can contract your view of a file by suppressing subheadings or data associated with one or more headings.

▶ **To contract a file heading:**

- Double-click the heading that contains the subheadings or data you want to hide (or select the heading and, from the View menu, choose Contract).

  You can also contract data elements associated with a heading by selecting one of the data elements and choosing the Contract Parent command on the View menu.

Moving Through a File

You can scroll through a file using the scroll bars or by using the UP ARROW and DOWN ARROW keys. Scrolling through a file doesn't move the selection cursor.

You can move the selection cursor by using commands on the View menu.

▶ **To move to and select the next heading on the same level:**

- From the View menu, choose Next.

▶ **To move to and select the previous heading on the same level:**

- From the View menu, choose Previous.

▶ **To move to and select the parent heading of the currently selected item:**

- From the View menu, choose Goto Parent.

▶ **To move to and select an item at a specific offset in the file:**

1. From the View menu, choose Goto Offset.

   The Go to Offset dialog box appears.

2. Enter the offset, expressed in decimal, of the item you want.

3. Choose OK.

Note If the file heading that contains the offset is contracted, FileWalker expands it.

Getting Information About a File Item

You can view a brief description of each element and heading in a file.

▶ **To view a brief description of an item:**

1. Select the item you want information about.

2. From the View menu, choose Description.

   If there is a description of the item, it appears on your screen, as shown in the following example:

If there is no description, a "No description" message appears.

Editing Files

Once you move to the element of the file you want to edit and display the data for that element, you can begin editing.

When you edit, changes to the file can be made in memory. You can also make changes directly to disk, either to the file or to a backup copy. The editing method you use depends on the option you chose when you opened the file. For more information on these options, see "Opening Files," earlier in this chapter.

You can edit files in the following ways:

- Moving data between the file and the Clipboard

- Deleting data

- Editing individual data elements

- Inserting new lines in an array

- Adding RIFF chunks to RIFF files

Caution   When you make changes to one part of a file, FileWalker doesn't apply them to the rest of the file. For example, if you change the element in a bitmap file header that indicates the size of the bitmap, the actual size of the bitmap does not change. To make the rest of a file consistent with the changes you make, you must modify the file yourself.

Selecting Data to Edit

To edit data values, you must first select the data you want to edit. You can select an entire file element or an individual field.

▶   **To select an element for editing:**

- Click the element heading you want.

Some actions that modify high-level elements don't require you to display individual subelements. For example, a single edit action can add rows to a color table in a .DIB file without you having to identify individual values in each new row.

▶ **To select a field:**

■ Click the field you want.

▶ **To cancel a selection:**

■ Click the selected item (or click a different item).

Editing Data Using the Clipboard

Once you select an element or a field, you can use the Cut, Copy, Paste, Clear, and Copy Text commands on the Edit menu. As you use these commands, you should understand how they relate to the Clipboard. The Clipboard is an area of memory used for short-term storage of different objects, such as text and images. The following list explains how each of these commands work with the Clipboard:

Cut
Removes one or more selected items, and places a copy of the items on the Clipboard. When you choose Cut, a dialog box appears asking you to enter the number of items to remove. Items following the cut item(s) move up, and their offsets are adjusted. You cannot use Cut to remove an entire element at once.

Copy
Places a copy of one or more selected items on the Clipboard. When you choose Copy, a dialog box appears, asking you to enter the number of items to copy. If an element heading is selected, the entire element is copied. The selected item is not removed from the file.

Copy Text
Copies the outline of a file to the Clipboard; headings and expanded sections of the file (field labels and data arrays) that are part of the current view are copied to the Clipboard. Copy Text does not copy unexpanded portions of a file.

For example, the following illustration shows a view of PINNACLE.RDI and the Clipboard after using the Copy Text command. The contents of the BitmapFileHeader section (an expanded section) are copied to the Clipboard; the contents of the unexpanded BitmapInfoHeader section are not copied.

```
┌─────────────────────────────────────┐   ┌─────────────────────────────────────┐
│ ⊟  FileWalker - C:\DIB\PINNACLE.RDI ▼ ▲│  │ ⊟           Clipboard          ▼ ▲  │
│ File  Edit  View  Help               │   │ File  Edit  Display  Help          │
│ RIFF                                 │   │   <Untitled>                     ▲  │
│     FormHeader RDIB                  │   │      FormHeader RDIB               │
│     data                             │   │      data                          │
│         Win3DIBFile                  │   │         Win3DIBFile                 │
│             BitmapFileHeader         │   │            BitmapFileHeader         │
│                 Type      19778      │   │               Type    19778        │
│                 Size      86162      │   │               Size    86162        │
│                 Reserved1  0         │   │               Reserved1  0         │
│                 Reserved2  0         │   │               Reserved2 0          │
│                 OffsetBits 1078      │   │               OffsetBits 1078      │
│             BitmapInfoHeader         │   │            BitmapInfoHeader         │
│             Win3ColorTable           │   │            Win3ColorTable           │
│             Image                    │   │            Image                 ▼  │
│ ←  ▢                               → │   │ ←  ▢                             → │
└─────────────────────────────────────┘   └─────────────────────────────────────┘
```

Paste

> Places the contents of the Clipboard into the file following the selection cursor, overwriting existing data values. If the contents of the Clipboard originated from a file with a different format, FileWalker converts the information into a form appropriate for the file. If FileWalker cannot convert the contents, it displays a "Clipboard value in incorrect format" message.

Delete

> Deletes one or more selected items from a file; nothing is placed on the Clipboard. If a hexadecimal byte is selected, a dialog box appears, asking you to enter the number of items to remove. The items following the deleted item move up, and their offsets are adjusted.

Editing a Data Field

With FileWalker, you can edit individual data fields in an array. The procedure you use depends on the type of data in the field.

▶ **To edit a byte or a character representation of a byte:**

1. Select the field you want to edit.

2. From the Edit menu, choose Edit Component (or double-click the field).

   A cursor appears in the field, highlighting the first character of the value.

3. Enter the new value for the field.

    The cursor moves to the next field.

4. Continue to enter values for each field you want to change. Press TAB to move from one field to the next without making changes.

When you edit a stream of hexadecimal values, you can edit either individual bytes or the character representations of the bytes that appear to the right of the FileWalker window, as shown in the following illustration:

Changes made to hexadecimal bytes are reflected in the character representations. Any changes made to character representations are reflected in hexadecimal bytes.

▶ **To edit a numeric value or a form header:**

1. Select the field you want to edit.

2. From the Edit menu, choose Edit Component (or double-click the field).

    An edit box appears, highlighting the value or string.

3. In the edit box, enter the new information.

   If you're editing a form header, a new value shorter than the original value will be padded with null bytes (value of zero) to fill the original space. If the new form-header value is longer than the original value, the new value will be shortened to fit into the original space.

4. Press ENTER to confirm your changes.

   If you select a different field or perform another operation without pressing ENTER, FileWalker displays the following dialog box:

5. To confirm your changes, choose Yes; to discard your changes, choose No; or to continue editing the original field, choose Cancel.

▶ **To edit a field that contains an enumerated type:**

1. Select the field you want to edit.

2. From the Edit menu, choose Edit Component (or double-click the field).

   The Edit Enumerated Type dialog box appears.

3. Select a new value for the type.

4. Choose OK.

▶ **To edit a string field:**

1. Select the field you want to edit.

2. From the Edit menu, choose Edit Component (or double-click the field).
   The Edit String dialog box appears.

3. Enter a new value for the string.

4. Choose OK.

Inserting a Data Field

You can insert one or more fields into a data array or a stream of hexadecimal values. You can insert fields before or after a selected field or at the end of an element. The fields you insert have a value of zero.

Note In a data array, you can insert only rows of new fields, not individual fields.

▶ **To insert data fields:**

1. Select the field before or after which you want to insert new fields.

2. From the Edit menu, choose Insert Array Element.
   The Insert Array Element dialog box appears.

3. In the Number of Items to Insert box, enter the number of new fields you want to insert. If you're editing a data array, enter the number of new rows you want to insert.

4. In the Insertion Point area, select one of the following option buttons:

   • To insert new fields before the selected field, select Before.

   • To insert new fields after the selected field, select After.

   • To insert new elements of the selected array, select Inside.

5. Choose OK.

The new fields appear before or after the selected field. Existing fields following new fields move down.

▶ **To add fields to the end of an array:**

1. Select the heading for the element to which you want to add fields.

2. From the Edit menu, choose Insert Array Element.

   The Insert Array Element dialog box appears.

3. In the Number of Items to Insert box, enter the number of new fields you want to insert. If you're editing a data array, enter the number of new lines you want to insert.

4. Choose OK.

The new fields appear at the end of the selected element.

Inserting a RIFF Chunk

You can use FileWalker to insert a RIFF chunk into a RIFF file. This option is available only if the file you are editing is a RIFF file. For more information on RIFF chunks, see the *Programmer's Reference*.

▶ **To insert a RIFF chunk into a file:**

1. Select an element.

   You can insert a RIFF chunk before or after the selected element, or you can add a chunk to the list of element subheadings within this element.

2. From the Edit menu, choose Insert RIFF Chunk.

The Insert RIFF Chunk dialog box appears.

The Chunk ID area lists the RIFF IDs you can use. The boxes below the ID list show the selected ID in decimal, hexadecimal, and text form.

3. Select an ID from the list, or enter it in any of the three boxes in the appropriate form. If the RIFF ID you want does not appear in the list, enter it in one of the boxes in the appropriate form.

4. In the Chunk Text box, enter the chunk text. For information on RIFF chunk formats and values, see the *Programmer's Reference*.

5. Select one of the following option buttons in the Insertion Point area:

    *   To insert the chunk before the selected field, select Before.

    *   To insert the chunk after the selected element, select After.

    *   If the Inside option is available, select it to insert the chunk at the end of the list of headings below the selected element.

6. Choose OK.

Saving a File

If the Edit File in Memory or Edit Backup Copy of File option was selected when you opened a file, you must save your changes before you leave FileWalker. You can save the file using its original name, or you can give it a new name.

If the Edit File Directly option was selected when you opened a file, you don't need to save the file because your edits were made directly to the disk as you worked, although saving the file flushes the buffers internal to FileWalker.

▶ **To save a file using a new name:**

1. From the File menu, choose Save As.

   The Save dialog box appears.

2. Enter the name you want.

3. Choose OK.

▶ **To save a file using the same name:**

- From the File menu, choose Save.

Note   You should use the Save command regularly to ensure that your changes are made to the file on disk.

Quitting FileWalker

When you finish editing files, you can quit FileWalker.

▶ **To quit FileWalker:**

1. From the File menu, choose Exit.

   If the Edit File in Memory or Edit Backup Copy of File option was selected and you haven't yet saved your latest changes, the following dialog box appears:

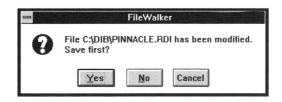

2. To save your changes, choose Yes; to exit without saving your changes, choose No; or to continue to work with FileWalker, choose Cancel.

Questions and Answers About Preparing Bitmaps, Palettes, and Sound Files

Previous chapters in this guide presented information about editing files with the Multimedia Development Kit tools. This chapter assumes a broader perspective, involving procedures that use a variety of commands, offering tips for capabilities that might not be obvious, and contrasting commands in the Multimedia Development Kit tools.

The first section addresses digital images—working with bitmaps and their associated palettes. The second section discusses editing waveform files.

Preparing Bitmaps and Palettes

This section contains information on preparing bitmaps and color palettes for your multimedia application. The major topic addressed in this section is a *composite palette*—a palette that works with more than one bitmap. Other topics contrast alternate methods of performing tasks or identify procedures involving more than one command.

Q **What bitmap-cropping techniques are available?**

A BitEdit provides the following commands you can use to crop an image:

- The Crop command on the Selection menu trims away the portion of a bitmap outside a selected area. This technique is useful for trimming unwanted areas from an image, however, it is less precise than using the Resize Image command to determine the frame size.

- The Resize Image command on the Options menu crops a bitmap to a specified frame size. This command places the crop frame in the upper-left corner of the bitmap; you then adjust the right and lower edges of the crop frame to the desired frame size. To crop an image, specify a frame size and clear the Scaling Resize check box.

Note   For additional information on the Crop and Resize Image commands, see Chapter 13, "Editing Bitmaps Using BitEdit."

Q   **How do I adjust the colors in a bitmap or palette?**

A   PalEdit and BitEdit include several commands you can use to change color definitions of one or more colors in a palette. PalEdit provides the most color-editing commands; however, BitEdit provides a Color Reduction command that produces an optimal palette for the current image. The following color-editing commands are available in PalEdit and BitEdit:

Add Color (PalEdit)
   Introduces a color into a palette by defining the RGB components of the color.

Add Selected Color (PalEdit)
   Adds (or subtracts) RGB values of a specified color to all palette colors.

Adjust Brightness (PalEdit)
   Increases or decreases brightness of all colors in a palette.

Adjust Contrast (PalEdit)
   Increases or decreases the distinction of dark and light colors in a palette.

Color Reduction (BitEdit)
   Reduces the number of colors in a palette by blending similar colors, producing an optimal palette for the bitmap displayed in BitEdit.

Cycle Palette (PalEdit)
   Swaps color definitions among a block of palette color cells.

Cycle RGB (PalEdit)
   Changes colors in a palette according to two color sequences.

Edit Color (PalEdit)
Changes the RGB components of a specified color in a palette.

Fade to Palette (PalEdit)
Maps colors from one palette to similar colors in a replacement palette.

Fade to Selected Color (PalEdit)
Converges all palette colors to a specified color.

Merge Colors (PalEdit)
Blends selected colors by averaging their RGB values.

Q   Does BitEdit support 24-bit-per-pixel bitmaps?

A   When you open a 24-bit-per-pixel device-independent bitmap (.DIB), BitEdit
automatically converts its copy of the bitmap and palette to a depth of 8 bits per
pixel. When storing a bitmap, BitEdit stores bitmaps using palette depths of 1, 4,
and 8 bits per pixel.

Q   How do I draw a solid-color rectangle, circle, or ellipse?

A   In BitEdit, set the foreground and background colors to the same palette entry
using the Current Color tool in the tool window. Then select the appropriate
geometric drawing tool and draw a rectangle, circle, or ellipse.

Q   How do I reduce the number of colors in a palette?

A   You can reduce the number of color entries in a palette by using one of the
following methods:

- Select and cut the color cells from the palette. If your palette contains colors
  not used by any bitmap, you can delete these colors without affecting any
  bitmaps. To identify unused colors in a palette, use the Select Unused Color
  command on the PalEdit Edit menu.

- Blend (or merge) colors. You can blend selected colors by using the Merge Selected Colors command on the PalEdit Edit menu, producing one color whose RGB values are the average RGB values of the blended colors. This color-reduction method is effective when several similar shades of one color occupy a palette. To select a group of similar colors, use the Select Similar Colors command on the PalEdit Edit menu.

- Use the Color Reduction command on the Options menu in BitEdit. With this command, you can truncate a palette to a specified number of colors or create an optimal palette containing a specified number of colors. For additional information on the Color Reduction command, see Chapter 13, "Editing Bitmaps Using BitEdit."

Q   Is there a simple way to clean up large, dithered areas of a bitmap?

A   Yes. In BitEdit, you should expose portions of the dithered area that need editing by temporarily changing the main color of the area to a highly contrasting color. Then touch up the area using the Brush tool. When you finish touching up the area, change the area back to the original color.

Q   How do I copy an object from one bitmap to another?

A   You can copy objects between bitmaps by combining the use of the BitEdit Selection tool with commands that manipulate the Clipboard. To copy a rectangular area of a bitmap, frame the area using the Selection tool, and then use the Copy and Paste commands on the Edit menu to transfer the selection to the target bitmap.

Copying an irregularly shaped object is more complex; you must edit the selection, and then use the Use Transparency and Paste commands to transfer the object to the target bitmap. For more information on the Use Transparency command, see "Using Transparent Color" in Chapter 13, "Editing Bitmaps Using BitEdit."

Q **How do I display multiple bitmaps on screen?**

A Displaying bitmaps on screen while maintaining consistent colors can be done as follows (note that both aspects must be considered):

- To display multiple bitmaps concurrently on screen, you must open each bitmap into its own window and then display the window.

- To obtain consistent colors for bitmaps that display concurrently and for bitmaps that use pieces from other bitmaps, you must use a composite palette containing colors used by each bitmap.

Windows with Multimedia uses one palette to display the current active window. This same palette provides color definitions for the desktop and other windows while the current window remains active. When another window becomes active, Windows loads the palette for the new window and reassigns color definitions for all bitmaps to the new palette. Using one palette for several bitmaps provides consistent color definitions for several windows and improves performance in the following ways:

- When the user switches to another window on the desktop, Windows with Multimedia does not load the composite palette for the active window.

- When the active window changes, Windows with Multimedia does not adjust the screen for a new color palette.

Q **How do I build a composite, or merged, palette?**

A Building a composite palette consists of identifying the most important colors for each bitmap and inserting those colors into one palette.

▶ **To build a merged palette:**

1. Start one copy of BitEdit to edit the bitmaps (cropping, sizing, and reducing colors used by the bitmap).

2. Start one copy of PalEdit from BitEdit (start this copy of PalEdit by using the Show Palette command on the BitEdit Options menu). Use this copy of PalEdit to select and copy palette colors used by the bitmaps.

3. Start one copy of PalEdit from the Program Manager or the File Manager. Use this copy of PalEdit to build and edit the composite palette. The composite palette initially is not associated with any bitmap.

The following illustration shows (in icon form) the applications you use to build a composite palette:

4. Select the images that will share the merged palette and rate the images according to their importance. Colors for the most important image are merged into the palette first; colors for the least important image are merged last.

5. Crop and size the images to dimensions appropriate for your application. You can reduce the number of colors needed in the palette by trimming unwanted areas and by resizing each bitmap.

6. Copy each bitmap. One instance of each bitmap will be used in the application; the second (working) copy of each bitmap will be used to build the merged palette. In the following example, the original, cropped bitmaps are stored in the C:\DIB\ORIGINAL subdirectory; temporary working copies of the same bitmaps are stored in the C:\DIB\TEMPCOPY subdirectory.

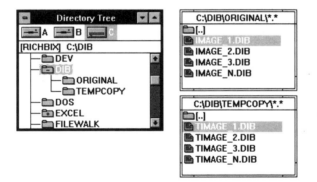

7. Open the working copy of each image in BitEdit. To preserve the quality of the more important images, work from the most important bitmap to the least important.

8. Reduce the number of colors used in the bitmap by using the Color Reduction command on the Options menu in BitEdit. Generally, you can reduce most bitmaps to less than 50 colors without adversely affecting the image.

9. Copy the bitmap palette to the Clipboard. Then switch the active window to the composite palette and paste the Clipboard palette entries into the composite palette.

10. Open the next bitmap in BitEdit and repeat steps 8 and 9.

The interaction of the bitmap in BitEdit, the bitmap palette in PalEdit, the composite palette in the second copy of PalEdit, and the Clipboard in steps 8, 9, and 10 is depicted in the following illustration:

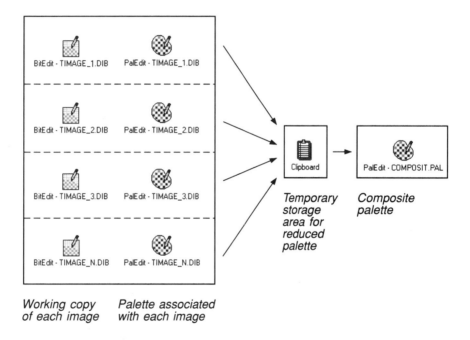

11. When you finish building the composite palette, use the Save As command to save the composite palette in its own file.

Note   If the composite palette becomes full, you must reduce the number of entries in the palette before continuing. Reorder the palette view by color to organize the palette display. Then use the Select Similar Colors and Merge Selected Colors commands on the Edit menu to merge similar colors.

Q How do I test a bitmap using a composite palette?

A You can visually test the compatibility of a palette and bitmap by opening the bitmap in BitEdit, then using the Fade to Palette command from the PalEdit Effects menu. The test allows you switch between the original palette and the replacement (composite) palette while you view the bitmap through BitEdit. Areas of the bitmap that change significantly during the test contain colors that are not in the replacement palette.

▶ **To test a bitmap and composite palette:**

1. Open the bitmap in BitEdit.

2. From the BitEdit Options menu, choose Show Palette.

3. From the PalEdit Effects menu, choose Fade to Palette.

4. Identify the replacement (composite) palette for the test.

5. In the Fade to Palette dialog box, move the scroll box right or left to examine the bitmap with each palette.

6. To exit the test, choose Cancel.

Q How do I adjust a composite palette for a new bitmap?

A For a bitmap that needs a few colors added to a composite palette, simply copy the necessary colors to the Clipboard and paste them into the composite palette.

▶ **To identify colors in BitEdit and copy them into a composite palette:**

1. Open the bitmap in BitEdit.

2. Test the bitmap with the composite palette by using the Fade to Palette command on the Effects menu (for more information on testing a bitmap, see the previous question).

3. Select an area in the bitmap that is adversely affected by the composite bitmap, and then use the Select in PalEdit command on the BitEdit Edit menu to identify the colors to add to the palette.

4. Make the bitmap palette the active window and copy the colors to the Clipboard by using the Copy command on the Edit menu.

5. Make the composite palette the active window and paste the colors into the composite palette.

Q How do I link more than one bitmap to a composite palette?

A You can link a bitmap to a composite palette by using the following procedure (note that this procedure involves both BitEdit and PalEdit).

▶ **To link a bitmap:**

1. Open the bitmap in BitEdit.
2. From the Options menu, choose Show Palette.
3. Make the bitmap palette the active window.
4. From the File menu, choose Apply From in PalEdit and specify the composite palette file as the replacement palette.

To link several bitmaps to one composite palette, repeat this procedure for each bitmap that uses the composite palette.

Q Can I change the maximum number of colors used in a bitmap?

A Yes. The BitEdit Resize Image command on the Options menu includes an area called Colors that lets you set the palette depth (1 bit, 4 bit, and 8 bit) for any bitmap. You can increase the palette depth to hold 16 or 256 colors, or you can decrease the palette depth to 2 or 16 colors.

▶ **To increase the palette depth:**

■ From the Options menu, choose Resize Image and specify a larger bits-per-pixel value in the Colors area.

▶ **To decrease the palette depth to 2 or 16 colors:**

1. Reduce the number of colors in the bitmap. From the Options menu, choose Color Reduction. In the Color Reduction dialog box, specify 2 or 16 for the number of colors in the resulting palette and select Optimal Palette for the color reduction method. Choose the Dither button to reduce the palette.
2. From the Options menu, choose Resize Image to decrease the palette depth.

   If you reduce the palette to two colors, specify 1 bit per pixel in the Colors area of the Resize Image dialog box. If you reduce the palette to 16 colors, specify 4 bits per pixel.

Q   Can BitEdit store images in compressed format?

A   Yes. BitEdit can read and save images in 4-bit and 8-bit RLE formats.

▶ **To compress the disk version of your bitmaps:**

1. Resize the bitmap palette depth to 4 bits per pixel or 8 bits per pixel by using the Resize Image command on the Options menu.

    When you save a bitmap in compressed format, BitEdit examines the palette depth and automatically uses the appropriate (4-bit or 8-bit) RLE format. For information on the Resize Image command, see Chapter 13, "Editing Bitmaps Using BitEdit."

    To save a monochrome bitmap in RLE format, increase the palette depth to 4 bits per pixel.

2. Use the Save As command on the File menu and specify the file type as either Microsoft RLE DIB or Microsoft RIFF RLE DIB. BitEdit examines the palette depth and stores the image using the appropriate (4-bit or 8-bit) RLE format.

Editing Waveform Files

Waveform data editing requires more than just using WaveEdit commands. Special effects enrich sounds played in your applications. This section contains information on how to include special effects in your sound files, as well as how to build a sound file of a specific length. The Zoom command and the Zoom scroll bar are also discussed.

Q   How do I create a waveform file of a specific size?

A   Creating a waveform file of a specific size consists of three steps.

▶ **To create a waveform file:**

1. Clear your work area by using the New command on the File menu. Then identify the number of channels, the sample size, and the sampling frequency in the New File Data Format dialog box.

2. Select the appropriate view for the waveform (the view you use sets the type of units you'll use to specify the file length). To express the new waveform in

time units, use the Milliseconds command on the View menu; to express the new waveform as a number of sound samples, use the Samples command.

3. Insert a specified amount of silence into the work area, building the working area to the proper size. Using the Insert Silence command on the Effects menu, and in the Insert Silence dialog box, specify the length of silence you want (milliseconds or samples).

Q   **How do I create a MIDI file?**

A   Windows with Multimedia does not include a MIDI editor. You must create the MIDI file by using another tool.

Q   **How do I create an echo?**

A   An echo is a copy of a waveform that has reduced volume. To create an echo, you make a copy of an original waveform, reduce the volume of the copy, and then mix the copied waveform into the original file after a specific time lag.

▶   **To create and add an echo to your waveform files:**

1. From the WaveEdit Edit menu, choose Select All, then choose Copy to copy the waveform to the Clipboard.

2. From the File menu, choose Run WaveEdit to start a second copy of WaveEdit. With this copy of WaveEdit, you'll copy and reduce the waveform amplitude.

3. In the second copy of WaveEdit, from the Edit menu, choose Paste.

4. From the Effects menu, choose Amplify.

   In the Change Amplitude dialog box, enter 50% and choose OK to decrease the volume of the waveform.

5. From the Edit menu, choose Copy to copy the reduced-volume waveform to the Clipboard.

6. In the first window, place the cursor in the waveform where you want to start the echo. Typically, an echo lags behind the original waveform 10 to 200 milliseconds.

7. From the Edit menu, choose Mix Paste to add the echo to the file.

To test the echo, play the entire waveform. To move the echo to another offset, use the Undo command on the Edit menu, and then repeat steps 4 and 5.

Q What is the difference between the Zoom command and the Zoom scroll bar?

A The Zoom scroll bar controls the level of detail displayed in the Edit area of the WaveEdit window. Moving the scroll box to the left in the Zoom scroll bar expands the view, providing more detail. Moving the scroll box to the right contracts the view, providing a better qualitative perspective of the waveform. The current position in the waveform file and the current selection remain unchanged when the Zoom scroll bar is used.

In contrast, the Zoom command on the View menu fills the Edit area with the currently selected portion of the waveform. The Zoom command places the left edge of the selection at the left edge of the Edit area and adjusts the detail level of the selection to fill the Edit area.

Q What is the significance of the Change Characteristics command?

A With the Change Characteristics command on the Effects menu, you can control the fidelity level of a waveform by adjusting the number of sound channels (mono or stereo), the dynamic range of the samples (8 or 16 bits), and the sampling frequency (the number of sound samples captured each second). The characteristics you select determine the amount of storage needed to preserve the waveform on disk or CD-ROM. The following table contains the range of file sizes needed for storing 1 second of sound:

Channel	Sample Size	Frequency (kHz)	File Size (bytes)
Mono	8 bits	11	11070
Stereo	8 bits	11	22094
Mono	16 bits	22	44144
Stereo	16 bits	44	176444

Note Lowering characteristics degrades waveform sound quality, but increasing the characteristics of an existing waveform has no effect on sound quality. When you record sound you should use higher settings, and then lower the characteristics to an appropriate level for the specific application.

Q   **How can I find a specific sample in a file?**

A   The following procedures can be used to find a specific sample.

▶   **To find a sample that plays a specific number of milliseconds:**

1. From the View menu, choose Millisecond to select the time reference.

2. Identify the sample in the waveform data by specifying the start sample and the size of the selection. In the Select Start spin box, specify (in milliseconds) the time interval from the beginning of the file to the sample. In the Select Size spin box, specify a size greater than or equal to 1 to include the sample in the selection.

3. Scroll through the waveform data. The selected portion of the waveform contains the specified sample.

▶   **To find a sample using the sample number as a reference:**

1. From the View menu, choose Samples to use waveform sample reference numbers.

2. Identify the sample in the waveform data. In the Select Start spin box, specify the position of the sample from the beginning of the file. In the Select Size spin box, specify a size greater than or equal to 1 to include the sample in the selection.

3. Scroll through the waveform data. The selected portion of the waveform contains the specified sample.

Q   **Can I edit a single channel of a stereo waveform?**

A   Windows with Multimedia does not let you edit individual channels in a stereo waveform file. You must use another tool to perform this edit.

Q   How can I fade a waveform so the sounds at the end of the fade are still distinguishable?

A   The Fade Down and Fade Up commands use scales of 0% through 100% and 100% through 0% to fade a waveform selection. If you temporarily add an interval of silence to a waveform and include silence in the selection when you fade the waveform, you can retain some sound at the low end of the fade.

▶ **To perform a partial fade:**

1. Insert an appropriate amount of silence in the waveform as follows:

    • To decrease the volume (Fade Down), insert silence to the right of the waveform section you want to fade.

    • To increase the volume (Fade Up), insert silence to the left of the waveform section you want to fade.

2. Select the interval of silence and the portion of the waveform you want to fade.

3. From the Effects menu, choose Fade Down or Fade Up.

4. Remove the interval of silence you created in step 1.

Q   How do I repeat segments of a waveform (individual sounds)?

A   You can use the following procedure to replicate sounds in a waveform.

▶ **To add repeated sounds:**

1. Identify where the repeated sounds will occur in the waveform.

2. Select the portion of the waveform to be repeated and copy the selection to the Clipboard.

3. Paste the contents of the Clipboard into the waveform file where the sounds will occur (for additional replication, repeat the paste operation).

Index

A

Access time, CD-ROM, 4-4, 5-7
Adaptive Differential Pulse Code Modulation
 See PCM files
Add Color command, in PalEdit, 14-16
Add dialog box, in Convert, 12-7
Add Selected Color command, in PalEdit, 14-19
Adjust Brightness command, in PalEdit, 14-17
Adjust Contrast command, in PalEdit, 14-18
Amplify command, in WaveEdit, 15-16
Amplitude
 clipping, 6-12
 decreasing, 15-16
 fading, 15-15 to 15-16
 increasing, 15-16
 partial fading, 17-14
 viewing, 15-3
 waveform, 6-2
 zero (silence), 15-15
Analog-to-digital converter, 1-3, 6-11
ANSI character equivalents
 in structured file, 16-9
 in unstructured file, 16-7
Apple Macintosh files
 AIFF conversion format, 12-1
 AIFF files in WaveEdit, 15-1, 15-19
 AIFF file format, 6-13
 PICT conversion formats, 12-2, 13-2
Apply From File command, in PalEdit, 14-32
Archival media, 3-3
ASCII text files, 8-1, 8-9
Aspect ratio, 5-5, 5-20
Asymetrix ToolBook authoring tool, 2-6, 9-3
Audio files
 conversion formats, 12-1
 converting, 12-5
 WaveEdit formats, 15-1
 Windows with Multimedia file formats, 11-3
AutoCAD Import files
 conversion format, 12-2, 13-2
 Select Bitmap Size dialog box, 12-11

B

Background color
 definition, 13-10
 and Ellipse tool, 13-14
 filling deleted areas with, 13-21
 in freehand drawing, 13-12
 in solid-color objects, 17-3
 and Line tool, 13-14
 and rectangle tools, 13-13
 replacing bitmap color with, 13-14 to 13-15
 replacing foreground color with, 13-15
 selecting from bitmap, 13-12
 selecting from palette, 13-11
 transparent, 13-30 to 13-33
Backup media, 3-4
Base-level synthesizer, 7-5, 7-16
BitEdit
 converting images, 5-22
 file formats, 5-11 to 5-12, 13-2
 menus, 13-4 to 13-6
 multiple instances of, 13-23
 quitting, 13-37
 setting defaults, 13-8 to 13-9
 starting, 13-2 to 13-3
 starting PalEdit from, 14-2 to 14-3
BitEdit Preferences dialog box, 13-8 to 13-9
BitEdit tools
 Brush, 13-12
 Brush Shape, 13-13
 Color Dropper, 13-12
 Color Eraser, 13-15
 Current Color, 13-10 to 13-11
 described, 13-6 to 13-7
 Ellipse, 13-14, 13-33
 Flood Fill, 13-14 to 13-15
 Line, 13-14
 Line Size, 13-12
 Rectangle, 13-13, 13-33
 Rounded Rectangle, 13-13
 selecting, 13-6
 Selection, 13-17
 Zoom Control, 13-15 to 13-16

BitEdit window
  customizing, 13-8 to 13-9
  resizing, 13-8 to 13-9
  scroll bars, 13-3
  selection coordinates, 13-17
  status bar, 13-3
  tool window, 13-3, 13-9 to 13-10
  zooming, 13-15 to 13-16
Bitmap files
  BitEdit formats, 13-2
  compressed format, 17-10
  conversion formats, 12-2, 13-2
  converting in BitEdit, 13-8
  converting in Convert, 12-5
  converting to greyscale, 12-14
  creating, 13-34
  FileWalker formats, 16-2
  opening in BitEdit, 13-7 to 13-8
  saving, 13-36
  saving palette changes, 14-15
  24-bit DIBs in BitEdit, 17-3
  Windows with Multimedia formats, 11-3
Bitmap Occurrence palette view, 14-9
Bitmaps
  BitEdit and Convert conversion formats, 5-11 to 5-12
  Clipboard editing commands, 13-20 to 13-21
  and color cell order, 14-24
  coloring area, 13-14 to 13-15
  copying selection, 13-20, 13-31 to 13-32, 17-4
  cropping, 13-24, 13-34, 17-1 to 17-2
  cycling colors, 14-27 to 14-29
  deleting selection, 13-21
  described, 5-4
  disk space, 3-2
  displaying multiple, 17-5
  dithered, 5-6, 13-28 to 13-29, 17-4
  drawing freehand, 13-12, 17-3
  file size, 5-7
  foreground/background colors, 13-10
  image depth, 5-5 to 5-6, 13-34 to 13-35, 14-2, 17-9
  inverting, 13-24 to 13-25
  memory when editing, 13-9
  in movie, 9-16
  moving selection, 13-18
  optimal size, 13-33
  and palette changes, 14-13
  palette for multiple, 13-28, 14-7, 17-8 to 17-9
  palette for new, 13-36
  palette, applying to, 14-31 to 14-32
  palette, replacing for, 13-21, 13-27 to 13-28
  pasting from Clipboard, 13-22 to 13-23
  resizing, 13-33 to 13-34
  resolution, 5-5

  rotating, 13-25 to 13-26
  saving changes to, 13-36
  canceling selection, 13-18
  selecting, 13-17 to 13-18
  transparent background, 13-30 to 13-33
  transposing, 13-24 to 13-25
  undoing changes to, 13-16
  Windows DIB format, 5-11 to 5-12, 5-22
  zooming, 13-15 to 13-16
Brightness palette view, 14-9
Browse sequences, 2-8
Brush Shape tool, 13-13
Brush tool
  dithered areas, 17-4
  drawing color, 13-12
  drawing with, 13-12
  shape of, 13-13
  width of, 13-12
Byte, editing, 16-15

C

C structure
  copying selection, 16-14
  deleting selection, 16-14 to 16-15
  displaying data fields, 16-8
  editing field, 16-15, 16-18
  moving between fields, 16-16
  moving selection, 16-14
  canceling selection, 16-14
  selecting field, 16-13 to 16-14
Cables, for recording audio, 6-11
Cache, with CD-ROM, 4-4
Camera stand, 5-15
Cast, 9-2
Cast members
  CPU processing, 9-16
  described, 9-2
  supported by Movie Player, 9-5
  transitions, 9-17
Cast window, 9-2
Cast-based animation, 9-2
CD-ROM, 11-2 to 11-3
  archiving data, 3-3
  capacity, 4-3
  data transfer rate, 4-4
  data transfer rate, bitmap, 5-7
  directory structure, 4-3
  distributing title on, 4-5
  mastering title, 4-7
  premastering title, 4-5 to 4-6
  Red Book audio, 6-5 to 6-6
  replicating discs for distribution, 4-7

CD-ROM (*continued*)
   seek time, 4-4, 5-7
   technology described, 4-2
CGM Import Filter dialog box, in Convert, 12-12
Change Amplitude dialog box, in WaveEdit, 15-16
Change Characteristics command, in WaveEdit, 15-14 to
   15-15, 17-12
Channel mapping, 7-2 to 7-3, 7-15
Channels, waveform
   and disk space, 15-14
   and file size, 17-12
   hiding, 15-10
   setting at file conversion, 12-15
   setting for existing file, 15-14
   setting when creating file, 15-6
   stereo, 17-13
Clear command, in FileWalker, 16-15
Clipboard
   in BitEdit, 13-20, 13-23
   in FileWalker, 16-14 to 16-15
   in PalEdit, 14-4 to 14-5, 14-26 to 14-27
   in WaveEdit, 15-13
Clipping, 6-12
Color cells
   adding from Clipboard palette, 13-22
   adding new, 14-16
   canceling selection, 13-30, 14-11
   See also Color definitions
   creating from bitmap color, 17-8
   default order, 14-23
   deleting, 13-28 to 13-29, 14-25, 17-3 to 17-4
   editing, 14-13
   HSL values, 14-14 to 14-16
   in identity palette, 14-29
   merging, 14-27
   moving, 14-24 to 14-25
   optimal for bitmap, 13-28
   pasting from Clipboard, 14-26 to 14-27
   relative importance in bitmap, 13-29, 14-13,
      14-23 to 14-24
   reordering, 13-29 to 13-30, 14-23
   RGB values, 14-14 to 14-16
   saving changes to, 14-15
   flashing selected, 14-13
   selecting from bitmap, 13-30, 14-12
   selecting in PalEdit, 14-10 to 14-12
   system-defined, 14-29
   unused, 14-12
Color definitions
   bitmap color median values, 13-28
   brightness, 14-17
   contrast, 14-18
   defining new color, 14-16

   editing, 14-13
   editing commands, 17-2 to 17-3
   editing methods, 17-2
   fading, 14-20 to 14-21
   filtering, 14-20
   HSL values, 14-14 to 14-16
   merging cell colors, 14-27
   RGB values, 14-14 to 14-16
   saving, 14-15
   shifting, 14-22
   tinting, 14-19
Color depth
   and image depth, 14-2
   setting from bitmap, 13-34 to 13-35, 17-9
Color Dropper tool, 13-12
Color Eraser tool, 13-15
Color palettes
   See Palettes
Color Reduction command
   in BitEdit, 13-28 to 13-29
   in BitEdit with PalEdit, 14-29
   in Convert, 12-13 to 12-14
Color shift sequences, 14-22
Color Sort palette view, 14-9
Color table
   displaying color offsets, 16-9
   expanded headings (illustration), 16-8
   inserting row, 16-18 to 16-19
Common palette, 14-7
Compact Disc-Read Only Memory
   See CD-ROM
Composite palette
   creating, 13-28 to 13-29, 17-5 to 17-8
   displaying multiple bitmaps, 17-5
   linking to bitmap, 17-9
   testing with bitmap, 5-14
Composite video input, 5-14
CompuServe GIF files, 5-12, 12-2, 13-2
Computer Graphics Metafile (CGM) image format, 5-12
Computer Graphics Metafiles
   image format, 5-12, 12-2, 13-2
   Import Filter dialog box, 12-12
   Select Bitmap Size dialog box, 12-11
Contents topic, 2-7
Contract command, in FileWalker, 16-11
Contract Parent command, in FileWalker, 16-11
Convert
   audio file conversion, 6-9 to 6-13
   buttons, 12-4
   file formats, 12-1 to 12-3
   image file conversion, 5-11 to 5-12
   quitting, 12-15
   starting, 12-3

Convert window
  Destination area, 12-4
  options, 12-4
  Source area, 12-4
Copy command
  in BitEdit, 13-21
  in FileWalker, 16-14
  in PalEdit, 14-4, 14-26 to 14-27
  in WaveEdit, 15-13
Copy Text command, in FileWalker, 16-14
Copy View command, in PalEdit, 14-23
Copyright issues, 2-11, 5-8, 6-12
CPU
  audio data processing, 6-10
  image processing, 5-13
  Red Book audio, 6-5 to 6-6
  text scanning, 8-5
Crop command
  in BitEdit, 13-23
  compared to Resize Image command, 17-1 to 17-2
Cross-topic jumps, 2-8
Current Color tool, 13-10 to 13-11
Cut command
  in BitEdit, 13-21
  in FileWalker, 16-14
  in PalEdit, 14-4
  in WaveEdit, 15-13
Cycle Palette command, in PalEdit, 14-27 to 14-29
Cycle RGB command, in PalEdit, 14-22

D

Darkness palette view, 14-9
Data array
  appending field to, 16-19
  copying selection, 16-14
  deleting selection, 16-14 to 16-15
  editing field, 16-15, 16-18
  inserting row, 16-18 to 16-19
  moving between fields, 16-16
  moving selection, 16-14
  canceling selection, 16-14
  selecting data in, 16-13 to 16-14
  viewing in structured file, 16-8
Data management systems, 3-7
Data storage
  CD-ROM, 4-3
  digital audio tape (DAT), 3-4
  hard disks, 3-3
  optical discs, 3-3
  tape drives, 3-4

Data stream
  character representations, 16-16
  copying selection, 16-14
  deleting selection, 16-14 to 16-15
  editing bytes, 16-15 to 16-18
  inserting value, 16-18 to 16-19
  moving between values, 16-16
  moving selection, 16-14
  canceling selection, 16-14
  selecting data in, 16-13
  viewing in structured file, 16-9
Data transfer systems, 3-4, 3-7
Database, managing resources with, 3-8 to 3-11
Delete command
  in BitEdit, 13-21
  in PalEdit, 14-5
  in WaveEdit, 15-13
Description command, in FileWalker, 16-12
Desktop audio recording system, 6-7
Device-independent bitmap. See Bitmap files
Digital audio
  analog-to-digital converter, 1-3, 6-11
  compared to waveform and MIDI audio, 7-7
  converting from other audio formats, 6-13
  CPU performance, 6-10
  DAT (digital audio tape)
    backup media, 3-4
    recording audio, 6-11
    storing audio, 6-14
  described, 6-2
  digital sound studio, 6-8
  digital-to-analog converter, 1-3, 6-11
  disk space, 3-2, 6-4 to 6-5, 6-10, 6-14
  editing, 6-13
  fidelity level, 6-6 to 6-7
  recording, 6-12 to 6-13
  red book audio, 6-7
  redbook audio, 6-5
  sound libraries, 6-7 to 6-8
  sound preparation software, 6-8 to 6-9
  sound processing hardware, 6-10 to 6-11
  translating from analog, 6-3
Digital images, 5-2
Digital Signal Processor (DSP), 7-3, 7-6
Digital-to-analog converter, 1-3, 6-11
Digitizer
  digitizing images, 5-19 to 5-21
  frame-grabber, 5-9
  purchasing, 5-14 to 5-15
  software, 5-10

Directory structure
    CD-ROM, 4-3
    data management, 3-9
Disk space
    archiving data, 3-3
    audio formats compared, 7-7
    CD-ROM, 4-1
    digital audio, 6-14
    digital audio recording, 6-10 to 6-11
    hard disk capacity, 3-3
    MIDI audio, 7-7
    movie file size, 9-16
    Red Book audio, 6-6 to 6-7
    waveform audio, 6-4 to 6-5
Display Offsets command, in FileWalker, 16-9 to 16-10
Dithering, 5-23
Draw programs, 5-3
DRW Import Filter dialog box, in Convert, 12-13
Dynamic range, waveform, 6-4

E

Echo, waveform, 17-11
Edit Color command, in PalEdit, 14-13 to 14-15
Edit Component command, in FileWalker, 16-15, 16-18
Edit Enumerated Type dialog box, in FileWalker, 16-17
Edit String dialog box, in FileWalker, 16-18
Ellipse tool, 13-14
    drawing hollow ellipse, 13-33
    drawing solid-color ellipse, 17-3
Encapsulated PostScript files, 5-12, 12-2, 13-2
Enumerated type, 16-17
Exit command
    in BitEdit, 13-37
    in FileWalker, 16-21
    in PalEdit, 14-32
    in WaveEdit, 15-20
Expand command, in FileWalker, 16-10
Extended synthesizer, 7-5, 7-16
Extensible, definition, 12-1

F

Fade Down command, in WaveEdit, 15-15 to 15-16
Fade to Palette command, in PalEdit, 14-20
Fade to Selected Color command, in PalEdit, 14-20
Fade Up command, in WaveEdit, 15-15 to 15-16
Fidelity level, digital audio, 6-6 to 6-7
File editor, 16-1
File extensions, default, 12-1

File formats
    BitEdit, 13-2
    compressed bitmap (RLE), 17-10
    conversion, 12-1, 12-3
    FileWalker, 16-2
    WaveEdit, 15-1
    Windows with Multimedia, 11-3
File headings
    contracting, 16-11
    expanding, 16-8 to 16-10
    getting description, 16-12
    moving between, 16-11
    outline form, 16-8
    selecting, 16-13
FileWalker
    file formats, 16-2
    menus, 16-3 to 16-5
    quitting, 16-21
    starting, 16-2
FileWalker window
    file display format, 16-7
    offsets, 16-10
    scroll bars, 16-11
    selection cursor, 16-11
    title bar, 16-3
Flash Selected Colors command, in PalEdit, 14-13
Flat-bed scanner, 5-13, 8-5
Flip Horizontal command, in BitEdit, 13-24 to 13-25
Flip Vertical command, in BitEdit, 13-24 to 13-25
Flood Fill tool, 13-14 to 13-15
Fonts, screen design, 2-9
Foreground color
    definition, 13-10
    and Ellipse tool, 13-14
    in freehand drawing, 13-12
    and Line tool, 13-14
    and rectangle tools, 13-13
    replacing background color with, 13-15
    replacing bitmap color with, 13-14 to 13-15
    selecting from bitmap, 13-12
    selecting from palette, 13-10 to 13-11
Form header, editing, 16-16
Frame-based animation, 9-2
Frame-grabber, 5-9
Frequency
    described, 6-2
    and disk space, 6-4
    and file size, 17-12
    setting at file conversion, 12-15
    setting for sample, 15-15
    setting when creating file, 15-6

G

GIF image format, 5-12
Goto Offset command, in FileWalker, 16-12
Goto Parent command, in FileWalker, 16-11
Greyscale
    converting image to, 12-14
    palette, 14-18
Group
    See C structure, 10-1

H

Hard disk
    backup media, 3-4
    capacity, 3-3
    digital audio, 6-10 to 6-14
    for image development, 5-13
    Multimedia PC specification, 1-3
Hardware
    analog-to-digital converter, 6-11
    authoring system, 1-4
    CD-ROM, 4-1
    desktop audio recording system, 6-7
    digital-to-analog converter, 6-11
    hard disks, 3-3, 6-10
    CPU for image development, 5-13
    image digitizing board, 5-9, 5-15
    image digitizing camera, 5-14 to 5-15
    image display monitor, 5-15
    MIDI cables and ports, 7-4
    MIDI keyboard, 7-11
    MIDI synthesizer, 7-10
    movie playback, 9-4
    Multimedia PC specification, 1-3
    OCR scanner, 8-4 to 8-5
    premastering equipment, 4-6
    removable media drives, 3-6
    scanner, 5-13
    SCSI interface, 3-4 to 3-5
    synthesizers, 7-5
    tape drives, 3-4
    text preparation, 8-11
Hardware, required, 10-7
Hewlett-Packard Graphic Language files
    conversion format, 12-2, 13-2
    image format, 5-12
    Select Bitmap Size dialog box, 12-11
Hex Bytes format, in FileWalker, 16-7
Hexadecimal file editor, 16-1
Hi8 video camera, 5-14

H (continued)

HSL values
    color cell, 14-14, 14-16
    cycling sequences, 14-22

I

Identity palette, 14-29
Image depth
    affect on bitmap, 13-34
    and compressed format, 17-10
    definition, 14-2
    setting, 13-34, 17-9
    setting when creating bitmap, 13-35
    supported, 14-2
Images
    acquiring, 5-8 to 5-9
    bitmap, 5-4
    converting, 12-5
    converting in BitEdit, 13-8
    converting to Windows DIB format, 5-11 to 5-12
    creating, 5-8 to 5-9
    digitizing, 5-9, 5-19 to 5-21
    editing, 5-10 to 5-11, 5-21 to 5-23
    image depth, 5-5 to 5-6
    resolution, 5-5
    scanning, 5-9, 5-17 to 5-19
    selecting for a title, 5-16
    vector graphic, 5-2 to 5-3
    Windows DIB format, 5-12
    Windows metafile format, 5-3
    Windows with Multimedia file formats, 11-3
Inks, in movie, 9-5 to 9-8
Input DATA Format dialog box, in Convert, 12-14 to 12-15
Input level, waveform, 15-18
Insert Array Element command, in FileWalker, 16-18 to 16-19
Insert RIFF Chunk command, in FileWalker, 16-19 to 16-20
Insert Silence command, in WaveEdit, 15-15
Interleave format, 4-5

K

Key assignments, 7-18
Keyboard-synthesizer, 7-11

L

Left Channel command, in WaveEdit, 15-10
Line Size tool, 13-12
Line tool, 13-14
Lingo, 9-5
Load Palette From dialog box, in PalEdit, 14-21
Local area networks, 3-6 to 3-7

Lotus 1-2-3 PICT files, 5-12, 12-11 to 12-2, 13-2
Luminance, 14-14, 14-16
LUX value, 5-14

M

MacroMind Director, 11-5
    Clean Up Cast command, 9-15
    Convert to Bitmap command, 9-16
    converting movie files, 9-18
    creating movies for title, 9-2
    features supported in Movie Player, 9-5
    files, 11-5 graphics tools, 9-16
    testing features on PC, 9-4
Make Identity Palette command, in PalEdit, 14-29
Master keyboard, 7-11
MCI (Media Control Interface)
    movie script channel commands, 9-10, 9-14
    streaming audio in movie, 9-9 to 9-10
MCI Wave Audio Driver, default time, 15-19
Media Player, 9-3
Memory, reserving for waveforms, 15-19
Merge Selected Colors command, in PalEdit, 14-27
Merge Selected Colors, in PalEdit, 14-30
Micrografx Designer/Draw files
    image format, 5-12 conversion format, 12-2, 13-2
    Import Filter dialog box, 12-13
    Select Bitmap Size dialog box, 12-11
Microphone, 6-11
MIDI audio
    acquiring scores, 7-8
    authoring device-independent, 7-14 to 7-18
    cables, 7-4
    channel numbers, 7-2
    compared to Red Book and waveform audio, 7-7
    converting for Windows with Multimedia, 12-3 to 12-5,
        7-13 to 7-14
    device-independent, 7-15
    editing in FileWalker, 16-2
    equipment for, 7-4
    message processing, 7-6
    MIDI specification, 7-4
    in movie, 9-9 to 9-10
    ports, 7-4
    recording, 7-11 to 7-13
    recording hardware, 7-10 to 7-11
    recording software, 7-9 to 7-10
    synthesizers, 7-5, 7-10
    technology and terms, 7-2 to 7-3
    Windows with Multimedia file formats, 7-13, 11-3

MIDI Mapper
    configuring, 7-5
    patch mapping, 7-10
Milliseconds command, in WaveEdit, 15-10
Mirror image, of bitmap, 13-24
Mix Paste command, in WaveEdit, 15-13
Mixed mode CD-ROM title, 6-6
MMP.DLL, 9-3
Mono channel. *See* Channels, waveform
Monochrome bitmap
    converting file to, 12-14
    image depth, 14-2
    saving in compressed format, 17-10
Movie Converter
    converting MacroMind Director files, 9-18
    waveform sound cast members, 9-9 to 9-10
Movie Player
    authoring guidelines for movie playback, 9-4, 9-8
    movie playback, 9-3
    script-channel commands, 9-9 to 9-10, 9-14
    supported MacroMind Director features, 9-5
Movies
    controlling MCI devices from, 9-9
    converting from MacroMind Director, 9-18
    creating for Windows environment, 9-2
    editing in MacroMind Director, 9-16
    file format, 9-1
    file size, 9-15 to 9-16
    fonts on Macintosh and PC, 9-16
    MacroMind Director files, 11-5
    MCI commands in, 9-10, 9-14
    minimizing cast member processing, 9-16
    Movie Player authoring guidelines, 9-4 to 9-5
    palette effects, 9-8
    playback methods, 9-3
    previewing, 14-27, 14-29
    scanning frame sequence, 5-20
    script-channel commands, 9-9 to 9-14
    sound cast members, 9-9 to 9-10, 9-15
    sound channel, 9-9 to 9-10
    streaming audio, 9-9
    synchronizing effects, 9-10
    testing under Windows, 9-4
    transitions, 9-17
    VGA display and palette colors, 9-6 to 9-8
    Windows with Multimedia file formats, 11-3
Multimedia Development Kit, 1-4, 2-12, 10-2
Multimedia extensions to Windows, 1-2

Multimedia PC
   authoring system
      CD-ROM, 4-3 to 4-4
      CD-ROM title distribution, 4-5 to 4-7
      creating movies, 9-2
      data sharing system, 3-4 to 3-5, 3-7
      data storage system, 3-2 to 3-4
      data transfer system, 3-5
      database to manage resources, 3-8 to 3-11
      digital audio recording system, 6-7 to 6-11
      Draw programs, 5-3
      image preparation system, 5-4
      image processing system, 5-10 to 5-11, 5-15
      MIDI audio system, 7-4 to 7-5
      MIDI recording system, 7-9 to 7-11
      multimedia authoring software, 2-11
      Multimedia Development Kit, 1-4
      recommended hardware, 1-4
      text preparation system, 8-4 to 8-6, 8-11
      title authoring tools, 2-12
   end-user system, 5-7
      audio fidelity level, 6-6
      base configuration, 1-3
      image depth and seek time, 5-7
      image depth and VGA display, 5-5 to 5-6
      MIDI authoring considerations, 7-12 to 7-14
      movie file size, 9-15
      movie playback, 9-3 to 9-4
      movie playback frame size, 5-20
      video display and movie colors, 9-6 to 9-8
Multimedia Producer's Legal Survival Guide, 2-11
Musical Instrument Digital Interface
   See MIDI files

N

New Bitmap dialog box, in BitEdit, 13-35
New command
   in BitEdit, 13-35
   in PalEdit, 14-7
   in WaveEdit, 15-6
New File Data Format dialog box, in WaveEdit, 15-6 to 15-17
New Palette dialog box, in PalEdit, 14-7
Next command, in FileWalker, 16-11
Numeric values, editing in FileWalker, 16-16

O

Offsets
   displaying, 16-9 to 16-10
   numbering system, 16-10
   searching for, 16-12
Open Bitmap dialog box, in BitEdit, 13-8

Open command
   in BitEdit, 13-8
   in FileWalker, 16-5 to 16-6
   in PalEdit, 14-7
   in WaveEdit, 15-7 to 15-8
Open File dialog box, in FileWalker, 16-5 to 16-6
Open Palette dialog box, in PalEdit, 14-32
Open Wave File dialog box, in WaveEdit, 15-7
Optical character recognition (OCR), 8-3 to 8-6
Optical media, 3-3

P

Paint programs
   creating images with, 5-8
   DIB file format, 5-4
   image editing, 5-10 to 5-11
PalEdit
   color cube, 14-14
   color selection cursor, 14-15
   menus, 14-4 to 14-6
   quitting, 14-32
   setting defaults, 14-8 to 14-9
   starting, 14-2 to 14-3
   starting from BitEdit, 14-2 to 14-3
PalEdit Preferences dialog box, 14-8 to 14-9
Palette views
   Bitmap Occurrence, 14-9
   Brightness, 14-9
   changing, 14-9 to 14-10
   Color Sort, 14-9
   Darkness, 14-9
   dual-view mode, 14-8
   moving cells between, 14-25
   palette order, 14-3, 14-9, 14-23
   reordering palette to match, 14-23
Palettes
   adding Clipboard palette colors to, 13-22
   applying to bitmap, 14-31 to 14-32
   and active bitmap, 14-7
   applying to bitmap, 14-31
   bitmap cast members, 9-15
   color cell order, 14-3
   See also Color cells
   color depth, 13-34 to 13-35, 14-2, 17-3, 17-9
   color sequences, cycling, 14-27 to 14-29
   combining, 14-26 to 14-27
   common palette, 14-7
   composite, 13-28, 17-5 to 17-9
   converting, 12-3, 12-5
   copying to Clipboard, 13-21
   creating, 13-28 to 13-29, 14-7 to 14-20, 14-26 to 14-30
   default, 14-6

Palettes (*continued*)
    editing in FileWalker, 16-2
    identity palette, 14-29 to 14-30
    included with MDK, 14-31
    Macintosh and Windows colors, 9-6
    opening file, 14-7
    palette effects in movie, 9-8
    reducing colors in, 13-28 to 13-29, 13-34, 17-3 to 17-4
    reordering color cells, 13-29 to 13-30, 14-23
    replacing in bitmap, 13-21, 13-27 to 13-28
    saving changes to, 14-15, 14-30
    separate file from bitmap, 14-3, 14-7
    truncating, 13-28
    updating bitmap changes, 14-8 to 14-9
Paste command
    in BitEdit, 13-22 to 13-23, 13-30, 13-32
    in FileWalker, 16-15
    in PalEdit, 14-5, 14-26 to 14-27
    in WaveEdit, 15-13
Paste Palette command, in BitEdit, 13-21, 13-27
Paste Without Color command, in BitEdit, 13-23
Patch mapping
    common patch definitions, 7-14
    device-independent MIDI files, 7-15
    MIDI file conversion, 7-13
    MIDI Mapper, 7-10
    Patch Mapper, 7-3
    standard MIDI assignments, 7-16 to 7-17
PC Paintbrush files
    conversion color palette, 13-2
    conversion formats, 12-2, 13-2
PCM files
    audio format, 6-13 conversion format, 12-1
    editing in WaveEdit, 15-19
    WaveEdit format, 15-1
PCX image format, 5-12
Percussion instrument
    percussive channels in MIDI files, 7-15
    standard MIDI key assignments, 7-18
Photographs
    converting to bitmaps, 14-2
    scanning and digitizing, 5-9
Pixel resolution, 5-5
Polyphony
    channel mapping, 7-15
    defined, 7-3
    polyphonic synthesizer, 7-6
    synthesizer capabilities, 7-5
Ports, Multimedia PC specification, 1-3
PostScript files
    See Encapsulated PostScript files

Preferences command
    in BitEdit, 13-8 to 13-9
    in PalEdit, 14-8 to 14-9
Previous command, in FileWalker, 16-11
Program-change message, mapping, 7-15

R

Read-only file protection, 16-6
Record dialog box, in WaveEdit, 15-17, 15-19
Rectangle tool
    drawing hollow rectangles, 13-33
    drawing solid-color rectangle, 17-3
    using, 13-13
Red Book audio, 6-6 to 6-8
    compared to MIDI and waveform audio, 7-7
    described, 6-5 to 6-6
    fidelity level and disk space, 6-7
    file size, 6-3
    in movie, 9-9 to 9-10
Red, Green, Blue. *See* RGB values
Removable media drives, 3-6
Reorder Palette as View command, in PalEdit, 14-23
Resize Bitmap dialog box, in BitEdit, 13-33 to 13-34
Resize Image command
    compared to Crop command, 17-1 to 17-2
    in BitEdit, 13-33 to 13-34
Resource Interchange File Format
    See RIFF files
RGB values
    adding a value to all cells, 14-19
    brightness, 14-17
    color cell, 14-14, 14-16
    cycling, 14-22
    filling deleted color cells, 14-25
    median bitmap, 13-28
    removing a value from all cells, 14-19
    selecting cells with similar, 14-11
Rich Text Format (RTF), 8-1, 8-10
RIFF DIB image format, 5-12
RIFF files
    conversion formats, 12-1
    FileWalker format, 16-2
    inserting RIFF chunk, 16-19 to 16-20
    multimedia Windows file formats, 11-3
RIFF movie format, 9-1
Right Channel command, in WaveEdit, 15-10
RLE DIB image format, 5-12
RLE file format (bitmap), 17-10
RLE RIFF DIB image format, 5-12
RMMP movie format, 9-1
Roller-fed scanner, 8-5

Rotate command, in BitEdit, 13-25 to 13-26
Rounded Rectangle tool
    drawing hollow rectangles, 13-33
    drawing solid-color rectangle, 17-3
    using, 13-13
Run-Length Encoding (RLE), 5-7

S

S-Video input, 5-14
Sample
    and file size, 17-12
    searching for, 17-13
    setting size, 12-15, 15-6, 15-14
Samples command, WaveEdit, 15-10
Saturation, 14-14 to 14-16
Save As command
    in BitEdit, 13-36 to 13-37
    in FileWalker, 16-21
    in PalEdit, 14-31
    in WaveEdit, 15-20
Save command
    in BitEdit, 13-36 to 13-37
    in FileWalker, 16-21
    in PalEdit, 14-31
    in WaveEdit, 15-19
Save To File command, in PalEdit, 14-30
Scanner
    OCR for scanning text, 8-3 to 8-6
    post-scanning image enhancement, 5-21
    production cycle considerations, 5-9
    purchasing, 5-13
    scanning images, 5-17 to 5-19
Screen design
    Contents topic, 2-7
    fonts, 2-9
    graphics, 2-10
    topic screens, 2-9
Screen resolution, 5-5
Script-channel commands (movie), 9-9 to 9-14
SCSI interface, 3-4 to 3-6
Seek time
    CD-ROM, 4-4
    image file size, 5-7
Select All command
    in BitEdit, 13-18
    in PalEdit, 14-11
    in WaveEdit, 15-12
Select Bitmap Size dialog box, in Convert, 12-11
Select In PalEdit command, in BitEdit, 13-30, 14-12
Select Similar Colors command, in PalEdit, 14-11
Select Size spin box, in WaveEdit, 15-11
Select Start spin box, in WaveEdit, 15-11

Select Unused Colors command, in PalEdit, 14-12
Selected Colors First command, in BitEdit, 13-30
Selection tool, 13-17
Sequencer
    channel mapping, 7-15
    definition, 7-2
    recommended capabilities, 7-9
    sending MIDI messages, 7-6
Serial port data transfer, 3-6
SGML formatting, 8-7
Show Palette command, in BitEdit, 14-2 to 14-3
Silence command, in WaveEdit, 15-15
Slide scanner, 5-13
Software
    audio file conversion, 6-13
    database to manage resources, 3-8 to 3-11
    digital audio recording, 6-8 to 6-9
    Draw programs, 5-3
    image processing, 5-10 to 5-12
    Media Player, 9-3
    MIDI patch mapper, 7-10
    MIDI sequencer, 7-2, 7-9
    Movie Converter, 9-18
    movie playback, 9-3
    Movie Player, 9-5
    multimedia authoring tools, 2-12
    Multimedia Development Kit, 1-4, 2-12
    OCR scanning, 8-5
    Paint programs, 5-8 to 5-9, 5-11
    required, 10-7
    sound editing, 6-13
    text preparation, 8-11
    Viewer authoring tool, 2-12
    word processors, 8-9 to 8-10
Sound cast members, 9-9 to 9-10, 9-15
Sound libraries, 6-7 to 6-8
Standard Generalized Markup Language (SGML), 8-7
Standard MIDI assignments, 7-16 to 7-18
STANDARD.PAL, 14-6
Stereo channel. *See* Channels, waveform
Stream of hexadecimal bytes
    See Data stream
Streamed audio, in movie, 9-9 to 9-10
String values, editing, 16-18
Structured files
    displaying, 16-8 to 16-9
    displaying offsets, 16-9 to 16-10
    editing backup copy, 16-6
    editing data, 16-15 to 16-19
    editing in memory, 16-6, 16-20
    editing original file, 16-6
    editing with Clipboard, 16-14 to 16-15
    elements of, 16-8, 16-12

file headings, 16-10 to 16-11
Structured files (*continued*)
    opening in FileWalker, 16-5 to 16-6
    outline form, 16-8
    outline, copying, 16-14
    positioning cursor in, 16-11 to 16-12
    saving, 16-20 to 16-21
    canceling selection, 16-14
    selecting data in, 16-13 to 16-14
Stutter, waveform, 17-14
SVHS video camera, 5-14
Synchronization, in movie, 9-10
Syntax checkers, 8-10
Synthesizer
    base-level, 7-5, 7-10
    definition, 7-3
    extended, 7-5
    keyboard, 7-11
    MIDI file channel mapping, 7-14 to 7-15
    Multimedia PC specification, 1-3
    polyphonic, 7-6
    timbre, 7-3, 7-6
System palette, 9-6

T

Tagged Image File Format (TIFF), 5-12
Tape drives, 3-4
Text files
    converting for Windows with Multimedia, 8-6, 8-10
    scanning text, 8-3 to 8-6
    typing text, 8-2
    typing services, 8-2
    Windows with Multimedia formats, 8-1, 11-3
Tiffany TIFF files
    conversion format, 12-2
    Select Bitmap Size dialog box, 12-11
Timbre, 7-3, 7-6
Time span, waveform, 15-8
Title
    acquiring audio, 6-7 to 6-8
    acquiring images, 5-8 to 5-9
    acquiring MIDI scores, 7-8
    acquiring text, 8-1
    applications, 2-2 to 2-5
    authoring tools, 2-11 to 2-12
    CD-ROM based, 4-3
    data management, 3-1
    data preparation, 2-10 to 2-11
    design, 2-9 to 2-10
    directory structure, 3-9
    distributing on CD-ROM, 4-5 to 4-7
    including movies, 9-1

screen design, 2-7 to 2-9
    structuring data in, 2-5 to 2-8
Topics
    contents topic, 2-7
    cross-topic jumps, 2-8
    grouping in browse sequences, 2-8
    user interface design, 2-9 to 2-10
Transitions (movie), 9-17
Transparent background, 13-30 to 13-33
Truevision TGA files
    Color Reduction Options dialog box, 12-13 to 12-14
    conversion format, 12-2
    image format, 5-12
Typesetting codes, 8-6 to 8-7, 8-11

U

Undo command
    disabling in BitEdit, 13-9
    in BitEdit, 13-16
    in PalEdit, 14-4
    in WaveEdit, 15-16
Unstructured files
    displaying, 16-7
    editing backup copy, 16-6
    editing data, 16-15 to 16-16
    editing in memory, 16-6, 16-20
    editing original file, 16-6
    editing with Clipboard, 16-14 to 16-15
    opening in FileWalker, 16-5 to 16-6
    positioning cursor in, 16-11
    saving, 16-20 to 16-21
    canceling selection, 16-14
    selecting data in, 16-13 to 16-14
Use Transparency command, in BitEdit, 13-30, 13-33

V

Vector graphics
    described, 5-2 to 5-3
    in movie, 9-16
VGA display
    bitmap image depth and resolution, 5-5
    drivers, 1-2
    image development, 5-13
    movie inks, 9-6 to 9-8
    Multimedia PC specification, 1-3
    256-color movies, 9-4
VGA.PAL, 12-14, 14-6
Video camera, 5-14 to 5-15, 5-19
Video digitizing equipment, 5-9
Viewer authoring tool, 2-6, 2-12
Volume, viewing waveform, 15-8

Volume-controller messages
    main volume controller value, 7-15
    relative patch volume, 7-15

W

WaveEdit
    file formats, 15-1
    menus, 15-3, 15-5
    Play button, 15-17
    quitting, 15-20
    Rec button, 15-17
    starting, 15-2
    Stop button, 15-17
WaveEdit window
    Edit area, 15-3, 15-8
    File Characteristics area, 15-3
    measurement scale, 15-10
    opening multiple, 15-8
    spin boxes, 15-11
    time span, 15-8
    waveform amplitude, 15-3, 15-8
    waveform time span, 15-3
    Zoom scroll bar, 15-3, 15-9, 17-12
Waveform audio
    analog-to-digital, 6-3, 6-10 to 6-11
    compared to Red Book and MIDI audio, 7-7
    converting from other audio formats, 6-13
    described, 6-2
    disk space, 6-4 to 6-5
    editing, 6-13
    in movie, 9-9 to 9-10
Waveform files
    channels, setting, 15-6, 15-14
    conversion data formatting, 12-15
    conversion formats, 12-1
    converting, 12-5
    creating, 15-6 to 15-7, 15-17
    creating specific size, 17-10 to 17-11
    file size, 17-12
    FileWalker format, 16-2
    frequency, setting, 15-6, 15-15
    opening in WaveEdit, 15-7 to 15-8
    playing, 15-17
    recording, 15-17 to 15-18
    sample size, setting, 15-6, 15-14
    sample, searching for, 17-13
    saving, 15-19
    WaveEdit formats, 15-1
    Windows with Multimedia file formats, 11-3

Waveforms
    amplitude, setting, 15-15 to 15-16
    amplitude, viewing, 15-8
    channels, hiding, 15-10
    copying, 15-13
    deleting, 15-13
    displaying segment, 15-11
    echoing, 17-11
    editing with Clipboard commands, 15-13
    partial fading, 17-14
    inserting, 15-13
    mixing, 15-13
    overwriting, 15-13
    playing, 15-17
    recording, 15-17 to 15-19
    sample scale, 15-10
    selecting, 15-10 to 15-12
    size, 15-11
    stutter, 17-14
    time scale, 15-10
    time span, 15-8
    undoing last edit, 15-16
    zooming, 15-9, 15-12, 17-12
Windows with Multimedia extensions, 1-2
Word for Windows
    RTF (Rich Text Format), 8-1
    text conversion capabilities, 8-10
WORM disc, 3-2 to 3-3

Z

Zoom command
    compared to Zoom scroll bar, 17-12
    in WaveEdit, 15-12

PROGRAMMING WINDOWS,™ 2nd ed.

Charles Petzold

This is *the* Microsoft-authorized guide to writing applications for Windows 3 for both new and seasoned Windows programmers. Now completely updated and revised, this thorough resource is packed with tested programming advice, scores of new sample programs, and straightforward explanations of the Microsoft Windows programming environment. New chapters detail virtual memory, multitasking, Dynamic Data Exchange (DDE), Multiple Document Interface (MDI), and Dynamic Link Library (DLL).

950 pages, softcover   7 ³/₈ x 9 ¹/₄ $29.95
Order Code: PRWI2

Contents:

Section One: A Windows backgrounder.

Section Two: Working with input from the keyboard; using the timer; using the mouse; using child window controls.

Section Three: Understanding memory management; working with icons, cursors, bitmaps, and strings; working with menus, accelerators, and dialog boxes.

Section Four: Introduction to GDI; drawing graphics; manipulating graphical information with bits and metafiles; working with text and fonts; using printers.

Section V: Dynamic Data Exchange (DDE); Multiple Document Interface (MDI); Dynamic Link Library (DLL).

Index.

Microsoft® Windows™ Multimedia Programmer's Library

(See back cover for more information)

MICROSOFT® WINDOWS™ MULTIMEDIA PROGRAMMER'S REFERENCE	MICROSOFT® WINDOWS™ MULTIMEDIA PROGRAMMER'S WORKBOOK	MICROSOFT® WINDOWS™ MULTIMEDIA AUTHORING AND TOOLS GUIDE

To order, call 1-800-MSPRESS or mail this order form:*

Quantity	Order Code	Title	Price	Total Price
_____	WIGUPR	Microsoft Windows Guide to Programming	$29.95	$_____
_____	WIPRRE	Microsoft Windows Programmer's Reference	$39.95	$_____
_____	WIPRTO	Microsoft Windows Programming Tools	$24.95	$_____
_____	PRWI2	Programming Windows, 2nd ed.	$29.95	$_____
_____	MMPRRE	Microsoft Windows Multimedia Programmer's Ref.	$27.95	$_____
_____	MMPRWO	Microsoft Windows Multimedia Programmer's Workbook	$22.95	$_____
_____	MMAUGU	Microsoft Windows Multimedia Authoring and Tools Guide	$24.95	$_____

SALES TAX CHART	**SHIPPING**
Add the applicable sales tax for the following states: AZ, CA, CO, CT, DC, FL, GA, HI, ID, IL, IN, IA, KS, KY, ME, MD, MA, MI, MN, MO, NE, NV, NJ, NM, NY, NC, PA, OH, OK, RI, SC, TN, TX, VA, WA, WV, WI.	One book .... $2.50 Two books .... $3.25 Each additional book .... $.75

SUBTOTAL $_____

Sales Tax $_____

Shipping $_____

TOTAL $_____

BHE

NAME
_____

COMPANY (if applicable)
_____

STREET (No P.O. Boxes)
_____

CITY _____ STATE ____ ZIP _____

DAYTIME PHONE
_____

CREDIT CARD NUMBER _____ EXP. DATE _____

CARDHOLDER SIGNATURE
_____

PAYMENT:

☐ Check/Money Order (U.S. funds)

☐ **VISA** VISA (13 or 16 digits)

☐ MasterCard MasterCard (16 digits)

☐ American Express (15 digits)

FOR FASTER SERVICE CALL
1-800-MSPRESS
(8AM to 5PM Central Time)
and place your credit card order. Refer to campaign **BHE**.
All orders shipped RPS or UPS.

No P.O. Boxes please. Allow 2–3 weeks for delivery.

* In Canada, contact Macmillan Canada,
    Attn: Microsoft Press Dept., 164 Commander Blvd.,
    Agincourt, Ontario, Canada M1S 3C7   416-293-8141

In the U.K., contact Microsoft Press,
27 Wrights Lane, London W8 5TZ